Yacht and Small Craft Construction
Design Decisions

Yacht and Small Craft Construction

Design Decisions

Gordon Trower

The Crowood Press

First published in 1999 by
The Crowood Press Ltd
Ramsbury, Marlborough
Wiltshire SN8 2HR

British Library Cataloguing-in-Publication Data

A catalogue record for this book is available from the British Library.

ISBN 1 86126 118 7

Picture credits
All line drawings by Gordon Trower
Photographs by Gordon and Nola Trower,
except Figs 49, 50, 83 and 85 by Charlie Erasmus

Thoughout this book, 'Lloyd's Rules' has been used as a convenient shorthand for 'Lloyd's Register Rules
and Regulations'.

Photograph previous page: Boat building in the Australian bush – a 21.5m (70ft) yacht hull constructed
from aluminium alloy. The hull has just been completed and wheeled outside the building shed. The
client's specification was for a lightweight construction and this was achieved by using closely spaced
frames and plating for only 4.5mm and 6mm thickness, graduated from the topsides to the bottom. The
resulting weight of all-aluminium alloy work for the hull, deck, superstructure, cockpit, keel (without
ballast), and rudder was a low 4.5 tonnes.

Front cover main photograph by Nola Trower of a chine dinghy design, computer-developed by the author
to illustrate the degree of developability of the hull panels from blue (fully developable) to red (difficult to
form, thus producing high stress).

Front cover subsidiary photograph by Bob Rowse, showing the complex, framed structure of an
aluminium alloy yacht's hull and superstructure under construction.

Back cover photograph by Tim Hope of a lightweight racing yacht built from an advanced fibre-resin
composite in which the hull has broken in two.

Typeset by Textype Typesetters, Cambridge
Printed and bound in Great Britain by Redwood Books, Trowbridge

Contents

Acknowledgements

I should like to thank the following people for their help in the preparation of this book:

My wife, Nola, for giving me a break from typing, for proof-reading, making sensible criticism and shutting herself in the darkroom for days on end.

Colin Edmunds for his editing extravaganza (If there's anything wrong, it's Colin's fault!).

Bob Rowse for relating his experiences about cut-and-shut foam sandwich building in Indonesia, and for lots of photographs from Holland.

Greg Carroll for digging out some really interesting articles and papers.

Ernie Bird for proof reading at short notice, despite BP Shipping's demands on his time.

Charlie and Deon Erasmus for a mass of photographs that came through customs unscathed from South Africa.

Tim Hope for proof reading whilst burning the midnight oil at Chris Gunter Designs.

Martin Keeble for putting up with the photographic disruptions at the Performance Sailcraft factory.

Sue Frazer, a work colleague, for her help in assembling the further reading list and with everything book-wise.

Bob Curry of the American Bureau of Shipping for his advice.

Paul Randall, of Walnut Boats, for his patience in waiting for preliminary drawings for a trailer sailer whilst I was finishing the book.

Geoff Williams, surveyor, of R. Pearce and Co., for his helpful review of my comments about regulations.

Phil Samuel for his photogenic qualities, as always.

Introduction

We can set out to design the structure of a boat so that failure is prevented under just about any circumstance. The solution is to over-build, the result being excessive weight, of course. But head towards the lightweight, ultra-light or feather-light and the risk of failure increases.

Decisions about strength, weight, and, indeed, how much flexibility or stretch is tolerable or desirable, are based upon the judgements boat designers and builders make.

There are no final answers, any more than when racing we can be sure that a chosen course will get us to the next mark in the least time. Logic and experience play a part, as when sailing inshore to avoid the tide rather than taking a direct line.

Similarly, logic (or analysis) and experience (or tradition) inform the decision-making process for the boat designer and the boat builder. To pop rivet my colours to the mast, this book deals with the former. The intention is to provide a thinking approach to boat construction.

Although this focus falls principally within the province of the designer, there is an overlap with that of the boat builder. Both need to be aware of how materials behave structurally; how structures resist loads; how failure is likely to occur; and how materials can be put together to create boats.

Both designer and builder are problem-solvers, though their approaches may differ. The designer is likely to be more analytically focused while the builder is more naturally led by practical experience.

It is my hope that this book will be of value to those who have an interest in boat design or building, or are boat experienced, as a means of enhancing their understanding of the structural concepts of boats. I also hope that this aspiration may be extended to those who don't know their bow from their stern.

As such, the book attempts a multi-level style. Calculations and explanatory notes are separated from the main text so that the body of the book can be read with or without amplification, and for a presentation that is more bite-sized.

Instead of dealing extensively with theory and then working through examples, case studies are given prominence and theory is introduced as needed in order to develop each case study. Hopefully, this makes the theory more palatable. For consistency, all calculations employ SI units, though the problem and solution are expressed in the most comprehensible metric units. Also, to make understanding a little easier, words initially in italics are defined in the glossary for reference purposes when used elsewhere.

My thought is to express a complex subject simply, and I am aware that some simplifications are not wholly accurate, nor provide an adequate model for the structural design of yacht and small craft. To the real experts in the field, I apologize.

Yacht and Small Craft Construction – Design

Decisions is a companion volume to my *Yacht and Small Craft Construction*, also published by The Crowood Press.

The companion volume makes a complementary study of boat designs as it relates to form. Aerodynamics and hydrodynamics present a focus, the behaviour and interaction of the hull, sails, keel and rudder being explored. The book also takes in the creative aspects of design, together with the techniques for producing a lines plan and the hydrostatic calculations involved.

Like *Yacht and Small Craft Construction – Design Decisions, Yacht and Small Craft Construction* culminates in a dedicated step-by-step procedure for design.

Chapter 1

Borrowing Structural Theory

Design Approaches

Tradition versus analysis

There are two principal approaches to designing the *structure* of a boat. The construction may be based upon examples that have already been built, that is, on tradition, or by considering the forces acting on the boat and its response, a process of analysis. A third method, of a sort, is by the application of rules prescribed by regulatory authorities which dictate the dimensions of the parts of the construction in order to meet *strength* requirements. Arguably this is not a distinct system at all because regulatory authorities base their rules upon both tradition and analysis.

Each approach has its merits. **Tradition signifies a quality which is solid but perhaps stolid – guaranteed to work but unimaginative; strong but unnecessarily heavy. Analysis implies the use of calculation, theory and reasoning.**

An evolutionary example

By way of example we may consider the possible evolution of a *deck beam*, a significant structural part of a boat. Suppose that it is constructed from wood with the objective of supporting the deck. The beam spans the width of the deck and rests on the wooden *beam shelf*, bent round each side of the boat. The first stage of development is when the boat builder 'tests' the beam he has just fashioned and fastened into position. He jumps up and

down on it. It flexes and he feels in his bones that it will not be strong enough, so he replaces it with a beam of larger cross-section.

The deck is laid from fore and aft planks fastened into position and, as the boat is launched, the sides of the hull spread. The laid deck is not effective in preventing this and, while the deck beam is excellent for jumping up and down on, it fails to restrain the beam shelf. It is obvious that the beams need to do more than just support the deck, so, in turn, a joint is created between the beam and the beam shelf to prevent them from pulling apart.

Time passes, the beam stands up well and everyone claps the boat builder on the back. Then, one day, a rather large wave lands on the deck and the beam breaks at its middle. Fearing for his reputation, the boat builder thinks that he must avoid a repetition of this.

He constructs a beam of heavier section still, but, noting that the failure occurred in the middle, he makes this area of the beam quite massive. He does not feel that he can be concerned that people will hit their heads on his beam as they go forward. He sails the boat in the roughest seas he can find and his beam does not break. He gets a commission from the king (who is, fortunately, quite short), makes his fortune from boat and beam building and lives happily ever after.

Accounting for waves

Well, for the rest of his days anyway. A century later, the boat builder is resting in peace with a serene smile on his face, the result of knowing that his beams had withstood the test of time. Then one of his beams breaks. The conditions under which this happens are horrendous, the wave which engulfs the boat being the highest recorded for over a hundred years.

Possibilities for the builder's successors now emerge: strengthen future beams further where the beam broke, lighten them where it did not break, or sit down and ponder how often waves of this magnitude come along. Wave heights are often categorized in terms of the statistical frequency of occurrence. Thus if a wave reaches or exceeds a particular height ten times in a thousand years it is referred to as a one-hundred-year wave.

A one-hundred-year wave is likely to be very large, but the location of its occurrence is all important. At sea, waves of this magnitude could be at least 30m measured vertically from crest to trough. On a reservoir the hundred-year wave might be 1.5m high.

The designer is faced with a quandary. **To design seagoing craft to withstand rarely occurring waves may seem to be producing craft having excessive strength.** Why not design for a fifty-year, a twenty-year or even a one-year wave, rather than a one-hundred year wave, particularly for a boat not intended for a century of service?

The drawback is that a one-hundred-year wave could occur this week, and then there could be another one along as soon as next month, and there is a possibility there could be a third before the year is out. It may be agreed that all this is unlikely, but then so is winning the national lottery, and yet some people win.

Overdesigning the structure

Who knows? Things could be worse. The poor deck beam might already be straining under the weight of a number of drums of oil, planned for the calming of the seas. Monster waves are not calmed readily, however, and it could just happen that a school of dolphins becomes caught up in the wave and thuds on

to the deck just as one hundred years of wave crash down.

The largest wave ever recorded was 34m high. But to design for the most extreme circumstance may be to overdesign. Designing the deck beam to withstand 34m of water plus the oil drums plus the dolphins is not a problem – although it could mean that the arrangement and the depth of the deck beams result in a boat which has little accommodation space and, in the extreme, is virtually solid!

Secondary problems ensue from over-designing, such as an increase of weight which in itself can place demands on the structure. Building costs also become higher and performance and efficiency lower.

Guaranteed construction

The obvious advantage of basing a boat's construction on what has gone before is that it is pretty well guaranteed to be satisfactory. It is likely to be strong enough, not excessively flexible, long-lasting, unlikely to leak or rot and generally user-friendly. **The downside of the traditional approach is that we do not know if, structurally speaking, the construction is in any way optimized.** It may be much too strong, for instance.

Construction defined by tradition becomes the precedent or standard, and this presents a limit or paradigm. Paradigms inhibit breakthroughs. What is interesting about breakthroughs is that once they have occurred there is a band-wagon effect.

Value of analysis

Traditional approaches do not encourage the use of, for example, advanced composites or space-framed structures in boat construction, although their adoption becomes archetypal in time. **By contrast, the analytical approach can lead to breakthroughs and would appear to be the necessary tool for unusual forms of construction or where high performance is called for.**

Nevertheless, this attitude may readily be criticized for its theoretical starting point. There is no guarantee that a structure will prove satisfactory. It is all too easy to make an indifferent assessment of the loadings and of the way in which the structure will withstand these. Although numbers possess a quality of certainty, the assumptions that may be made before moving to the numerical are not infallible.

Providing reserves

Whether the design of the construction is based upon tradition or upon estimation of the forces imposed by mega-waves and the like, a decision must be made about the level of risk that is to be accepted. Traditional approaches deal with such decisions by practicality and as a result of common agreement. **The analytical style is one of considering the loads commonly encountered under working conditions, and then applying what may be described as a** *factor of safety.*

A factor of safety is a mysterious, make-everything-right number. It multiplies the *working load*, perhaps at a 'normal' maximum, to provide a *design load*. This represents the load we assume in the design of the structure; predictably the load the structure can only just withstand under extreme circumstances.

For example, the normal maximum load to serve as the basis for the design of a rowing dinghy *thwart* might be the weight of a heavy person sitting or standing in the middle of the thwart. In order to allow for contingencies,

such as a crew laden with baggage jumping down on to it or unknown material defects, a factor of safety of perhaps six might be applied. This means that the thwart and its associated fixing would be designed with sufficient strength to support six heavy persons all in the middle of the thwart.

Fig 1 *'Now, if you could just pass the rest of the bags, the inflatable dinghy, the gas bottle. . .'*

Factor of safety

An adage in engineering is that it is not possible to be certain that all loadings on the structure have been accounted for. For example, it may not occur to the designer that the dinghy (perhaps when partly filled with water) could be lifted by the thwart at its middle. The factor of safety, it is hoped, allows for this possible omission.

Usually, the factor of safety chosen would be low where the consequences of failure are likely not to be serious and weight is a major disadvantage. Where the result of failure is likely to be disastrous, and weight is of little or no concern, the factor of safety would be high. Life risk usually demands factors of safety of twelve or so.

Factors of safety, therefore, may range from just above one, up to perhaps twenty. Typical values are often fairly low. The rig of a yacht might be designed on the basis of a factor of safety of two to four because weight aloft adversely affects stability.

For *ballast keel bolts*, a relatively high factor of safety of ten to fifteen might be applied, since it is really bad news if the ballast keel detaches itself from the hull. Also, the additional weight resulting from the reserve strength built into the bolts is not detrimental, unless the designer is paranoid about achieving a super-low *centre of gravity*.

Design loadings

The approach in determining the design loading for the rig involves a consideration of the loads imposed by strong wind conditions, and multiplying these loadings by a number between two and four. The diameter of keel bolts is defined on the basis of a design loading ten to fourteen times greater than the load occurring under reasonably maximum load conditions, such as occur when the yacht is heeled through 90 degrees.

Other, less significant aspects that the factor of safety should account for include the loss of strength of the material resulting from corrosion or other forms of deterioration. Intrinsic faults, such as knots in wood and materials which are not as strong as expected, also fall into this category.

In a way, the factor of safety represents the application of trial and error or experience. **Certainly the value of the factor of safety applied is judgemental.**

Composite view

Thus it seems that even where the dimensions of a boat's constructional elements are calculated on the basis of the loadings thought likely to occur, an allowance for generations of experience is then made in the form of a factor of safety. Evolution tends to display a mix of tradition and analysis. Testing and thinking why failure happens indicate a system of analysis, albeit at a primitive level, although it is perfectly valid for all that. Continuing to build beams to established dimensions demonstrates tradition at work.

Perhaps it is obvious that most design work possesses features of both the traditional and the analytical approach. We all are structural designers when involved in screwing a shelf to

---

Supplementary Note

Sometimes the factor of safety may have a value of less than one. For example, a dinghy outboard motor propeller may be reasonably expected to stir up the beach at times and strike the occasional rock. But this places the transmission at risk of breakage. A *shear pin* acts as a *fail-safe* so that any undue loading breaks the pin rather than a more expensive or difficult-to-replace part.

Supplementary Note

There is, however, a small trap that may creep into the evolutionary process. This has been identified as *engineering towards failure*. The classic case of this is where the design of one component, which has given excellent service for a long time in a particular system, is considered to be overweight, and a quick analysis of the component's primary function comes up with the result that it could be made lighter. The analysis, however, has only looked at the primary and not at any secondary function it may be fulfilling.

Another example is the very evolutionary nature of traditional design, where a component is refined and refined, because it has always worked well before, until the inevitable happens and a little too much is pared away from the margin of safety. When this happens, the first set of operating conditions out of the ordinary finds the weakness and designers go back a few steps.

An example of this process is given by the (unconfirmed) story concerning the French tunny fishing fleet. This comprised big, gaff-rigged boats that fished well out to sea and thus had to be very fast. They evolved a fine run aft which gave them an elegant *counter stern*. It is said that, over a long time, the stern became finer and finer and the counter longer and longer, such that the buoyancy and long lever caused the counter to break off in following seas.

the wall or repairing a chair in the home, or adding a cleat, or wedging a mast on a boat, or even tying up alongside. But we do tend towards one or other of the styles.

In practice, therefore, constructional design embodies the principles of both tradition and analysis, with a major emphasis on the latter nowadays, due to the proliferation of new materials.

Major Loadings

Understanding loadings

Failure of the construction and components is not uncommon. Cleats pull out of decks; halyards break; propshafts bend; centreboards fracture; hulls are holed; sails tear; shackles pull apart; lead ballast keels deform; decks crack. **Understanding the nature of the**

SUMMARY: DESIGN APPROACHES

1. In order to ensure satisfactory service, the construction of boats and many of their components is the subject of structural design which, in the extreme, may be based upon either tradition or analysis.

2. Designing for loadings that occur only in the most extreme conditions, as with rarely occurring waves or in unusual accidents, may be over-cautious and lead to excessive weight in the structure.

3. Applied factors of safety depend principally upon the consequences of failure, but ultimately are judgemental and the product of experience, and therefore are essentially derivative.

4. Structural design of an innovative nature usually relies strongly upon an analytical approach, but more generally analysis is tempered by the design of previous, accepted construction, the dictate of tradition.

loadings to which marine craft are subjected
is a first step in their structural design.

Powering effects

Significant loadings on the hull and its
associated structural elements occur as a result
of the driving force, for both power and sail.
As far as powered craft are concerned, thrust
from the propeller pushes the boat forward
and is resisted by the engine beds or a thrust
block. There also is a twisting or *torsional* force
occurring on the propeller shaft, resulting from
the rotation of the propeller. This tends to lift
the engine on one side and depress it on the
other, the loadings being transmitted through
the engine beds to the main structure of the
hull.

Unstayed rig loading

For sailing craft, the loadings from the sails'
driving force are complex. The simplest rig
layout is probably the *una rig* carried on an
unstayed mast. This type of rig comprises a
single sail set on a mast without rigging. The
mast is subjected to a *bending* load as a result of
the wind in the sail, and there are side forces
on both the deck and keel, the mast being
supported at both points.

The direction of these side forces depends
upon the direction of the wind. When the boat
is sailing *upwind* the side force at the deck is
largely athwartships. When sailing *downwind*
the force on the sail, and hence on the deck, is
primarily forwards.

The loadings in the deck in these directions
are largely *compressive* and therefore are
transmitted to the side of the boat or to the
stem in the line of the force. The appreciation
of the nature of these loadings leads to the
design of a suitable structural configuration,
with, of course, a factor of safety for good
measure.

The knock-on effects do need to be
recognized however. For instance, a
compression member – a *strut* – could be used

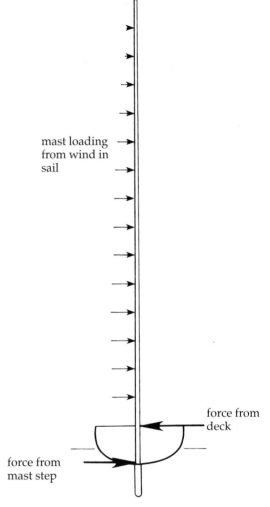

mast loading
from wind in
sail

force from
deck

force from
mast step

*Fig 2 The deck structure and mast step counteract
the unstayed mast load. The force exerted by the
deck is equal to the force of the mast step plus the
mast load.*

to bridge the gap between mast and *gunwale*
(which reinforces the side of the boat at the
deck edge similarly to the beam shelf). The
strut would bear upon the gunwale, thus
attempting to bend it and distort the deck. In
turn, the gunwale would tug on the adjacent
deck beams, which in turn would deform the
gunwale on the other side of the boat, and so
on.

Loadings at the keel are similar. Here, the side force is likely to be resisted by a *mast step* which distributes the loading over several regular, transverse, hull structural members, known as *floors*, a term not to be confused with the cabin sole.

Stayed rig loadings

A *stayed rig* enables the mast to be lighter owing to the support of the rigging. If a *foresail* is carried, the most common arrangement, the use of a stayed rig is virtually inevitable, the foresail being carried on a *forestay*. **However, the network of loadings on the hull becomes very complex with stayed rigs.**

A primary requirement for this type of rig, most particularly for high-performance dinghies and yachts, is that the *luff* of the foresail (its leading edge) should remain as straight as possible. In practice, the wind and sheeting loads cause the forestay, and hence the foresail, to sag. This reduces upwind performance because the sail shape lacks stability.

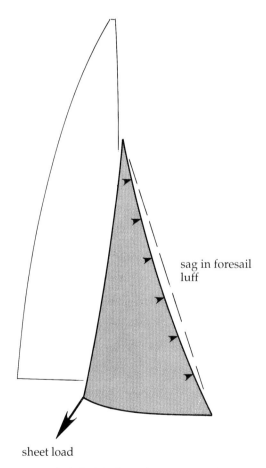

sag in foresail luff

sheet load

Fig 3 Sag in the luff of the foresail is caused by the sheet and wind loads.

Supplementary Note

With a slack forestay, the foresail tends to swing around when sailing in waves. The severe movement, exaggerated aloft, upsets the flow of air over the sail. Furthermore, in gusts the sail becomes fuller, thus increasing side force and heel, the opposite of what is required for efficiency.

Maintaining a near straight luff relies upon a forestay which is under a high level of *tension*. It is not possible to achieve a perfectly straight luff because, however small the side load, some deflection of the *catenary*, as this structural arrangement is termed, will occur. An example of a catenary is that of an anchor chain in use, which sags due to its weight even when highly loaded, a fortunate occurrence in this case, the chain pulling along the bottom.

When sailing, the *backstay, running backstays* or *backswept shrouds*, depending upon the layout, struggle to achieve adequate tension in the forestay. The net result is a considerable downward force on the mast, compounded by the tension occurring in the shrouds from the side force of the wind in the sails. **Every rigging wire which is under tension produces compression in the mast, which is therefore loaded as a strut.**

Hull bending

In consequence, the hull of a yacht with

Fig 4 *Backswept rig without running backstays.*

backstay and forestay is deflected downwards under the mast and upwards at its ends. The amount of deflection may be considerable. Tensioning the backstay may pull up the stern (and also the bow, by reaction) by perhaps 50mm.

The bending of the hull has a tendency to cause the *topsides* to spread outwards, although the shrouds do provide a measure of restraint, and *bulkheads* would all but eliminate this distortion. Otherwise, it is seen that the deck, *coachroof* sides and top are subjected to a tensile load which seeks to straighten the cross-section.

Under the bending load caused by the stays pulling up the ends of the hull and the mast pushing downwards, the deck and the coachroof would also be subject to

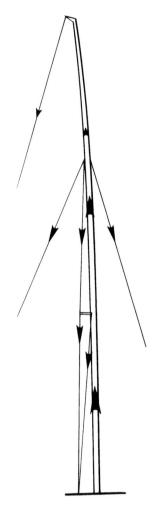

Fig 5 *The shrouds and stays all produce compression in the mast.*

compression and the hull bottom to tension. These would both be in the fore and aft direction. Again, changes in the line of the coachroof would reduce its ability to deal with the compressive load, although the compression is also distributed along the deck on either side of the coachroof.

This compression is sometimes evident in decks of relatively thin, aluminium-alloy plate. Slight bulging may occur between each deck beam when the rig is loaded.

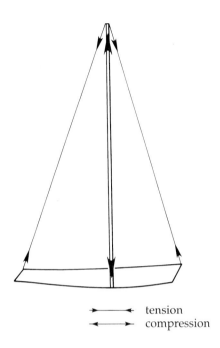

tension

compression

Fig 6 Bending of the hull results from the mast compression and stay tensions. Note the system for representing compression and tension.

Topside shear stress

The hull may be likened to a *trussed structure*, such as the jib of a crane, which also experiences bending loads. A key feature of this structure is that it is built using diagonals which link the top and the bottom panel of the jib. The *shear* loadings are dealt with by the diagonals.

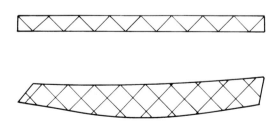

Fig 7 Representation of the trussed jib of a crane (top) and the diagonal reinforcement in a hull (bottom).

Similarly, the topsides of the hull are loaded in this diagonal fashion. It is best to think of these diagonal loadings on the hull as multiple or numerous rather than from one interconnection to the next, as for a crane jib. **In designing the hull structure attention needs to be given to these loadings, so that appropriate orientation of reinforcement of the materials may be effected during construction.**

Sagging and hogging

In principle, the hull is loaded as a beam because under these rig loadings the hull is subjected to bending. **In the same way, bending of the hull occurs when it is supported unevenly, such as by waves.** When waves support the boat by the bow and stern, the loadings compound those resulting from the backstay, forestay and mast combination, though it is likely that the rig loadings are the more dominant.

Powered craft fare better, having only wave loadings to contend with, although as hull size increases so does the problem of hull bending. Ships have been known to break their backs at sea, as they would if chocked in dry dock without middle body support.

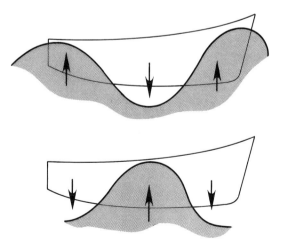

Fig 8 Waves result in sagging (top) and hogging (bottom).

Not surprisingly, this manner of bending is known as *sagging*. When the hull is supported by a wave amidships it suffers *hogging*, which also fairly well describes the condition.

Water pressure

Other factors must be taken into account in the design of the hull. Its capacity to withstand the *pressure* of the water is a significant one. When the boat is in a marina the loadings on the hull caused by water pressure are relatively low. The *head* of water, which in this case is given by the depth from the *waterline* to the hull bottom, determines the water pressure.

In waves the head increases at times as the water level rises above the waterline, and therefore so does the pressure.To design the hull so that it would survive being consumed fully by a one-hundred-year wave, or a one-

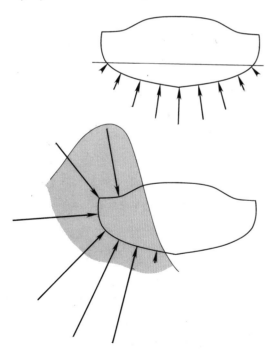

Fig 9 Water pressure increases with the head of water: shown when a boat floats in still water (top) and in waves (bottom); the length of the arrows represents the pressure.

year wave for that matter, would produce a much over-built hull. In practice, the hull is picked up by the wave rather than being engulfed totally. To assume a head of the same height as the wave is therefore excessive.

It serves well enough to assume a maximum head which is two or three times the hull depth, with some variation according to purpose or expected sea conditions.

Dynamic loads

Similarly, the hull bottom of a planing craft must be able to withstand water pressure. But the cause of this pressure arises principally when the hull meets the water at speed and from slamming in waves. These are hydrodynamic loads which are generated when the hull moves at speed through or on the surface of water. The loads described earlier, whichrelate to water depth, are hydrostatic in nature.

Nevertheless, it would be feasible to satisfy the requirements of the hull's structural integrity with respect to rig and water loads, and yet fail to meet another important criterion. **The need to withstand** *local loadings* **must also be addressed.**

Surviving impact

For example, a 30m vessel could be built with a complex, closely-spaced framework covered by aluminium baking foil. Given such a framework, the foil could be strong enough for any wave the sea could throw at it and the framework would be able to handle the *global loads*, in particular those producing hull bending (and hull torsion). The trouble is that the foil would not withstand the impact arising from a collision with a beer can, an inordinate number of which may be found littering our oceans.

While adequate provision must be made for possible impact, the questions about how large and angular an object, struck at what speed and where on the hull are imponderable.

Fig 10 A bow easily able to penetrate the water reduces the hydrodynamic loads.

Meeting up with an escaped shipping container on a dark night is likely to do grievous bodily harm to any hull, however thick the skin. But it is reasonable that the hull of a cruiser should be able to withstand crunching into the odd quay, pile or rock, and a dinghy hull should be strong enough to be bumped about on a launching trolley, as is their wont.

SUMMARY: MAJOR LOADINGS

1. An appreciation of the loadings to which boats are subjected is fundamental to their structural design.

2. Loadings resulting from the driving force are fairly easily dealt with in terms of the construction, but stayed rigs produce amplified loadings as a result of the rigging tension and mast compression.

3. Stayed rigs cause bending of the yacht hull, which places the bottom in tension, the bending being limited by a deck resistant to buckling and topsides that are diagonally reinforced.

4. Significant water pressure on the hull from wave and dynamic water loads produces both local and global loadings on the structure, but impact with solid objects has potentially more serious local consequences.

Physical Stress

Concept of stress

Stress in a structure can be likened to the use of the term at an everyday level. We may feel stressed when we are loaded, such as at work when required to complete yet another task, adding to our workload and putting us under additional pressure. (Not to be confused with being loaded in a financial or alcoholic sense, which tends toward a de-stressing effect!)

If we are used to handling extra work and completing additional tasks over and above our normal workload – our shoulders are broad – we may feel relatively little stress. **In parallel, the degree of stress in a structure relates to the loading and to the area of material resisting the load.** Increase the loading and the stress also is increased; but if the area involved is increased – like having broad shoulders – stress is correspondingly reduced.

Defining stress

Suppose a shroud is loaded by tightening the *bottlescrew* which attaches the shroud to the *chainplate* to the deck. The same level of tension seeks to pull apart the rigging wire at all positions along its length (like a mooring chain). Tightening the bottlescrew increases the tension and thus the stress. In fact,

doubling the loading doubles the tensile stress, tripling the loading triples the stress, and so on.

However, increasing the shroud's cross-sectional area by using a thicker wire would result in less stress. The relationship is similar to that described for the load, but in this case doubling the cross-sectional area halves the stress. Of course, the use of a thinner wire would increase the stress: half the area produces twice the stress.

Formally, stress is defined as the loading per unit area resisting the load. In the case of the shroud, we would assess its level of stress by the ratio of the loading to the cross-sectional area of the rigging wire.

Since the most commonly used rigging wire comprises nineteen stainless steel strands spirally bound to form a bundle, the cross-sectional area would not include the spaces between the strands. It can be seen that each strand would experience one-nineteenth of the total tension and, having one-nineteenth the area of the bundle, would be stressed to the same degree as the whole bundle.

Variation of stress

Although we normally make the assumption that the loading is shared evenly between all strands, in practice this may not be so. In reality, some strands may experience more

---

Supplementary Note

In terms of the calculation of stress, the unit of area may be the square inch, square foot, square metre or otherwise. The use of square millimetres (mm^2) adopts a metric stance, though to be Système International (SI) correct we should use square metres (m^2).

The formal unit of force or weight is the *newton* (N), named after the English physicist and mathematician Isaac Newton. Although load and weight are often expressed in *kilograms* (kg), strictly speaking this is a measure of *mass*, the quantity of matter in an object.

Weight may be thought to be the effect of mass. When a 100kg pig of ballast traps your finger, the weight of the ballast, which would be 981N, exerts a force of 981N on it. A medium-sized man weighs about 750N (12 stones or 168lb), a 10m (30ft) cruiser about 35,000N (or 35kN) and its anchor about 100N.

stress and others less. **Variations in stress are likely where the cross-sectional shape of a load-bearing structure changes, even if the cross-sectional area remains unchanged.** For example, *lenticular rod rigging*, which has a low windage cross-section, would have zones of stress variation as the cross-section changes towards the end of the attachments.

Stress variation is of no concern whilst the maximum stress is below the breaking strength. But when the loading increases, the area which is under greatest stress is sure to fail first, the less stressed areas not reaching their potential. It is better to spread the stress. **A target for the designer is to attempt to ensure a consistent level of stress throughout a structure, although for anything other than very simple structures this target is an elusive one.**

Stress in a sail

A sail is a relatively simple structure. The greatest tension occurs in the corners and radiates from these points so that in general the centre of the sail experiences least tension. If the sail were of uniform cloth weight and not reinforced, stress would be highest in the corners.

By reinforcing the corners, using *patches*, the stress level in these regions is reduced. Nevertheless, obtaining a uniform stress distribution is unlikely, if only because the patches comprise individual pieces of sail cloth, albeit well staggered, but not of continuously graduated weight. Of course, extra weight of sail cloth in certain areas which lowers the level of stress below the norm probably is of little disadvantage except that designers usually abhor redundancy. The areas of elevated stress are the cause of concern.

Mapping stress

A general appreciation of stress variation within a structure is a valuable skill to acquire. The designer with X-ray vision programmed

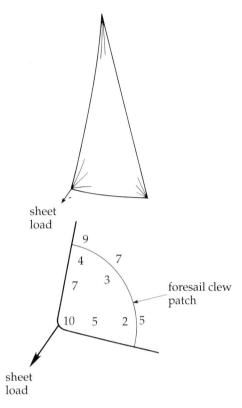

Fig 11 A representation of the stress in the corner of a sail (the clew) indicating the way in which the sheet load is distributed. Note the reduction of stress with distance from clew and the effect of the patch on the stress. A nominal value of 10 is used to represent the greatest stress.

to register the stress patterns occurring on a boat under working conditions would leap ahead of the competition.

In fact, computer programs are available to predict stress mapping by a process of *finite element analysis* but they work on much assumed information. It still remains for the designer to develop his good stress sense in order to design effectively.

Stress concentration

Stress is increased by way of *discontinuities*, such as at the corners of cockpits or hatches, or the openings in masts. These are termed *stress concentrations.* It helps to imagine lines of stress which have to squeeze around corners. The closeness of these lines indicate the level of stress, rather as steep gradient is shown by narrowed contours on an ordnance survey map.

Stress concentrations can be minimised by radiusing corners as far as possible, or compensated for by additional reinforcement in these areas. It is apparent that such irregularities of shape experience elevated stress when the corner is internal and tends to be opened under load, in which case the stress is tensile in nature. Under this condition, a crack may be formed, especially in materials that are non-*ductile.* Since a crack possesses an extremely sharp corner at its bottom, progressive failure is likely, notably for *brittle* materials and particularly at low temperatures when brittleness is exacerbated.

Optimising structures

Minimizing redundancy in a structure leads to an improvement in efficiency and usually a reduction in weight. The process can be depicted by the design of a dinghy thwart. When we sit in the middle of the thwart the greatest bend is where we sit (assuming the thwart is of constant cross-section) and this is where the stress is highest. The level of stress radiates from the middle of the thwart, decreasing towards the ends.

Stress is high if we are heavy and the thwart is thin, a principle developed earlier. However, a more regular stress distribution results if the

Supplementary Note

The extent to which stress is increased by a stress concentration is indicated by the *stress concentration factor,* effectively a multiplier of the stress that would exist without the presence of the stress concentration. For a small hole, the stress concentration factor is about 2, for a rounded V-notch about 3, while a crack in a ductile material is about 10. A crack in a brittle material pushes the stress upwards by anything from 100 to 1,000.

thwart is thickened in the middle or indeed tapered towards the ends. It should be added that whether this is worth doing depends upon the manufacturing process and whether the weight really is worth saving.

Material failure

The next very important question relates to the upper level of stress which is acceptable. Whatever the material, there is a level of stress which will cause it to fail. The stronger the material, the higher the level of stress it can tolerate. **Therefore the level of tolerable stress**

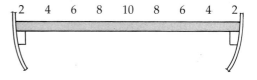

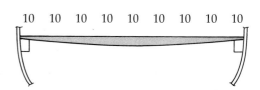

Fig 12 Representative stress in a parallel-sectioned thwart (top) and a tapered thwart (bottom), assuming a central load in both cases. A nominal value of 10 indicates the greatest stress.

has to be judged against the material to be used in the structure.

All the same, the level of stress in a structure is independent of the material used. It is the material strength which determines whether or not failure occurs. Returning to the analogy of personal strength, the nervous breakdown would equate with structural failure of the material, and indeed personality type defines proneness to stress, as material strength defines the capability to withstand stress.

Tensile stress

Stress comes in different shapes and sizes. Tensile stress is one of the simplest forms to analyse. It is to be noted that length does not affect tensile stress. Thus, a tensile member which is a kilometre long would be no more highly stressed than one of a metre length given the same loading.

Supplementary Note

The strength-to-weight ratio of thread is judged by considering the length which would support its own weight. This runs into kilometres for most threads and, presumably, would be assessed theoretically rather than practically because of the difficulty of hanging several kilometres of thread from a helicopter. Failure occurs when the tensile stress reaches the tensile strength of the thread and this, at least theoretically, would be at the point of suspension, the stress diminishing down the length of the thread.

Compressive stress

Compressive stress is perceived in a similar manner to tensile stress by regarding cross-sections along the length, but in the opposite sense. A strut which supports the superstructure on a motor cruiser would be subject to compressive stress. Again, length would not be an issue, although long struts

develop other stresses in addition if loaded so that they fail by buckling.

A mast step provides another example in which compressive stress occurs. Depending upon the mast step arrangement, the area over which the compression is distributed could be relatively large, in which case the stress would be higher in the vicinity of the mast heel and gradually reduce with distance from the heel. The determination of compressive stress (on the basis of the ratio of the load to area) would be inexact if the total area were considered because the stress is not uniform.

Shear stress

Shear stress is evident in the fastenings which bolt a traditional-type chainplate to the side of a yacht. Loading from the shroud is transmitted through the chainplate and onto the bolts (and in turn to the frame or local area of hull). The effect of the shear stress is a tendency to slice the bolts in two and would be assessed, as indicated for other forms of stress, by the ratio of the loading and the area tending to be sliced, in this case across the diameter of the bolts.

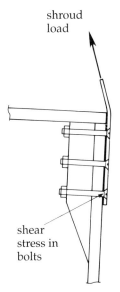

Fig 13 The shroud load places the chainplate bolts in single shear.

Fig 14 Examples of both single and double shear.

This form of shear, described as *single shear*, relies on reasonably tight fastenings. *Double shear* does not, as in the case of a rigging *toggle pin*, although the greater spacing of a *shackle* would produce bending in the pin. In the case of such double shear, the stress is calculated on the basis of twice the cross-sectional area of the pin.

Torsional stress

A propeller shaft experiences torsional stress, although more specifically the shaft is subject to shearing. The manner of shearing differs from that described for the fastening with the chainplate. As before, cross-sections can be considered, although the stress tends to twist adjacent cross-sections relative to each other.

The shaft can also be thought to comprise a

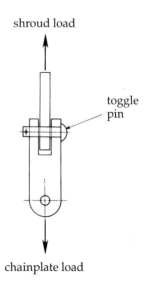

Fig 15 Double shear is demonstrated by the toggle pin.

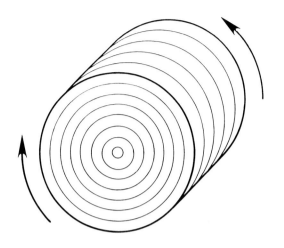

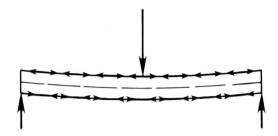

Fig 17 Tensile and compressive stresses resulting from bending loads.

Fig 16 Shear stress occurs in both adjacent cross-sections and representative concentric tubes.

stress towards the plane running along the centre of the beam (in fact the centre of gravity of the cross-section) and described as the *neutral surface*.

series of concentric tubes, the torsion tending to shear one relative to the next. Shear stress is greater for the larger diameter tubes, reaching a maximum at the surface of the shaft. It follows that, when the loading is sufficiently high, this is where failure is initiated, which then progresses towards the centre.

If the water is thought to flow in layers, each layer shears relative to the next because there is a small difference in speed. Towards the sandbank, the same differential occurs from flow in one direction to zero flow and then to flow in the opposite direction. **Analogously,**

Bending stress

Many parts of the structure of boats and their components are subject to bending, and therefore suffer bending stress. The stresses involved are complex however. Since a beam is curved under bending, the outside face is stretched to a small degree, implying a tensile stress, whilst on the inside the material is shortened slightly, indicating compressive stress, as discussed earlier.

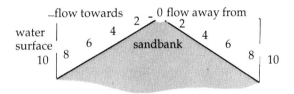

The nature of these stresses can be modelled by two rivers flowing in opposite directions and separated by a very narrow sandbank, the depth of the water increasing with distance from the sandbank. The fastest flow occurs where the water is deepest, corresponding to the greatest tensile and compressive stresses on the outside faces of the beam. Flow reduces gradually towards the sandbanks, as does the

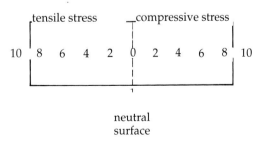

Fig 18 The varying tensile and compressive stress in a beam is analogous to a river's flow with varying depth.

the beam experiences shear stress at all planes parallel to the neutral surface. This principle is illustrated by considering the bending of a ream of weakly bonded paper, demonstrating interleaf shear stress. The adhesion between sheets fails as the sheets slide over each other.

Shear stress in a beam is also apparent as a result of the direct loadings, and acts perpendicularly to the neutral surface. Adjacent sections of the beam experience shear stress, one section being forced up and the other down, if the beam is assumed to be horizontal.

Both forms of shear stress are resisted by tension and compression loadings at plus and minus 45° to the planes of shearing. This explains the success of the lattice of the jib of a crane and indeed the diagonally-arranged reinforcement of the topsides of a yacht.

combining stresses

It is evident that bending stress can be visualized as an amalgam of different stresses. In a similar way, many structures are not the subject of a single stress type when loaded, as is the case for a shackle pin, which experiences both shear and bending.

Another example is the *stock* of a *spade rudder* (ie a rudder without a *skeg*), which suffers two *principal stresses* as a result of the hydrodynamic load. Significant bending stress in the stock is produced, the rudder not being supported at its bottom by a skeg. In addition, the torque from the tiller (or wheel) and from the rudder blade cause torsional stress in the stock.

For a simple approach, we might consider just the obviously major stress (eg the bending

stress), or, if unsure, determine the rudder stock diameter on the basis of each stress, opting for the larger diameter, and then allow a factor of safety to account for the other stress. The difficulty is that, although the stresses are additive, they are not so directly.

The simplest way of illustrating this is to make a gross simplification and envision the stresses as *vectors* in the same way we think of the forces that cause them.

Supplementary Note

A vector is the linear representation of a force and the direction in which it acts. We may suppose the torsional stress to be represented by one vector and the bending stress by another, the resultant being obtained geometrically or by calculation. The section on rig analysis in Chapter 5 deals extensively with vectors.

Consequentially, the resultant stress is greater than either the bending or torsional stress, but usually not by much! Still, for very low factors of safety, or to save a few grammes, the approach is worthy.

Structural Deformation

First concepts

Inevitably linked to the occurance of stress in a material is the *strain* which always accompanies it. In an everyday context, we often refer to the 'stresses and strains' of work,

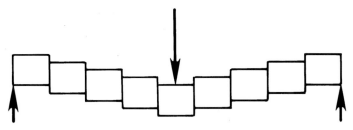

Fig 19 A representation of direct stress in a beam.

SUMMARY: PHYSICAL STRESS

1. Stress in a material is defined as the loading occurring over unit area of the stressed section, and is independent of material strength.

2. The achievement of uniform stress in a structure is a design ideal, and is often modelled as such, yet stress variation does occur, even for simple tensile and compressive members.

3. The level of stress occurring in a material is independent of the strength of the material, this property only defining the maximum stress the material can withstand.

4. Stress may be expressed in the form of tension, compression, shear, bending and torsion, many components experiencing more than one type, thus increasing the maximum stress.

relationships or life, although the distinction between the two terms is not clear. Since the concept belongs in the field of engineering, we may suppose that the individual is stretched under a work or other load, just as a material extends or deforms when loaded.

Nevertheless, expressing strain in terms of extension without a reference point reveals little about how the material is affected. For instance, if a shroud is 30m long and stretches 25mm, the implication is very different from a 5m shroud which stretches by the same amount.

Defining strain

In order to provide a sense of relativity, **strain is expressed as the ratio of the extension to the original length.** Thus the strain for the shorter shroud would be much higher than for the longer one. It is worth mentioning that calculated strain does not relate to whether the material has failed.

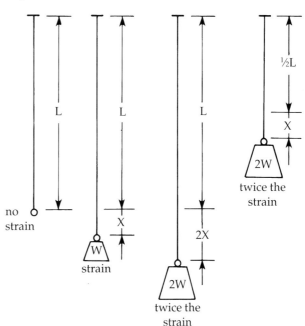

Fig 20 A doubling of the load results in a doubling of strain in the wire, regardless of its length.

For instance, it could be supposed that the 30m shroud stretches 15m, implying a strain of 0.5. Given that the shroud is of stainless steel and not of bungee elastic, it would have broken long before straining to this degree. In fact, stretch of about 100mm would bring the shroud to the point of failure.

Types of strain

Compressive strain has much the same features as tensile strain and is determined by the ratio of compression or length reduction to the original length.

Strain in shear is measured rather differently, however. In this case the *angle of shear* indicates the strain. The use of an angle is not as contrary as it seems. Consideration of the ratio of distortion under shear relative to the distance over which distortion occurs is very close to the angle of shear (if expressed in *radians*). **In the case of a propeller shaft the shear strain is expressed most simply by the ratio of the twist in the shaft to the length over which the twist is considered.**

Relationship with stress

In all cases, strain increases as the loading and stress increase. Of significance is the relationship between the two, which is a linear one. In the 1670s the British scientist Robert Hooke suggested that the extension of a spring is proportional to the load, up to a point of excessive strain.

The implication is that if a spring extends say 25mm with a suspended weight of 10N, increasing the weight to 20N produces an extension of 50mm, 30N results in 75mm extension, and so on. The ratio of the weight to the extension is constant, and when we plot the relationship we see that it is *linear*, that is, it produces a straight line.

Because strain relates *directly* to extension, we can say that strain also relates directly to loading and therefore stress. For example, doubling the stress doubles the strain.

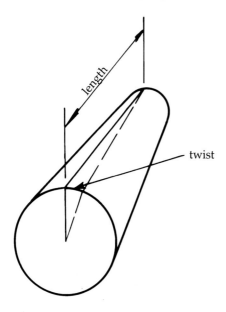

Fig 21 *A section of shaft can be imagined fixed at the far end and a torsional force applied at the near end. This produces a measurable amount of twist at the circumference of the shaft, the strain being indicated by the twist relative to the length of the section of shaft.*

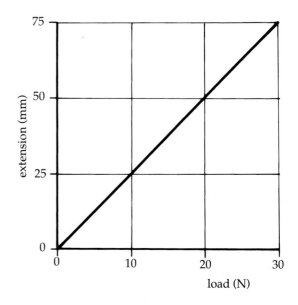

Fig 22 *Extension increases directly with load.*

In fact, the spring is strained in torsion because the weight unwinds the coils of the spring. The example of the shroud, used previously, portrays a tensile member which follows the same principle in which tension and strain are proportional to loading.

It follows that compressive strain also obeys this principle, provided buckling does not occur nor the column *barrels*. Perhaps surprisingly, the deflection of a beam under transverse loading describes the same linear relationship.

Stiffness and strength

The extent to which a beam or tensile member deflects or extends when loaded is indicative of the stiffness of the material. *Young's modulus of elasticity* (after Thomas Young, the British physicist) provides a measure of a material's stiffness: **the stiffer or more rigid the material, the higher the Young's modulus, despite the impression given that high numbers relate to high elasticity.**

The distinction between strength and stiffness is commonly not clear, just as stress and strain are confused. Given a number of lengths of wood of the same dimensions but of different species with the instruction to predict which is the strongest, most of us would bend each length across a knee. The final decision about relative strength would probably be based upon how far each bends with more or less the same pull and discomfort to the knee.

But this test, in fact, measures the comparative stiffness of each of the materials, not the strength. **Strength can only be measured by assessing the force required to break each sample.** Whilst it may be possible to wrap one sample right around the knee, this does not mean that this sample is the strongest.

Structural effectiveness

We do need to differentiate between the strength and stiffness of a material, and the strength and stiffness of the structure in which a material is used. It is quite possible that a structure comprising an assembly of components is weak and flexible even though the materials used are strong and stiff. Conversely, a strong, stiff structure can be achieved to some extent even where the materials are weak and flexible.

All structures need to be adequately strong. Components such as tillers, rudders, keels, cleats, toe straps and warps need to be so strong that breakage occurs only exceptionally. The requirement for stiffness is less certain. Low stretch in shrouds, for instance, is generally regarded as desirable because the mast falls less to leeward and the foresail better retains its shape.

Prioritizing stiffness

In the case of the shroud, a material having a high Young's modulus of elasticity would be used. Stainless steel is used in preference to nylon rope, for example. **However, increase in diameter of the stainless steel wire would also lead to a reduction of stretch and it may well be advantageous to use excessively strong wire.**

In this instance, the need for low stretch takes priority. Various other structural elements of a boat share this priority. A foredeck which is flexible may not be reassuring to work on and may give an impression of inadequate strength. Again, one solution would be to overbuild to provide sufficient stiffness, though more likely a stiffer method of construction would be employed, such as *sandwich construction* in which a *core* of lightweight material is sandwiched between two layers of high strength material such as GRP.

Low flexibility

A tiller needs to be stiff so that a boat can be steered precisely. Flexibility here, would would be like having worn steering components on a car. Like the foredeck, the

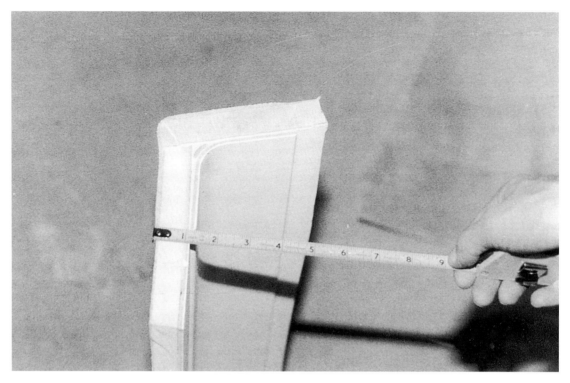

Fig 23 Example of a GRP/foam sandwich.

tiller could be designed by adopting a sandwich-type construction in the form of a box so that it possesses a high measure of stiffness.

The toe straps used on a dinghy, enabling the crew to maintain a sitting-out position, need to stretch as little as possible. Hull bottom panels need to be stiff so that distortion between frames is minimized, thus reducing disturbance to the water flow. Excessive deflection affects the performance at high speed, particularly, for planing craft, because of a seeming energy absorption.

But achieving zero deflection is an impossibility. A loading, however small, on a massively-built structure, using a material of enormous stiffness, always produces a deformation, if only a minute one. Any loading produces stress and hence strain inviolably.

Advantage of flexibility

In some instances, we seek to achieve flexibility or elasticity. A good example is an anchor warp, which should be able to stretch as it takes up a sudden load. This stretching absorbs the considerable kinetic energy that results when a wave picks up the vessel, which then snatches against the warp in extreme conditions.

The energy transferred to the warp is stored as *strain energy*, which is the product of the loading and the stretch in the warp. For a less elastic warp, the loading would be much higher for the same strain energy. **If the inelastic warp stretches half as much, it follows that the loading is twice as great, which may fail the warp or the deck cleat to which it is attached.**

Flexibility with strength

Whilst the warp is doing its stretching exercises, the bow topsides come in for a battering from wave impact. Again, designing in flexibility reduces the loading on the bow panels. Probably the best constructional solution is to omit frames and use thicker, essentially unsupported, hull panels in this area.

The trick to the successful incorporation of flexibility is to ensure that the structural configuration is such that it is able to respond to sudden loading. Unstayed masts and trees which bend to gusts are more likely to remain standing than stayed masts or trees. Staying does work very well, however, under constant wind strength and therefore load conditions.

Although it is obvious when given a moment's thought, perhaps it needs to be noted that reducing the diameter of a stay, shroud, or anchor warp just to give more flexibility would not improve strength under sudden loadings!

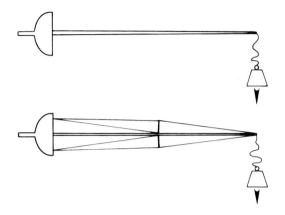

Fig 24 For the unstayed mast (top) the falling weight results in bend in the mast and a gradual absorption of the energy. The stayed mast (bottom) lacks this flexibility and is more likely to fail under a sudden load.

SUMMARY: STRUCTURAL DEFORMATION

1. Strain is defined as the extension or deformation of a structure relative to the original or some other base length, and correlates linearly with stress and therefore load, up to a limit.

2. Young's modulus of elasticity is used to measure the stiffness of a material, but its strength can only be appraised by the stress that causes failure.

3. Although adequate strength is always required of the structural elements of boats, low deflection or stretch may take precedence, leading to bulkier construction having excessive strength.

4. Flexibility enhances strength when sudden loadings are likely, such as in the case of the bow topsides which benefit from a construction employing a thick, non-stiffened skin, able to deform readily.

Chapter 2

Pursuing Case Studies

Analytical Processes

Intuition and analysis

Structural needs must be taken into account for the design of most parts of a boat. From a judgement of the likely loads and a general appreciation of the stress and strain with regard to the material to be used, a stab at the structural configuration may be taken. This implies an intuitive, semi-analytical approach arising from on-the-water experience and from a grasp of how structures and materials stand up to loading.

An analytical approach also proves invaluable to the designer. Some of the most effective structural solutions to boat design have come from engineers, especially aircraft designers who work in a closely related field which tends to keep several steps ahead of even the highly developed yacht racing scene. **Indeed, much may be borrowed from engineering structural theory, developed over a long period.**

Mathematical modelling

The process involves the construction of a *model* using engineering theory to represent the structural configuration. This kind of modelling involves a theoretical analogue and has nothing to do with building physical models. To attempt to predict the weight of a boat, using limited information, presents a non-structural example of modelling undertaken to avoid physically weighing the boat.

You may have noticed that when attempting to step off a dinghy on to a slipway or pontoon, the dinghy moves backwards, threatening to dunk you in the water. The effect is much less if the dinghy is laden or you are disembarking from a sizeable – and heavy – boat. We might propose that we measure how far the boat moves when a person of known weight walks a measured distance forward. The supposition is that the product of the person's weight and distance walked would equal the product of the boat's weight and the distance it moves. In this way we could, in principle, deduce the weight of the boat. The model is likely to be more accurate if the weight is low and the experiment is conducted on a calm day (if it works at all, that is – I haven't tried it …).

A quite different model could be constructed in which we measure the length waterline, the beam waterline and the draught of the boat, calculate the volume of a box of the same dimensions, estimate the volume occupied by the underwater part of the hull relative to the volume of the box (say 0.4), find the volume, and then the weight of water of this volume. By Archimedes' principle, the weight of the boat would equal the weight of this water.

Predictive capability

Both approaches sound complicated – analyses often are – and the solutions are likely to be only approximate. The effectiveness of the first model would need to be judged by conducting the test on several boats of known weight, perhaps building in a 'fudge factor' if the method consistently over- or under-estimates the weight. If consistency is not achievable, we need to look towards more direct measures, as is evident in the second model. In this approach the estimates of boat volume and box volume could lead to major error, though again knowledge of typical values of this factor (known as the *block coefficient*) for different boat types could produce a workable model.

Similarly, the use of engineering structural theory provides a useful starting point, if a sometimes inexact one, for the design of boat structures. Inexactitude occurs where the theory is an imperfect fit and where assumptions are made, for example, about the magnitude of the load experienced. **The quality of the prediction made by engineering theory also depends upon the complexity of the structure and its loadings.** Simple structures are simple, or at least simpler, to analyse.

SUMMARY: ANALYTICAL PROCESSES

1. Boat constructional design may be undertaken at a level that involves an intuitive appreciation of structural analysis.

2. Analysis relating to the structural design of small craft is widely based upon engineering theory.

3. The application of engineering theory to relevant structural design involves a process of constructing representative models.

4. Modelling demonstrates inexactitude where theory fits the structural situation imperfectly, especially when the latter is complex.

Rigging Size

Strength criteria

The analysis of structures subject to purely tensile stress is fairly straightforward. Stress is usually regarded as uniform across the cross-section. Although this is not strictly true, to predict the stress variation would be difficult.

As an example we can find the maximum loading which 8mm-diameter *carbon-fibre composite* rod rigging could withstand. Effectively, this is equivalent to the maximum weight which could be hung on the end of the rod. Although this is often termed its strength, the term is not to be confused with the strength of the material, known as the *ultimate tensile strength*, essentially the stress which would bring the material to the point of failure.

Supplementary Note

In order to express the ultimate tensile strength in SI units, it is necessary to specify the stress in terms of the number of newtons which would bring $1m^2$ of cross-sectional area to failure (though an area of $1mm^2$ is a much more manageable quantity).

Since a square measuring 1m by 1m, that is, 1,000mm by 1,000mm, has an area of $1,000,000mm^2$ (one million, or 10^6), a stress of $1,500N/mm^2$ would be the same as $1,500,000,000 \, N/m^2$, or $1,500 \times 10^6 \, N/m^2$. This may otherwise be expressed as $1,500,000 \, kN/m^2$ (since 1,000N is one kilonewton (1kN)), or as $1,500MN/m^2$ (since there are one million newtons in one meganewton, 1MN).

It will be seen that $1,500N/mm^2$ is equivalent to $1500MN/m^2$, that is, the two are numerically the same. Furthermore, calculation will show that $1,500MN/m^2$ is equivalent to $1.5GN/m^2$, where the GN is the giganewton, or 10^9N or one billion newtons.

The Appendix summarizes these equivalents and others.

The ultimate tensile strength of a material is derived from experiment. The object is to find the maximum tensile load which could be applied to the unit cross-sectional area of the material, such as 1mm² or 1m². It is more convenient to consider a cross-section of 1mm² and this could be represented by a square section. Thus the ultimate tensile strength of the carbon rod is assessed by the load which could be suspended from a 1mm by 1mm rod of the material.

Bearable loading

Experiment indicates that such a carbon rod could withstand about 1,500N. This is a very strong material; a very heavy person could be lifted by this sample.

Assuming a uniform stress distribution across the cross-section, it follows that its shape is unimportant. Thus a round section of the same area as a square one would have the same strength, the diameter of the round section being 1.13mm.

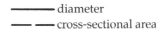

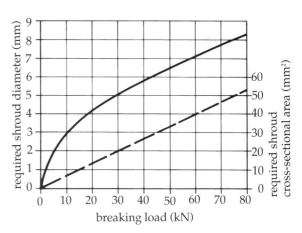

Fig 25 The required carbon-fibre composite shroud cross-sectional area and diameter for different breaking loads.

This may be scaled up for an 8mm-diameter shroud. Since its cross-sectional area would be 50.26mm² and we know that 1mm² could withstand 1,500N, then the strength of an 8mm shroud would be approximately 75,400N or 75.4kN. If we suppose the

---

Supplementary Calculation

The diameter of a shroud having a cross-sectional area of 1mm² (10^{-6}m²) is given by:

$$\text{cross-sectional area} = \frac{\pi \times (\text{diameter})^2}{4}$$

$$= 10^{-6} = \frac{\pi \times (\text{diameter})^2}{4}$$

$$= \text{diameter} = 1.13 \times 10^{-3}\text{m}$$

The shroud diameter would be 1.13mm.

For a diameter of 8mm the cross-sectional area of a single shroud may be found using the above expression, in which case:

$$\text{cross sectional area} = \frac{\pi \times (8 \times 10^{-6})^2}{4}$$

$$= 50.26 \times 10^{-6}\text{m}^2$$

Supplementary Calculation

The maximum tensile load that can be withstood by the 8mm-diameter carbon-fibre-resin composite rod shroud can be calculated given the ultimate tensile strength: 1.5GN/m² and the cross-sectional area: 50.26mm² (50.26 x 10^{-6}m²):

$$\text{tensile stress} = \frac{\text{tensile load}}{\text{cross-sectional area}}$$

$$\Rightarrow 1.5 \times 10^9 = \frac{\text{tensile load}}{50.26 \times 10^{-6}}$$

$$\Rightarrow \text{tensile load} = 75.4 \times 10^3\text{N}$$

The maximum tensile load the carbon-fibre–resin composite shroud can withstand is 75.4kN (7.5 tons).

reasonable maximum working load on the shroud is 25kN, the factor of safety implied is just over three.

Shroud stretch

Consideration of the amount of stretch in the shroud would normally be based upon working conditions, and so a load of 15kN might be assumed. However, the length of the shroud affects the elongation. Suppose the shroud is 10m long.

The other factor that affects the issue is the resistance to elongation of the material, namely Young's modulus. This is measured by the ratio of stress and strain under any loading condition within the *elastic limit*, beyond which the material deforms permanently. This relates to the ratio of loading to extension within the parameters of the cross-sectional area and the original length. Now, carbon rod is a fairly inextensible material. **The modulus of elasticity is about 200GN/m², in which case the resultant extension is 14.9mm, given a shroud length of 10m.**

In reality, it is unlikely that we would need to know the result this accurately, and therefore the stretch could be expressed as 15mm. Calculated figures should not be regarded too literally in any case. The modulus of elasticity used in the calculation could be different from that of the manufactured carbon-fibre composite rod and the quoted and measured diameters may be at variance. We also make an assumption about the working load which may not be especially realistic.

It would be more reasonable to suggest that the stretch in the shroud in strong winds would be between 15 and 20mm, with proportionally less stretch in lighter winds. Stretch of this order in a shroud seems large, particularly in relation to the mast fall-off it would permit. Given a simple rig layout and normal shroud base, the mast fall-off would be about 100mm, not a very healthy situation in terms of rig stability.

Rigging pre-tension

The position is improved by *pre-tensioning* the rig. The figure previously calculated for the sideways movement of the mast accounts for the shrouds without initial tension. **If the shrouds are tightened substantially, mast fall-off is significantly reduced.**

It may seem that pre-tensioning the rigging results in a higher working loading in the shrouds, the thinking being that wind load simply adds to the pre-tension in the shroud

---

Supplementary Calculation

The extension of the carbon rod shroud is calculated using the following data: shroud length: 10m; shroud diameter: 8mm (cross-sectional-area = 50.26 x 10^{-6}m²); Young's modulus: 200GN/m²; and load: 15kN.

By definition,

$$\text{Young's modulus of elasticity} = \frac{\text{stress}}{\text{strain}}$$

$$= \frac{\text{load}/(\text{cross-sectional area})}{\text{extension}/(\text{original length})}$$

$$\Rightarrow \quad 200 \times 10^9 = \frac{(15 \times 10^3)/(50.26 \times 10^{-6})}{\text{extension}/10}$$

$$\Rightarrow \quad \text{extension} = 1.492 \times 10^{-2}\text{m}$$

The carbon-fibre–resin composite shroud extends 14.9mm.

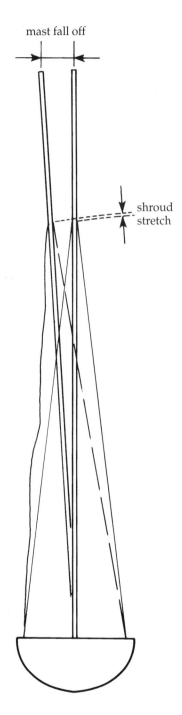

mast fall off

shroud
stretch

and compression in the mast, a concern in strong winds. However, this is not so, provided that the leeward shroud becomes slack when sailing upwind in these conditions. If slack, the leeward shroud cannot pull the mast to leeward, nor increase the tension in the windward shroud.

It is true that in lighter winds pre-tensioning may well result in residual tension in the leeward shroud and therefore increased rig loadings. But this is not of consequence because loadings in lighter winds are low anyway.

The solution generally adopted therefore is to pre-tension the shrouds up to the point where the leeward shroud remains just slack in fresh conditions. Any more and loading in the shroud is increased.

The design process

The foregoing presents an analysis of a yacht shroud and it has to be asked whether a designer actually goes through this process. Structurally speaking, the problem is a relatively trivial one that a designer or an engineer would complete quickly. At the same time, information about the properties of rigging wires and rods is readily available in catalogues such as that from Riggarna, which includes wide ranging specifications covering the tensile strength of rigging in a variety of materials, diameters and constructions. Ian Nicolson's *Boat Data Book* also provides much useful off-the-shelf information.

Certainly such information is convenient for the designer and makes his task easier. But it would be a mistake to rely totally upon such support. **Variations in design often demand an approach from first principles and the designer needs a broad understanding, certainly in order to design in an analytical style.**

Fig 26 Small shroud stretch results in a relatively large mast fall-off.

SUMMARY: RIGGING SIZE

1. The strength of a shroud, predictable by calculation, relates to but is to be contrasted with the ultimate tensile strength of the material, derived by experiment.

2. An 8mm-diameter carbon-fibre composite shroud would be expected to be able to withstand a maximum loading of about 75kN and its extension under a working load of 15kN would be about 15mm.

3. Pre-tensioning the shrouds significantly reduces mast fall-off and does not add to the loadings in the rig, provided that the leeward shrouds are just slack when sailing upwind in fresh conditions.

4. Data relating to shroud specification are readily available, but the prime requirement is a broad understanding of the principles of the structural design of small craft in order to deal with variances and new concepts.

Tiller Specification

Tiller loadings

The loading in a tiller is relatively simple. In normal use no directly compressive, tensile or torsional loads occur, except perhaps if the tiller is pushed or pulled along its length or twisted by accident, habit or frustration. The resultant stresses would be of little significance and the design of the tiller need not take into account these loadings.

An appreciation of the more significant stresses for many structures may be gauged by considering the structure to be built very lightly. In the case of an imaginary, wand-like tiller, bending is apparent as the boat is steered. **The greatest bend, producing the least radius of curvature in the tiller, occurs at the rudder end, the degree of bending decreasing towards the end held. This assumes that the tiller has a constant cross-section.**

Magnitude of loadings

The amount of bend relates to the side force on the tiller resulting from the helmsman's efforts to turn the boat or to keep it on course. At times, particularly with yachts, the force may be large, for example, when *reaching* with spinnaker set in fresh winds. Because of the yacht's heel the driving force from the sails is offset well to leeward, and so the yacht has a strong tendency to turn towards the wind. To hold the yacht on course *weather helm* must be applied.

Nevertheless, the force on the tiller can be no greater than the helmsman is physically able to apply and this provides a useful starting point. But other contingencies need to be taken into account, such as the possibility that the tiller could become tangled with a control line or a sheet, thus holding the tiller to windward, or a crew member could assist the helmsman in holding the boat on course, or a maladroit crewman could be steering.

Other possibilities of extreme loading include those of an accidental nature, such as someone's falling on the tiller from some height, though to design the tiller to withstand a 200kg person falling from the top of the mast or even from above the boom would be unrealistic. This accidental loading would subject the tiller to a vertical loading as opposed to the normal horizontal one and therefore would need to be analysed separately.

Bending moments

Loadings of this kind produce a bending moment. Looking at a typical horizontal loading, it is convenient to regard the rudder

Fig 27 The tiller for a small yacht. Note the taper and the reasonably square section.

as fixed, the helmsman then pulling or pushing sideways on the end of the tiller. **The bending moment at any point along the tiller comprises the force applied to the tiller multiplied by the distance from the force to that point.** Essentially, this is the *moment* producing bending; the greater the distance along the tiller from the force, the greater the bending moment.

The maximum bending moment occurs where the tiller is fixed to the rudder; this is most easily appreciated if the rudder is hung on the *transom* and the tiller is attached along the top of the rudder. Since the maximum bending moment indicates the greatest degree of bending, it is at this position that the tiller will break, assuming that it is of constant cross-section (parallel sided).

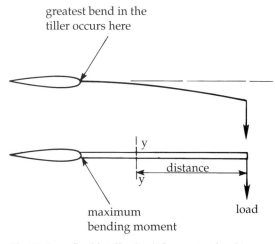

Fig 28 For a flexible tiller (top) the greatest bend is evident and this translates to the maximum bending moment (bottom). Bending moment at a section Y–Y is given by the product of the load and the distance.

Tiller stress

It is apparent that stress in the material will increase as the bending moment increases. **But the stress will also depend upon the size and the shape of the section of the tiller.** If the tiller were wand-like, stress would be correspondingly high.

Bending in the tiller results in half the tiller from the vertical neutral surface outwards being stretched and the other half being compressed. Considering a rectangular section, the degree of tensile and compressive stress which results will vary from the neutral surface outwards, the outer 'fibres' being more highly stretched or compressed than those towards the centreline.

Neutral surface

The assumption that the transition occurs along the surface which passes through the section's centroid (known as the *neutral axis*) is, strictly speaking, true only if the tiller material is equally flexible in both tension and compression. Otherwise the transitional surface shifts towards the stiffer mode. Certainly for metallic materials equal strain is realistic and the same assumption for non-metallic materials makes for a more straightforward calculation.

It follows that there would be equal stress in both tension and compression at a particular distance on either side of the neutral surface, the greatest stress occurring at the outer surface. **It is reasonable in analysing the tiller to consider the stress at one or other of the outer surfaces at the fixing with the tiller because this defines where material failure is likely to occur.**

Beam section

The expression for stress in a beam indicates increasing stress with bending moment and also with the distance from the neutral surface, since stress increases with strain. However, the size of the section has a significant and obvious effect. In general, the larger the section the less stress will result.

The size of the section, or more accurately its

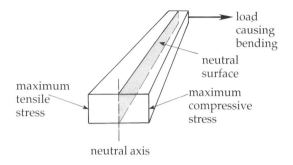

Fig 29 Given horizontal bending loads, and hence bending moment, the neutral surface is vertical and the maximum tensile and compressive stresses are indicated to be on the outer surface where the bending moment is at a maximum.

Supplementary Note

Consideration of strain implies that the neutral axis would pass through the centroid of the section, whatever the sectional shape. For example, the neutral axis for a triangular section would be perpendicular to the bending loads and one-third from the side.

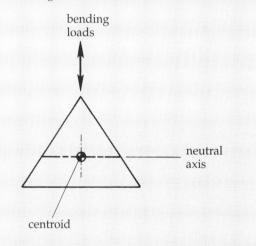

Fig 30 The neutral axis is perpendicular to the bending loads and passes through the centroid of the section. (This assumes that the material's strain characteristic is the same in both tension and compression.)

Supplementary Note

In order to support the argument that material is best placed at a distance from the neutral axis, we may suppose a tiller to be constructed from a combination of low- and high- strength material in a specific proportion, say 70:30, and these two materials to be bonded together effectively. If the cross-section of the tiller were rectangular and constant along its length, there are limitless variations in the disposition of the two materials.

We may consider four arrangements, the high-strength material being of darker shading. Although the natural choice for greatest bending strength might be section 1 or section 2, because it appears that the strong material is resisting bending, the strong material close to the neutral axis is not employed most effectively because it is not highly stressed. Sections 1 and 2 are of equal bending strength, 3 is superior and 4 the worst of all.

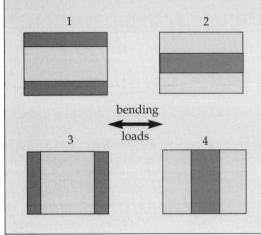

Fig 31 Strong material disposed at a distance from the neutral axis (best demonstrated by 3) lends the greatest bending strength.

resistance to bending, is expressed by the *second moment of area* of the section. The second moment of area of a floor joist measuring 50mm wide by 150mm deep is less than one of the same width by 200mm deep. Depth in the joist is much more significant than width in resisting bending from the floor loads. Similarly, for a side loading on the tiller, thickness (width) in the direction of loading (sideways) is more effective than great vertical height (depth) of the section in reducing stress.

In general, material arranged at a large distance from the neutral axis is more effective in creating bending strength than material close to it.

Calculating stress

There are a number of approaches in deciding upon the dimensions of the tiller section. Given stock sections, such as are available for aluminium and steel, one could start with a section felt to be adequate and then, given the loading and the tiller length, calculate the resultant stress. This could then be compared with the strength of the material. Alternatively, and perhaps too complex at this stage, the starting point could be the *allowable stress* in the material, from which the dimensions of the section may be derived, given the loading and the length as before.

Suppose then that the tiller is to be designed for a small yacht or powered craft and we feel that it should be able to withstand a load (pull or push)

Supplementary Note

For comparative purposes a range of possible sections for a tiller of just one material is drawn to scale, each having the same bending strength (consistency of length, material and loading is assumed). Because some sections are more effective than others there are differences in area and hence the ultimate weight of the tiller.

Regarding a solid tiller of round section as the starting point, the weight of each of the other tillers is expressed as a percentage of the round-sectioned one. It should be mentioned that no consideration is given to vertical loadings nor to practical aspects, such as holding the tiller.

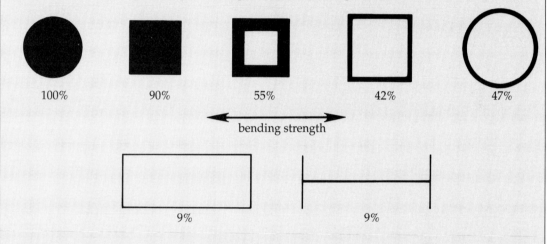

Fig 32 The representation of theoretical sections all having the same bending strength. The weight of each is expressed as a percentage of the solid round section. The benefits of width and hollowing are evident.

of 700N (about the weight of an average person) at its end. We may assume the length of the tiller to be 0.8m, from the rudder stock attachment to the point pulled or pushed. Suppose we wish to construct the tiller from solid wood so that it is straight and of constant rectangular section having a width of 40mm and depth of 30mm.

Beam theory **provides a model which predicts that the maximum stress occurring in the tiller would be 70MN/m².** Most timbers are able to withstand this level of stress, though the low-weight timbers such as balsa or western red cedar would fail if stressed to this extent.

Tapering the tiller

The level of stress would diminish with distance from the rudder stock because of the reduction of bending moment. Both stress and bending moment are related linearly to the distance from the loading, and therefore at a distance one-quarter of the length from the end held the stress would be one-quarter that at a maximum; at halfway it would be half the maximum, and so on.

This presents a means of calculating the taper of the tiller so that the stress in the tiller is more uniform along its length (and also because tapered structural components look structurally efficient). For example, **at a position 0.3m from the loading and with no change in the vertical dimension the width of the tiller could be reduced to 24.5mm for the same stress level it experiences at a maximum.**

Supplementary Calculation

The *maximum stress* occurring in the rectangular-sectioned tiller can be found, based upon the following data: end load: 700N; length: 0.8m; section dimension in line of loading: 40mm; section dimension perpendicular to loading: 30mm. For a rectangular section, the second moment of area is given by the principal dimensions of the section. The dimension in the same line as the loading increases the second moment of area significantly, and in turn the section's resistance to bending. The dimension at 90 degrees to the loading also improves resistance to bending, but to a lesser extent.

For a rectangular section,

$$\text{second moment of area} = \frac{(\text{dimension perpendicular to loading}) \times (\text{dimension in line of loading})^3}{12}$$

$$= \frac{0.030 \times 0.040^3}{12}$$

$$= 160 \times 10^{-9}\,\text{m}^4$$

For this structural configuration, essentially a *cantilever* (in which one end is 'built-in'),

Fig 33 A cantilever, one end being 'built in'.

$$\text{maximum bending moment} = \text{end load} \times \text{length}$$
$$= 700 \times 0.8$$
$$= 560\text{Nm}$$

Finally, for a beam in general,

$$\text{maximum stress} = \frac{(\text{bending moment}) \times (\text{distance from neutral axis to outer surface})}{\text{second moment of area}}$$

$$= \frac{560 \times 0.02}{160 \times 10^{-9}}$$

$$= 70 \times 10^{6}\,\text{N}/\text{m}^2$$

The maximum stress in the tiller is 70MN/m².

Supplementary Calculation

The width (that is, the dimension in the line of loading) of the section of the tiller can be found at a position 0.3m from the loading, given that the depth (the dimension perpendicular to loading) of the tiller and the other parameters remain unchanged: end loading: 700N; section depth: 30mm; stress: 70MN/m²:

$$\text{bending moment} = (\text{end load}) \times (\text{distance from load to 0.3m position})$$
$$= 700 \times 0.3$$
$$= 210\text{Nm}$$

and,

$$\text{maximum stress at 0.3m position} = \frac{(\text{bending moment}) \times (\text{distance from neutral axis to outer surface})}{(\text{second moment of area})}$$

$$\Rightarrow \qquad 70 \times 10^6 = \frac{210 \times (\text{width}/2)}{(0.03 \times (\text{width})^3)/12}$$

$$\Rightarrow \qquad \text{width} = 0.0245\text{m}$$

The required width of the tiller at a distance 0.3m from the loading is 24.5mm.

Continuing this line of thinking, it would seem that the tiller could be of zero width where the load is applied. This would not be easy to hold on to, however!

Other loadings

Consideration needs to be given to other forms of failure and, as has been mentioned already, someone's falling on the tiller is a possibility.

Supplementary Calculation

The vertical load on the end of the tiller which would result in a stress of 70MN/m², as before, may be found from the following: length: 0.8m; width: 40mm; depth: 30mm.

$$\text{second moment of area} = \frac{\text{width} \times (\text{depth})^3}{12}$$
$$= \frac{0.040 \times 0.030^3}{12}$$
$$= 90 \times 10^{-9}\text{m}^4$$

and, as before,

$$\text{maximum stress} = \frac{\left(\begin{array}{l}\text{maximum bending}\\\text{moment}\end{array}\right) \times \left(\begin{array}{l}\text{distance from neutral axis to outer}\\\text{surface}\end{array}\right)}{(\text{second moment of area})}$$

$$\Rightarrow \qquad 70 \times 10^6 = \frac{(\text{maximum bending moment}) \times 0.015}{90 \times 10^{-9}}$$

$$\Rightarrow \text{maximum bending moment} = 420\text{Nm}$$

since,

$$\text{maximum bending moment} = (\text{end load}) \times \text{length}$$
$$\Rightarrow \qquad 420 = (\text{end load}) \times 0.8$$
$$\Rightarrow \qquad \text{end load} = 525\text{N}$$

With a vertical end load to failure of 525N (118 lb) a lightweight person could sit on the tiller, but to fall on it is to be avoided.

The vertical load would be calculated as before except that the neutral surface would be horizontal rather than vertical.

Tiller flexibility

A further consideration in the design of the tiller relates to its degree of flexibility. **It could be that the tiller is strong enough but more flexible than is desirable.** Extreme spring in the tiller could result in imprecision in helming, although it could be argued that a flexible tiller helps to damp any sudden or excessive applications of helm. Nevertheless, most helmsmen would feel that a whippy tiller either is not strong enough or that the tiller seems remote from the rudder and lacks 'feel'.

The degree of flexibility may be measured in terms of the deflection at the end of the tiller when loaded. The difficulty lies in deciding how much deflection is acceptable. It is tempting to seek absolutely minimal deflection. However, the search for very low deflection in a beam such as the tiller is likely to result in an excessively large section.

Assessing flexibility

Flexibility needs to be assessed under working conditions. Determining the deflection in the tiller when loaded to failure is somewhat irrelevant. **For a working load of 75N applied horizontally, a deflection of about 7mm would result for the 40mm × 30mm section of wood having a flexural modulus of elasticity of 11GN/m².**

It may well be that a deflection of 7mm (which is 0.875 per cent of the length of the tiller) is felt to be excessive, although this would be a subjective decision based upon experience. The solution to improving stiffness is to increase the size of the section, in particular its width, thus increasing the second moment of area in the horizontal plane. Increasing the width by 10 per cent reduces deflection by 25 per cent, while a width increase of 20 per cent creates an impressive 42 per cent reduction in deflection. At the same time, the tiller becomes stronger than is necessary, the increases in width of 10 and 20 per cent indicating reductions in stress of 17 and 31 per cent, respectively, given the same loading.

Structural efficiency

Structurally speaking, the *efficiency* of the tiller would be improved by removing material which is close to the neutral surface and/or distributing additional material at a further distance from this surface. An alternative approach is to replace material close to the neutral surface with lighter weight material, the benefits of which have been

---

Supplementary Calculation

Deflection in the tiller may be found by using the following information: end load: 75N; length: 0.8m; second moment of area: 160×10^{-9} m⁴ (calculated previously); modulus of elasticity: 11GN/m². For a cantilever with a single, end load:

$$\text{deflection} = \frac{(\text{end load}) \times (\text{length})^3}{3 \times (\text{modulus of elasticity}) \times (\text{second moment of area})}$$

$$= \frac{75 \times 0.8^3}{3 \times (11 \times 10^9) \times (160 \times 10^{-9})}$$

$$= 7.27 \times 10^{-3}\text{m}$$

The resulting deflection in the tiller is 7.3mm.

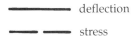

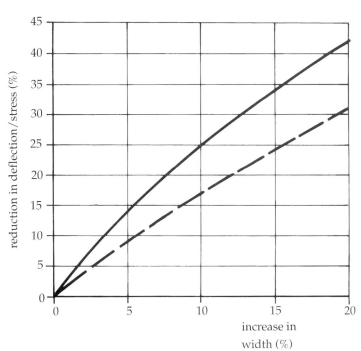

——— deflection

— — stress

reduction in deflection/stress (%)

increase in
width (%)

Fig 34 The reduction in stress and deflection are significant when the width of the tiller is increased. For a depth increase (not shown) the effect on both stress and deflection is direct. For instance, a 10 per cent increase in depth results in a 10 per cent reduction in both stress and deflection.

SUMMARY: TILLER SPECIFICATION

1. The maximum horizontal force on a tiller may be defined by the greatest force the helmsman is able to apply, although due allowance for extreme circumstances needs to be made.

2. The tiller can be modelled as a cantilever, the maximum bending moment and therefore stress occuring at the junction with the rudder head, enabling the tiller's sectional dimensions to be determined.

3. For a constant cross-section, stress in the tiller reduces with distance from the rudder end, in which case it is feasible to taper the tiller, calculated for consistent stress based upon second moment of area.

4. Even if it is strong enough, the tiller's flexibility may be unacceptable and may be corrected by increasing section width, with dramatic effect, leading to a greater strength than is deemed to be necessary.

outlined already. The former implies a hollow, box-like construction and the latter a sandwich construction.

Both have the effect of reducing weight for a given strength and stiffness or, of course, of improving strength and particularly stiffness for the same weight. The use of hollow sections is explored further with the next case study.

Boom Section

Creating a model

An example in which hollow sections prove effective is that of a sailing dinghy boom. The boom extends the *foot* of the *mainsail*. The mainsail outer corner, the clew, pulls on the outer end of the boom in the direction of the *leech* of the sail and the sail along its foot pulls upward on the boom, but to a minor extent.

Tension in the leech is created by the downward force of the *mainsheet*. Contributing to the downward force at the outer end of the boom, the *kicking strap* also produces a degree of compression in the boom and therefore thrust on the mast. A downward force on the *gooseneck* also results.

A simplified model could assume that the leech load is vertical and acts at the end of the boom; the mainsheet is downhauled from the midpoint of the boom; and the loadings produced by the kicking strap are omitted. The boom could then be analysed as a simple beam.

Fig 35 A dingy boom that uses a strut to hold down the boom. This arrangement produces different loadings in the mast and the boom compared with a kicking strap, the latter creating compression in both spans.

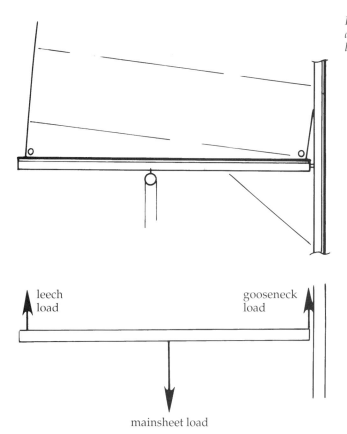

Fig 36 The actual forces on the boom (top) are represented by vertical, symmetrical loads (bottom).

leech
load

gooseneck
load

mainsheet load

Section choice

Following the principle in which we can improve efficiency by distributing material at a distance from the neutral axis, various hollow sections or an 'I' section could be utilized. Given that the loadings are vertical, the neutral surface would be horizontal; we therefore seek a deep section with a substantial wall thickness or thick flanges at top and bottom. Although an 'I' section would meet this criterion well, from the practical point of view the lower flange could prove an effective weapon for cracking skulls, so booms with more rounded contours are more appropriate for the sake of safety.

Analytical approach

To calculate the required dimensions for a hollow section given particular loadings is mathematically more involved than working from a possible section towards the loadings. For a given hollow section the second moment of area can be found and, knowing the boom length, the loadings which would produce a particular level of stress calculated. The stress may then be compared with the strength of the intended material. Similarly, the amount of bend in the boom this loading produces can be judged.

Wind loadings on the mainsail and their transfer to the boom are not easy to quantify and it is easier to start from the mainsheet loadings. The mainsail might be sheeted with a reasonably maximum pull of around 180N, which would be magnified by a *tackle*. For a tackle with a *velocity ratio* of 3, the downward loading on the boom would be 540N, neglecting friction in the system.

The bending moment reaches a maximum at the point of attachment of the mainsheet tackle, assumed to be at the midpoint of the boom. Since the downward loading at this position is assumed to be 540N, it follows that the upward loading on both the mainsail leech and the gooseneck would be 270N, the mainsheet tackle loading being shared equally between leech and gooseneck since the take-off is in the middle of the boom. **It also follows that the maximum bending moment is given by the product of one of the upward loads and the distance from one end to the middle of the boom.**

Stress and deflection

In order to calculate the stress in the boom we need to specify its length, the sectional dimensions and the constructional material. Suppose the **boom is 2.5m long and is constructed from a simple aluminium-alloy round tube of 75mm diameter and 1.5mm wall thickness, giving an internal diameter of 72mm.**

The second moment of area of a symmetrical, hollow section is found by subtracting the second moment of area of the hollow portion, assumed solid, from the second moment of area of the full section, also assumed solid. Both second moments of area are taken about the neutral axis.

The stress in the boom resulting from the 540N mainsheet take-off load is calculated to be 54.1MN/m². If the boom were constructed from wood (though the wall would be very vulnerable), or lower-strength GRP for that matter, the factor of safety implied would be insufficient. But since the *yield strength* of the aluminium alloy likely to be used for such an extrusion is about 180MN/m², a factor of safety of 3.3 is indicated. This order of factor should be adequate for extremes of loading either by enthusiastic oversheeting or large gusts.

Deflection in the boom is an important consideration and, under the load assumed which results from a mainsheet tension of 180N, the boom bends 11.4mm. This would seem to be within the realms of acceptability.

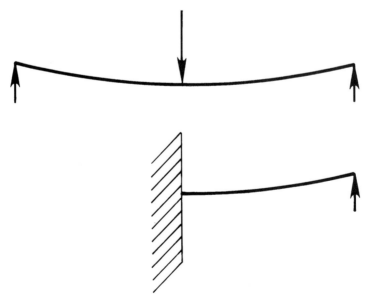

Fig 37 A simply supported beam with central point load results in the same maximum bending moment as the cantilever.

Supplementary Calculation

Maximum stress in the tubular round-sectioned boom can be derived in a similar manner to the approach used for the tiller: central loading: 540N; length of boom: 2.5m; external diameter: 75mm; internal diameter: 72mm.

$$\text{maximum bending moment} \quad = \quad \frac{(\text{central load})}{2} \times \frac{\text{length}}{2}$$

$$= \quad \frac{540}{2} \times \frac{2.5}{2}$$

$$= \quad 337.5\text{N}$$

Now, for a round section,

$$\text{second moment of area} \quad = \quad \frac{\pi \times (\text{diameter})^4}{64}$$

and for a round tube,

$$\text{second moment of area} \quad = \quad \frac{\pi \times (\text{external diameter})^4}{64} - \frac{\pi \times (\text{internal diameter})^4}{64}$$

$$= \quad \frac{\pi \times 0.075^4}{64} - \frac{\pi \times 0.072^4}{64}$$

$$= \quad 234 \times 10^{-9}\text{m}^4$$

As before,

$$\text{maximum stress} \quad = \quad \frac{(\text{maximum bending moment}) \times (\text{distance from neutral to outer surface})}{(\text{second moment of area})}$$

$$= \quad \frac{337.5 \times 0.0375}{234 \times 10^{-9}}$$

$$= \quad 54.1 \times 10^{6}\text{N}/\text{m}^2$$

The stress in the boom is 54.1MN/m².

Supplementary Calculation

The deflection in the middle of the boom can be found from the following data: central loading: 540N; length of boom: 2.5m; second moment of area: $234 \times 10^{-9}\text{m}^4$ (calculated previously); modulus of elasticity: 70GN/m².

For a simply supported, centrally loaded beam,

$$\text{deflection} \quad = \quad \frac{(\text{central load}) \times (\text{length})^3}{48 \times (\text{modulus of elasticity}) \times (\text{second moment of area})}$$

$$= \quad \frac{540 \times 2.5^3}{48 \times (70 \times 10^{9}) \times (234 \times 10^{-9})}$$

$$= \quad 11.4 \times 10^{-3}$$

The resulting deflection in the boom is 11.4mm.

Other sections

In order to give greater vertical bias to the boom, since the loadings in this plane are greater than those laterally, a deep rectangular box section could be employed, perhaps tapered towards the ends where the bending moment is low. Again, a section could be chosen and the stress then derived. For aluminium-alloy extrusions, this approach is sensible because manufacturers produce a limited range.

Often manufacturers specify the values of second moment of area for the sections extruded. These values usually are described by I_{xx} and I_{yy}, xx and yy representing the principal neutral axes. Although the calculation of second moment of area for round and rectangular sections is relatively simple, because the formulae are analytically derived and published, irregular sections, as commonly used for masts, require a first-principles, numerical approach. It is best to rely on the manufacturers' data.

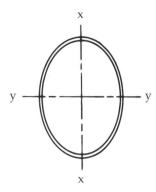

Fig 38 Neutral axes x–x and y–y.

Mast Pillar

Masting arrangements

For the most part, masts are stepped on the keel and therefore pass through the deck or coachroof; but deck-stepped, stayed masts are not uncommon. Deck-stepping simplifies the raising and lowering of the mast, facilitates the variation of *rake* while sailing and eliminates the ingress of water at this point. But it has to

---

SUMMARY: BOOM SECTION

1. A simplified model to describe the loads on a boom may be constructed by considering a central mainsheet load and vertical leech and gooseneck loads, implying a point-loaded, simply supported beam.

2. The bending moment is obtained by likening the beam to two cantilevers; and the second moment of area for a hollow section is given by the difference between the second moments of area of the solid and the hollow.

3. Adequacy of strength is most easily determined by selecting what is thought to be an appropriate boom section, calculating the load a boom of this section can withstand and revising the section choice iteratively.

4. Deflection in the boom affects performance and needs to be checked for acceptability, leading to the possibility of using deep sections, for which values of second moment of area are available from spar manufacturers.

be said that the reduced level of bracing which comes from locating the mast foot on deck is a structurally inferior arrangement to running the mast through to the keel and benefiting from the lateral support given by the deck or the coachroof.

The loadings resulting when masts are stayed tend to be high because the stays and the shrouds pull the mast downwards, resulting in considerable compression in the mast. **Typical compressive loadings approximate to the yacht's weight, without a factor of safety.** This provides a useful base for structural design. More accurate assessment of compressive loadings may be made by considering the specific loadings, and this is certainly necessary for sailing dinghies for which mast loadings are not closely related to all-up weight (assuming the crew to be excluded).

Beam or strut

Two differing solutions to supporting the deck-stepped masts of yachts present themselves. One is a heavy duty deck beam which transfers its loading via frames to the keel, offering a less obstructed interior space. The other is the provision of a *mast pillar* or strut, designed to support the full mast loading.

It is possible to use both beam and mast pillar together, but the low level of compressive flexibility of a strut compared with the relatively high flexibility of a beam, even with massive cross-section, means that the beam contributes little. It is most structurally efficient to employ a mast pillar only.

Buckling failure

It would appear sensible to employ a mast pillar of the same section as that of the mast on the grounds that compressive stress, like tensile stress, is a function of cross-sectional area. However, for compressive members of any length, failure does not occur as a result of compression as such, in which the material is crushed. Instead, failure occurs because the

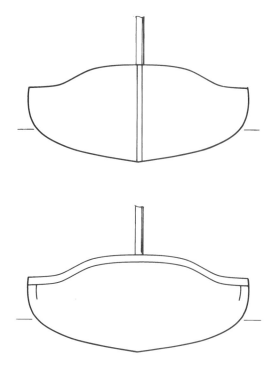

Fig 39 Mast support using a pillar (top) and a much more flexible beam (bottom).

strut buckles in much the same way that a sheet of plywood bends when you lean on one edge.

Theoretically, if the mast or strut were straight, that is, without any deviation, or the sheet of plywood flat, the compressive loading would be carried through to the support and buckling would not occur. In reality this is not achievable. The merest deviation, variation in

---

Supplementary Note

Compression failure resulting from crushing may be demonstrated by squeezing a short section of the mast in a vice. The load required to fail the sample would be high. For a small yacht mast, this would need a squeeze of perhaps 300kN (30 tons), some four or five times the loading which the mast, or mast pillar, would need to withstand.

---

material or asymmetry of end loads initiates buckling. A parallel could be drawn with the attempt to balance a ballpoint pen on its point. It ought to be possible but it is not.

Importance of stiffness

The factor which inhibits the buckling of an end-loaded strut is the resistance to deflection conferred by the section and also the stiffness of the material. Thus a strut of large section constructed from a material possessing a high Young's modulus is needed.

Interestingly, material strength is not relevant if pure compression is considered, because struts are deemed to have 'failed' when bent to a relatively small degree by the end loads. As the strut buckles further the end loads that the strut can withstand are reduced. Effectively, if a strut is subjected to an increasing load, a point will come at which the strut starts to buckle and then collapse.

Section properties

Resistance to buckling is measured by the second moment of area, as for a beam. The nature of the loading on a round strut means that it could buckle in any direction. However, if the strut is not round in section the number of directions in which it buckles is predictable. For example, lean on the end of a steel rule and it deforms in one or other of the directions in which it is thinner.

The key to defining which way buckling will occur for a strut lies in the least second moment of area. This would be determined by calculating the second moment of area about two axes at least. Mostly it is clear in which direction the least second moment of area will lie, as is the case for the steel rule, but for some sections, such as the square, this is not immediately obvious because the least second moment of area axis could be a diagonal one.

In terms of structural efficiency the round section is the clear winner. However, better than a solid section is the round tube, which has a higher ratio of second moment of area to weight than the solid section. For structural equivalence the diameter of the tube would be greater, which may be a drawback in some cases, but a considerable weight saving is effected.

Strut theory

It is evident that the greater the least second moment of area (and the larger the modulus of elasticity) the greater the load the strut can withstand. However, strut length has the opposite effect in that increasing the length reduces the potential load. Worse, **a doubling of the length results in a load capability of one-quarter.**

The relationship has been defined by the Swiss mathematician Leonhard Euler. This relationship is adapted if one or both ends of the strut are *fixed* (that is, 'built-in', as for a cantilever) since this affects the loading potential. **Euler proposed that, if one end is fixed, the constraint will have the effect of theoretically shortening the strut so that twice the load can be carried. It follows that if both ends are fixed the strut is good for four times the load.**

Practical solutions

It would seem to make sense to design the mast pillar so that it is fixed at both keel and deck head in contrast to adopting a *pin-ended* approach. In practical terms fixing the ends would involve using a substantial flange at both ends of the pillar, since there is not the

---

Supplementary Note

A 50mm diameter, 3mm walled tube has the same second moment of area, and therefore will withstand the same end loading, as a 39.8mm solid sectioned pillar of the same length and material, but the tube has only 36 per cent of the weight.

scope for sinking it either into the keel or the deck head. For a metal pillar this could involve welding a plate at top and bottom and then through-bolting.

Just how secure a fixity this would provide is worthy of some consideration. The question is whether, in the extreme, the flanges would constrain the pillar at each end so that the very ends remain in alignment. This would depend upon the thickness and the footprint of the flanges and also, significantly, on the resistance to flexing of the areas of the keel/hull and deck to which the flanges are bolted.

In order to ensure that the pillar is sensibly stronger than the mast we might take a rather pessimistic view and assume that the end fixings provide a multiplication factor of 1.5. This is higher than for the pin-ended strut and

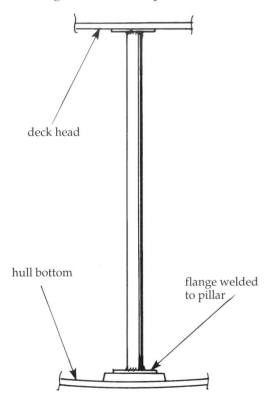

deck head

hull bottom

flange welded to pillar

Fig 40 Flanges welded to the pillar lend a measure of fixed-endedness.

considerably lower than for the perfectly fixed strut.

As an example, we could suppose a **mast pillar to be built from stainless-steel tube of 1.5mm wall thickness and flanged as described. Suppose the distance from the deck head to the keel is 1.8m and the design loading, allowing a factor of safety, is 80kN. The resultant diameter required is about 55mm.**

Propeller Shaft

Torsional stress
Like many components used on boats, the propeller shaft is subjected to several loadings. Thrust from the propeller results in compression in the shaft, while the weight of the propeller produces direct shear at the

---

SUMMARY: MAST PILLAR

1. The compressive loading in a yacht's stayed mast, either keel- or deck-stepped, is of the order of two to three times the yacht's weight and this loading is transmitted to the hull.

2. A deck-stepped mast may be supported by a mast pillar or a beam, the relatively large deflection of the latter indicating a less satisfactory solution.

3. The effectiveness of a mast pillar is defined by its resistance to buckling, a function of the second moment of area of the section and the stiffness (but not the strength) of the constructional material.

4. Fixing or partly fixing the ends of the mast pillar, for example by using end plates, has the same effect as shortening the strut, the length strongly affecting the maximum end loads the pillar can withstand.

Supplementary Calculation

The diameter of a mast pillar in round, stainless-steel tube can be found from the following data: strut length: 1.8m; strut wall thickness: 1.5mm; modulus of elasticity: 200GN/m²; mast loading under sailing conditions: 20kN. The design loading, accounting for a factor of safety of 4, would be 80kN. For a pin-ended strut, Euler suggests:

$$\text{maximum end load} = \frac{\pi^2 \times (\text{modulus of elasticity}) \times (\text{second moment of area})}{(\text{strut length})^2}$$

In order to make some allowance for the effect of the end flanges a multiplier of 1.5 may be applied, and so,

$$80 \times 10^3 = \frac{1.5 \times (\pi^2 \times (200 \times 10^9) \times (\text{second moment of area})}{1.8^2}$$

$$\Rightarrow \quad \text{second moment of area} = 87.54 \times 10^{-9} \text{m}^4$$

Now, for a round tube,

$$\text{second moment of area} = \frac{\pi \times (\text{outside diameter})^4}{64} - \frac{\pi \times (\text{inside diameter})^4}{64}$$

This is most easily solved by trial and error, particularly with a calculator having a programming capability or a computer. The target second moment of area is $87.54 \times 10^{-9}\text{m}^4$

Trial outside diameter (m)	Resultant second moment of area (m⁴)
0.050	67.2×10^{-9}
0.060	111.8×10^{-9}
0.054	85.3×10^{-9}
0.055	90.3×10^{-9}

With persistence, one can go further than this. To five significant figures, a diameter of 0.054455m is obtained, but such accuracy is not called for. Stainless-steel tube having an outside diameter of 55mm would appear to be adequate.

---

bearing and also bending, particularly if the shaft extends significantly beyond the bearing. However, the principal loading is clear cut. **As the engine rotates the propeller produces resistance to rotation leading to torsion in the shaft.**

The design of the propeller shaft, apart from the detail elements involving the end connections, relates to the shaft's section so that it will withstand the torsional stresses and, in turn, the other stresses mentioned. Torsion in the shaft produces shearing stress which increases with distance from the centre, reaching a maximum at the outer surface

Engine torque

The starting point to determine the shaft diameter is the establishment of the *torque*

Supplementary Note

Although the propeller shaft could be of square, triangular or any other section, the nature of the stress indicates that round sections are the most structurally efficient. From a practical point of view, corners on the shaft seem hazardous in terms of contact and could do serious damage to a sea-boot (and more) if the shaft were exposed in the bilge.

---

applied to the shaft by the engine. Torque provides a measure of turning effect, most easily appreciated when tightening a nut with a spanner. The product of the force applied to the spanner and the distance from the hand to the nut provides a measure of the torque.

Torque may be found at a particular engine speed if the *power* at that speed is known. This provides the means for establishing the propshaft torque. One difficulty is that we need to know the torque the engine produces at a maximum, since this would transmit the greatest torsional stress to the propeller shaft.

Diesel engines have fairly flat *torque curves* (that is, the torque does not change markedly with the engine speed) and therefore it is easy

---

Supplementary Calculation

An associated example is presented and may be likened to an engine. The torque and the power produced by a cyclist can be found by using the following data: force on pedal: 200N; pedal revs/sec: 1.33 (80rpm); crank length: 170mm.

Considering one revolution,

$$\text{pedalling speed} = \frac{\text{distance}}{\text{time}}$$

$$= \frac{2 \times \pi \times (\text{crank length})}{1/(\text{pedal revs/sec})}$$

$$= \frac{2 \times \pi \times 0.170}{1/1.33}$$

$$= 1.42\text{m/s}$$

now,

$$\text{torque} = (\text{force on pedal}) \times (\text{crank length})$$

$$= 200 \times 0.170$$

$$= 34\,\text{Nm}$$

and,

$$\text{power} = (\text{force on pedal}) \times (\text{pedalling speed})$$

$$= 200 \times 1.42$$

$$= 284\text{W}$$

The torque produced by the cyclist is 34Nm and the power 284W (0.38hp). The calculation may be simplified by expressing the formulae differently:

$$\text{power} = \text{force x (revs/sec)}$$

$$= \frac{\text{torque}}{\text{crank length}} \times \frac{2 \times \pi \times (\text{crank length})}{1/(\text{revs/sec})}$$

$$= 2 \times \pi \times \text{torque} \times \text{revs/sec}$$

---

to make a reasonable estimate. Even easier is to refer to the engine manufacturers' data sheets which often quote maximum torque.

Some allowance needs to be made for *mechanical losses* since power (specifically *brake power*) is generally quoted as *at the flywheel* and may exclude the energy losses caused by ancillaries and the transmission. Reduction gears, intended to reduce the rotational speed of the propeller so that the engine and propeller operate within their most efficient ranges, increase the torque in the shaft. A reduction ratio of two to one, for example, doubles the torque. This effect is evident to those who cycle or drive cars.

Alternatively, since the power delivered to the propeller shaft is equal to the engine's power less mechanical losses, the torque at the shaft can be found based upon its speed of rotation. Of course, another alternative is to ask the engine manufacturer.

Supplementary Calculation

The diameter of a bronze propeller shaft may be found from the following information: engine power at 50 revs/sec: 9000W; reduction ratio: 2:1; shaft shear strength: $250 MN/m^2$; factor of safety: 15.

Since,

	power	=	$2 \times \pi \times$ torque $\times$ (revs/sec)
$\Rightarrow$	9000	=	$2 \times \pi \times$ torque $\times 50$
$\Rightarrow$	torque	=	28.65 Nm

Allowing for the reduction gear,

	torque	=	28.65×2
		=	57.3 Nm

and, allowing for losses, assume that

	torque	=	50 Nm

Now, for a circular section,

$$\text{polar second moment of area (about centre)} = \frac{\pi \times (\text{diameter})^4}{32}$$

and,

$$\text{allowable stress} = \frac{(\text{material strength})}{(\text{factor of safety})}$$

$$= \frac{250 \times 10^6}{15}$$

$$= 16.7 \times 10^6 \, N/m^2$$

now,

$$\text{torsional stress} = \frac{\text{torque} \times (\text{shaft radius})}{(\text{polar second moment of area})}$$

$$\Rightarrow \quad 16.7 \times 10^6 = \frac{50 \times (\text{shaft diameter})/2}{(\pi \times (\text{shaft diameter})^4)/4}$$

$$\Rightarrow \quad \text{shaft diameter} = 24.8 \times 10^{-3} m$$

The required propeller shaft diameter is 24.8mm.

Shaft diameter

As an example, we could suppose that an engine produces 9kW (12hp) at 50 revolutions per second (3,000 rpm), at which rotational speed we could suppose maximum torque results. This calculates to be 28.65Nm. If a 2:1 reduction is used, the torque is multiplied to 57.3Nm. Allowing for losses, a **reasonable torque figure in the shaft might be 50Nm. If the shaft is to be in bronze of maximum shear (torsional) strength 250MN/m2, and a factor of safety of 15 is allowed, the required diameter would be 24.8mm.**

Polar second moment

The expression for torsional stress is similar to the formula for bending stress. Torque may be related to bending moment, the distance to the outer surface contrasted with the shaft radius, and instead of the second moment of area about the neutral axis, the *polar second moment of area* of the shaft's section is considered about the centre.

Effectively this provides a measure of the resistance of the shaft's section to rotational shear. Material further away from the centre presents greater resistance to twist and this is reflected in the expression for the polar second moment of area, likened to the beam's second moment of area. A doubling of the shaft diameter would increase the polar second moment of area by a factor of sixteen.

Principal stresses

The analysis has neglected stresses other than torsional, though a factor of safety of 15 builds confidence in making such an omission. **Compression and direct shear are trivial, but if the propeller is heavy and overhangs the bearing significantly, the resulting bending stress justifies inclusion in the analysis.**

The approach used is to combine stresses, the expression looking not unlike Pythagoras's theorem, in which the hypotenuse represents the resultant from the torque and the bending

moment vector. The resultant is described as the *equivalent torque.*

Equivalent torque may be found most satisfactorily if the *Poisson's ratio* of the material is considered. This is the ratio of the contraction across the width of a sample of the material to its elongation when stretched. The ratio for rubber is about 0.5, but most engineering materials have a value of about 0.3.

Suppose the propeller weighs 80N and its centre of gravity extends 0.1m beyond the bearing. The propeller's bending moment is therefore 8Nm. (We could also take account of the overhanging weight of the propeller shaft, but this would have minimal effect on the bending moment.) Given a propshaft torque of 50Nm, as previously, the equivalent torque is calculated to be about 51Nm. This implies that the effect of bending is to increase the torque by 1Nm (2 per cent). The large factor of safety used with the simpler analysis, in which bending was neglected, validates the omission.

For a seriously heavy propeller of 150N and a highly vulnerable overhang of 0.25m the equivalent torque is calculated as 68Nm. At this level of effective torque increase (that is, 36 per cent), the effect of the bending moment bears consideration. It would make sense to calculate the propeller shaft diameter on the basis of the equivalent torque in this case.

Shaft twist

The foregoing leads towards the ensuring of adequate strength in the propeller shaft; but some consideration also needs to be given to flexibility. While flexibility would lead to shaft *wind* as a result of the torque, and consequently would give some capability for absorbing sudden loadings such as result when the propeller is fouled, a criterion to limit shaft wind is usually applied. **The limit typically set is that the shaft should twist no more than 1 degree over a length of the shaft of twenty times its diameter under maximum torque**

Supplementary Calculation

Equivalent torque, which incorporates the bending effect of the propeller in addition to the torque produced by the engine, may be resolved given the following data: torque in shaft: 50Nm; weight of propeller: 80N; propeller overhang: 100mm; Poisson's ratio: 0.3.
The beam type can be regarded as a cantilever. Thus:

$$\text{bending moment} = (\text{weight of propeller}) \times (\text{propeller overhang})$$
$$= 80 \times 0.1$$
$$= 8\,\text{Nm}$$

now,
$$\text{equivalent torque} = \sqrt{\frac{2 \times (\text{bending moment})^2 + (\text{torque})^2}{1 + (\text{Poisson's ratio})}}$$
$$= \sqrt{\frac{(2 \times 8^2) + 50^2}{(1 + 0.3)}}$$
$$= 51.0\,\text{Nm}$$

The equivalent torque is 51.0Nm.

conditions, the factor of safety not being applied.

Twist in the shaft is also a function of the resistance of the shaft material to distortion in shear, described as the *modulus of rigidity* – not to be confused with the modulus of elasticity, which is a measure of the stiffness of a material under tension or compression (or bending). The modulus of rigidity assesses the ability of the material to resist twisting or shearing specifically.

Calculating twist

Assuming a shaft diameter of 24.8mm (found to be sufficient to keep the shear stress below a tolerable upper limit, neglecting the propeller's bending moment), the twist in the shaft is found to be 1.03 degrees over a length of 496mm (twenty times the diameter).

Although marginally over the one degree criterion, this would appear satisfactory, particularly as the adoption of a nominal

SUMMARY: PROPELLER SHAFT

1. The most significant loading in a propeller shaft results from torsion caused by the torque produced by the engine in conjunction with the propeller.

2. Engine torque relates to engine power and rotational speed, although, unlike power, torque does not vary markedly with speed and therefore maximum torque can be specified readily.

3. Torque produces shear stress in the propeller shaft, permitting the calculation of its diameter, but a more thorough approach is given by considering the principal stresses.

4. The degree of twist in the shaft relates to the modulus of rigidity of the material and should lie within a nominal 1 degree over a length twenty times the shaft diameter under maximum torque.

Supplementary Calculation

In order to find the twist in the shaft over a length twenty times its diameter, we require the following background information: shaft diameter: 24.8mm; shear stress: 6.7MN/m^2; modulus of rigidity of bronze: 37GN/m^2.

Under torsion,

$$\text{modulus of rigidity} = \frac{\text{shear stress}}{\text{shear strain}}$$

$$\Rightarrow \quad 37 \times 10^9 = \frac{16.7 \times 10^6}{\text{shear strain}}$$

$$\Rightarrow \quad \text{shear strain} = 451.4 \times 10^{-6}$$

The shear strain indicates the ratio of the amount of twist, expressed as a distance around the outer surface, relative to the shaft length over which the twist is considered. For a length equal to twenty times the shaft diameter, that is 0.496m,

$$\text{shear strain} = \frac{\text{twist}}{\text{shaft length}}$$

$$\Rightarrow \quad 451.4 \times 10^{-6} = \frac{\text{twist}}{0.496}$$

$$\Rightarrow \quad \text{twist} = 223.9 \times 10^{-6}\text{m}$$

Now, the ratio of the twist relative to the circumference of the shaft will be the same as the ratio of the angle of twist and the angle described by the circumference, that is 360 degrees.

Thus,

$$\frac{\text{twist}}{\text{circumference}} = \frac{\text{angle of twist}}{360}$$

Since
circumference = π x diameter,

$$\Rightarrow \quad \frac{223.9 \times 10^{-6}}{\pi \times 0.0248} = \frac{\text{angle of twist}}{360}$$

$$\Rightarrow \quad \text{angle of twist} = 1.03 \text{ degrees}$$

The angle of twist in the shaft is 1.03 degrees over a length twenty times the diameter.

diameter of 25mm or 25.4mm (1in) would bring the twist closer to the magic one degree and also make some concession to a moderate propeller bending moment.

Chapter 3

Appreciating Construction Materials

Material Dating

Natural materials

Early history defines different periods according to the materials then available, principally for the making of tools. Thus the Stone Age, the Bronze Age and the Iron Age, spanning a period from about 3.5 million to 2,500 years ago, provide a clue to the developing lifestyle of the human race.

Symbolic though each term might be in terms of 'breakthrough' materials, only iron appears significant as far as boat building (strictly ship building) is concerned, with the construction of iron ships in the early 1800s. As for other boat building materials, wood and the animal skins used to build the coracle belong in the Stone Age.

Because of its connotations, many owners and builders of wooden boats would object to describing wood as a Stone Age material and perhaps this era would better have been defined as the 'ready-to-hand-natural-materials age'. In terms of its use for boat building, there was a major paradigm shift from the dugout to the assembling of boats from separate pieces of timber.

The second stage is the more interesting, perhaps even more so for boat builders than historians. **Wood boats can be assembled with fastenings to hold the constituent parts together, a system often termed** *traditional wood construction.* **By contrast, modern construction makes use of resin adhesives and coatings to hold the parts of wood together**

and also to seal it. This type of construction is usually referred to as *modern wood construction.*

The plastics age

Although resins occur naturally – pine trees exude copious amounts – the resins used for modern wood construction are *synthetic*, and their development shifted wood boat building out of the Stone Age. **A new age, which could be termed the Plastics Age, was heralded in the 1930s** when *polyethylene* (trade name Polythene) was discovered by accident when the chemical reaction between ethylene and benzaldehyde was being examined at extreme pressure and elevated temperature.

Some would say that the biggest contribution of polyethylene to boat building has been in the buckets used to mix the resin for GRP boats, but the creation of polyethylene provided a kick start. The early term *fibreglass* poorly described this modern boat building material since it is a product of both synthetic resin, usually *polyester* resin, and glass-fibre reinforcement.

The resins used are *thermosets*, unlike polyethylene which is a *thermoplastic*. Resins have developed significantly since the 1940s, in particular with respect to the *epoxy* and later the *vinyl ester* resins.

Major developments in reinforcement materials have advanced the building of lighter weight boats. Of significance is carbon or *graphite* reinforcement, a seemingly even less likely material than glass.

In order to conjure up a generic term to

Fig 41 Not really Stone Age boat building – the tools look pretty current!

account for the variety of reinforcements available and also the different resins that may be used, the term *reinforced plastic* is well enough known. An alternative, because more than one material is involved, is the term *composite*, though this can be confused with the same term used to describe, in the traditional wood boat construction age, wood yachts with steel floors, used to tie together the bottom. Fibre composite, or perhaps better, *fibre–resin composite* seems apt.

Modern metallic alloys

The concept of the composite has been widely exploited in so far as metals are concerned. Pure metals are rarely used for structural purposes, the properties of the parent metal being enhanced significantly by the addition of small proportions of other metals or non-metallic elements to produce *alloys*. Steel, an alloy of iron, was developed in the middle 1800s, the aluminium alloys following later.

Further alloys – such as high strength *Duralumin* and *stainless steel* – were created in the early 1900s, followed by the gradual development of higher strength alloys. **Despite the introduction of metals such as titanium, the rise of the metals has made less impact than have the fibre-resin composites.**

As for the future, ceramic composites could become important in boat construction. But one thing is for sure: novel materials appear nowadays with greater rapidity than ever before. And who knows what boats will be made from in fifty years' time – neural-networked-grown whiskers in a modified pasta matrix, perhaps?

Wood Characteristics

The allure of wood

In the early 1960s 60 per cent of the boats exhibited at the London Boat Show were built using wood as the main construction material. Nowadays most major manu-facturers specialise in GRP. Modern wood construction remains a minor feature, but true traditional wood construction is a comparative rarity.

Despite its labour-intensive and therefore costly production, wood boats continue to be alluring and bring out the romantic in many people. With the use of epoxy resins in particular modern wood construction has fought back since the 1970s. It retains its boatyard credibility as a system of construction which is structurally efficient, and its yacht club credibility for its aesthetic and affective appeal.

Micro-structure

In term of its micro-structure, wood could be likened to a fibre–resin composite. The nature of a tree's growth is such that tube-like cells occur along the trunk, carrying sap and nutrients from the roots in order to aid growth. These cells are held together by the substances lignin and hemicellulose which are natural polymers that may be likened to the plastic matrix used to bind an engineered composite. The characteristic of the cellulose wood cells resembles the directional reinforcement in the composite.

This basic micro-structure describes all woods although variations occur. The cell structure of *hardwoods* is different from that of *softwoods*. Hardwoods are produced by broad-leaved trees that are *deciduous* if from temperate climates and *evergreen* if tropical. The evergreen *coniferous* trees with needle-like leaves produce softwoods, as example being the fir trees we decorate at Christmas. These only shed their leaves during the festive season because the trees have been cut down in their prime.

Hardwoods do tend to be harder than softwoods, but there are exceptions, examples being balsa and jelutong which are in fact

---

SUMMARY: MATERIAL DATING

1. Developments in the construction of boats have been characterized by significant changes brought about by advances in both techniques and materials.

2. Paradigms in wood boat construction have been evident with respect to the dugout; traditional wood (in which construction members are fastened together); and modern wood (involving resin adhesives).

3. The development of GRP signified a major shift in boat construction, the fibre–resin composite providing desirable structural properties; the same is true for metal alloys.

4. Advanced reinforcements, such as carbon fibre, have transformed the capabilities of composites, in particular in terms of stiffness but also as regards strength for weight.

hardwoods, despite being soft and easily damaged. The softwoods pitch pine and yew are also unrepresentatively hard. Other common characteristics of hardwoods in comparison with softwoods include higher density (and they are therefore heavier for the same volume) and darker colour. Other correlations, such as resistance to rot and the ability to bend to a tight radius, are found, but only if one is selective in the timbers chosen for comparison.

Moisture content

Wood needs to be *seasoned* before being used for boat construction. This involves the removal of the sap from the cells, a process taking naturally about six months for softwoods and a year for hardwoods, although other systems such as *kiln drying* speed up the process considerably. As a result of seasoning the density just about halves.

If wood is soaked for a long period the cells tend to fill with water, which, of course, raises its density. The weight of moisture contained in the wood, expressed as a percentage of the wood's dry weight, is known as the *moisture content*. **Under normal atmospheric conditions wood dries, or indeed absorbs moisture, to an equilibrium moisture content of about 12 per cent.** This obviously depends upon the ambient humidity. **The strength of wood improves as it dries, though it has been**

Fig 42 Samples of woods. From the top, left to right: afrormosia, agba, ash, elm, Douglas fir, iroko, jelutong, keruing, parana pine, African mahogany, Brazilian mahogany, English oak, sycamore, teak and utile. The sample, far right, is lignum vitae, a very hard wood, the lighter coloured portion being sapwood, in contrast to the darker-coloured heartwood

argued that kiln drying, which can bring the moisture content down to about 3 per cent, denatures it.

Wood movement

The tendency for wood to change its moisture content if it is submerged, or even if the weather looks like rain, is of significance for boat designers, builders and users. When dried, wood shrinks and, when soaked, it expands. For boats of traditional construction, allowance is made for the wood's expansion when wet, for example, when planking. Boats in which the planks are edge *butted* require several days after launching for the planks to *take up* and become (reasonably) leak-proof.

Joints in large sections of wood are bolted together so that swelling should improve the fit. And, just to be on the safe side, a softwood dowel, appropriately named a *stopwater*, is fitted into the joint line.

Limiting movement

Generally, traditional wood construction deforms and conforms, but such deformation may prove the undoing of modern wood construction. **Since all joints are glued, movement tends to break the glue joints.** This allows further water penetration which exacerbates the situation.

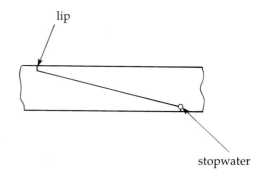

Fig 43 A lipped scarph which includes a stopwater.

Fig 44 *The laminations of the rudder are arranged so that the movement of one strip offsets that of the adjacent one, resulting in good overall stability.*

The solution is to use smaller sections of wood having different grain directions that balance each other and are restrained by the adhesive. Modern wood construction tends to consist of extensive laminates in order to build thickness and so that curves may be fabricated, such as for deck beams. Another requirement for low movement is that the surface should be fully sealed subsequently to prevent water ingress.

Differential movement

The problems associated with movement are made worse because it is not consistent in all directions, unlike a metal when it is expanded by heat. In a *tangential direction*, that is along the *annular growth rings* evident in the cross-

section of a tree trunk, movement is higher than in the *radial* direction, considered perpendicular to the rings.

Typically the movement in the tangential direction is one-and-a-half times to twice the movement radially. The standard approach to assessing movement is by considering the percentage change in dimensions both tangentially and radially for a change in atmospheric humidity from 90 to 60 per cent. **Classification rests upon the sum of the tangential and the radial percentage: 3 per cent representing a timber of low movement, 3 to 4.5 per cent medium movement and over 4.5 per cent large movement.** Clearly, the precision engineering available with metals is not relevant.

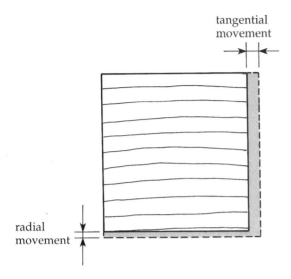

Fig 45 Tangential movement is greater than radial movement.

Plank distortion

One of the undesirable aspects of differential movement is that, depending upon the grain structure, planks may distort badly. If a plank is *plain sawn* such that the annular rings run across the width it will tend to *cup* on one face or the other depending upon whether the moisture content rises or falls. **When dried a plank tends to shrink in such a manner that** the annular rings become straighter. Conversely, if the moisture content rises, the curvature of the rings is exaggerated.

The manner of *converting* the tree to produce planks therefore affects the distortion which tends to occur in service. Planks in which the rings run parallel to the thickness suffer little distortion. Those having this grain orientation are known as *quarter-sawn* and are highly favoured in wood boat-building.

Resistance to rot

Added to the to-be-favoured list are woods which do not decay or rot easily, in which case they are described as *durable*. Generally these woods contain natural resins which inhibit attack by the fungi that encourage decay. The means of assessing a wood's durability is the *graveyard test*. Samples are buried in good soil and the time they take to decay measured.

Woods lasting less than five years are classed as *perishable*; five to ten years as *non-durable*; ten to fifteen years as *moderately durable*; fifteen to twenty years as durable and the expectation for the *very durable* is at least twenty-five years. For traditional wood construction the need to use durable timber is apparent, especially as the moisture content of the wood used to build the hull of a boat kept

---

Supplementary Note

By way of example, for a humidity change from 90 to 60 per cent, African mahogany exhibits 1.8 per cent shrinkage tangentially and 1.3 per cent radially, a total of 3.1 per cent. A 50mm square section would shrink 0.9mm along the annular rings, assumed parallel to one face, and 0.65mm in the perpendicular direction. By contrast, imported western red cedar indicates lower movement of some 0.9 and 0.5 per cent, respectively.

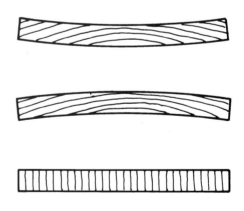

Fig 46 Reduced moisture content (top) and increased moisture content (middle) produce different plank cupping. Quarter-sawn planks (bottom) tend not to cup.

afloat through the season may well be above 30 per cent. The generally regarded limit above which decay may occur is 20 per cent.

The more durable woods tend to be those which are darker in colour and more commonly are hardwoods. Some of the lighter-coloured hardwoods, such as rock elm, are non-durable, but nevertheless bend very well and therefore may be used for parts of the boat where extreme bends are required.

Two-part adhesives

When bends are achieved by laminating the expectation is that the wood will fail rather than the glue itself or its bond to the wood. The property of being waterproof goes without saying. Another requirement, particularly for general jointing, is that the adhesive should be *gap-filling*. Most manufacturers claim that no loss of strength occurs for joint gaps even when they are somewhat greater than 1mm.

Resorcinol formaldehyde glue is the time-served, fully-waterproof, gap-filling adhesive. An alternative, but somewhat less waterproof product, is *urea formaldehyde* which does have the advantage of producing virtually transparent joint lines, which is better under varnish than the dark brown of resorcinol formaldehyde.

Also having stood the test of time are the epoxy adhesives, commonly used now for modern wood construction. **Possessing the potential for 6mm gap-filling, one may wonder whether chain-saw boat-building is feasible.** Epoxies have not stood up well in tests involving boiling samples in water, but this is not especially significant in regard to boats. **Nevertheless, performance of the adhesive in tropical conditions does introduce a small question mark as to their use.**

One-part adhesives

The adhesives described so far are used in two-part form in one way or another such that the combining of the components initiates *curing*,

---

Supplementary Note

One type of urea formaldehyde adhesive is available as a single powder. Both components are contained within the powder, the addition of water activating the crystallized acid component. Whether this is a one- or a two-part adhesive is a matter of definition. Certainly the characteristic is that of a resin adhesive.

---

in which a chemical reaction causes the adhesive to harden. This feature describes the essence of a synthetic resin adhesive, unlike natural glues such as the casein-based or the glutinous mess that results from rendering animal bone and hide. Such glues become effective as they air-dry when water evaporates from the surface. They are not waterproof.

Polyurethane adhesive is an interesting, recently introduced synthetic. It is of one- rather than two-part form and is moisture-cured, atmospheric humidity providing sufficient moisture. **Flexibility is the key difference with this adhesive, which in some circumstances provides a bonus.** However, if this flexibility causes the surface finish to be broken, local water saturation then produces movement in the wood leading to further water penetration, in a cyclical fashion. Concern has also been expressed about the capability of this adhesive when subject to long-term wet conditions, and also to stress because of the possibility of creep which causes wood fabrications to distort gradually.

Low-solvent finishes

The need to ensure that water does not penetrate the wood has been made apparent. But the minor abrasions and digs from the boat tender, other boats, quays and so on make this inconvenient for boats which lie afloat, particularly as retouching the surface finish is more difficult than is possible for dinghies kept ashore. Another problem is the finish itself.

No finish is totally waterproof. Conventional paints and varnishes are *solvent-based* and hardening occurs in part by solvent evaporation. **Because of this process, the solvent tracks through the paint or varnish, the result being a semi-porous coating through which water can pass.**

The advantage of finishes which cure in the same fashion as the resin adhesives described is that the solvent in the coating is minimized thus reducing its porosity. A goal for the manufacturers of epoxies, used increasingly as waterproofing coatings, is to achieve a resin with an ultra-low solvent content, yet a low enough viscosity so that a level of resin absorption into the wood fibres may be achieved.

Coatings which are just that provide less effective mechanical adhesion with the wood surface. Relatively minor breaks in the surface permit water to be absorbed readily, and, not being able to escape easily, cause the detachment of the surface film, possibly even in a single sheet. Early polyurethanes sometimes suffered in this way.

Sealed or porous

With modern wood construction, the principle is that the surface should be sealed with a highly waterproof synthetic material which is able to soak into the wood to a reasonable degree so that minor abrasions do not expose water-hungry fibres. It follows that all surfaces should be treated, both inside and out.

An alternative approach is needed for traditional construction, for which movement of the wood is inevitable. This demands the use of relatively porous finishes specifically now available. Some boat builders go so far as to leave the bilges unpainted.

Metallic Materials

Marine metals

For largish commercial craft and yachts where robustness is called for, steel is regarded as the unbeatable constructional material. For large yachts, aluminium alloy is the choice. For deck hardware and many other components, metals such as stainless steel and *phosphor bronze* are ubiquitous.

Alloys

It is rare that the metals used are pure. Even the lead for a ballast keel is likely to have a

---

SUMMARY: WOOD CHARACTERISTICS

1. Wood may be likened to a natural fibre–resin composite and may be classified as either a hardwood or a softwood, the distinction being botanical rather than physical.

2. The process of seasoning reduces moisture content to a typically ambient 12 per cent, improving the strength of the wood, though changes in moisture content in service result in movement, the extent varying with the wood type and the grain direction.

3. Durability varies with natural resistance to fungi, hardwoods commonly being more durable than softwoods, as measured by the time taken for samples buried in rich soil to decay.

4. Gap-filling resin adhesives are used to bond wood parts, thus restraining movement, and waterproof resins are used to seal the surfaces of boats of modern wood construction, in contrast to traditional construction that relies upon the swelling of the planks for water-tightness.

---

small percentage of antimony added so that the keel will be stronger, even though there is some loss in weight. In the same way boats are not constructed from pure iron or pure aluminium. **The strength properties of both metals are significantly enhanced by the addition to the molten base metal of relatively small proportions of other elements.**

Thus the addition to iron of carbon at a rate of about 0.2 per cent and manganese at about 0.5 per cent by weight, with one or two other minor inclusions, produces steel, termed *mild steel*, which describes its properties fairly well. Alternative descriptions are *plain* or *low-carbon steel*, which also serve adequately. Increasing the percentage of carbon, within limits, raises the strength of the steel, but leads to difficulties in welding.

Enhancing strength

Several other elements may be incorporated to produce varying properties. Very high strength steels result from the use of non-carbon alloying elements up to about 5 per cent by weight. Additions of chromium and molybdenum, for instance, produce steels two to three times stronger than mild steel, but such alloys have no place in boat construction.

Cost is a disadvantage for such exotic steels and therefore contrary to the ethos in using steel for the main construction in the first place. High strength steels are *heat treatable*, which means that they can be and are heat treated, a process involving heating followed by rapid cooling. This technique locks in the high strength by changing the structure of the metal. However, any attempt at welding it, with its associated high temperature, reduces the strength in the vicinity of the weld.

A halfway measure comes in the form of a steel developed in the USA and classified as ASTM A-242, its trade name being *Cor-Ten*. This alloy has about 5–10 per cent greater strength than mild steel and yet is easily welded. The inclusion of chromium and

copper in the alloy provides a measure of resistance to corrosion, but, while effective in the atmosphere, the improvement in corrosion resistance over that of mild steel is more marginal in sea water.

Corrosion of steel

Pure metals dull when exposed to the air, the result of the development of an oxidized surface from contact with oxygen. This layer inhibits corrosion. **The surface of steel also oxidizes, but the *ferric oxide* layer produced (the rust) is porous and tends to expand as it is formed, creating breaks in the surface.** The potential for a steel boat to corrode is one of the main disadvantages of the material.

Nevertheless, for rust to occur there is a need for moisture to be present – steel does not rust if exposed to air with a relative humidity below 60 per cent. Sea water strongly encourages corrosion. The moisture or water, and oxygen from the air or dissolved in the water, penetrate the rust layer and rusting continues unabated. The condition producing the fiercest corrosion is around the waterline, where both sea water and oxygen from the air are present.

Corrosion protection

The addition of chromium as an alloying element in steel results in a chromium oxide layer which is not self-destructive. In order

Supplementary Note

A high level of resistance to corrosion in a marine environment is given by stainless steel of type 316, having a typical composition, in addition to iron, of chromium 17 per cent; nickel 12 per cent; molybdenum 3 per cent; manganese 3 per cent; silicon 1 per cent; and carbon 0.08 per cent.

that corrosion is limited at least 11 per cent of chromium is required, and this heads towards the material's being classified as stainless steel. On cost grounds stainless steel is not practicable for boat construction, but for fittings generally the material is admirable.

The *metallizing* of steel hulls does provide a viable alternative in the battle against corrosion. In this process molten zinc is sprayed on to the heated hull surface. Even when scratched through, any rusting is inhibited because the zinc has a protective function.

Galvanic corrosion

Bimetallic or *galvanic corrosion* results when two dissimilar metals such as zinc and steel are in close proximity in an *electrolyte*, a solution which has the potential to conduct electricity, sea water providing a splendid example. A cell is formed in which the zinc is *anodic* and so goes into solution in preference to the steel. In fact, the mild steel will not rust while zinc remains near a scratch. However, the metallizing process does not negate the need for surface coatings.

Similar sacrificial protection is provided by the attachment to the hull of sacrificial anodes, which are substantial lumps of metal, usually zinc. Although particularly necessary for steel hulls, there is a need to fit such anodes irrespective of the hull material because any dissimilarity of metal, such as between the propeller shaft, the propeller and its retaining nut and split pin, will produce galvanic corrosion.

In fact, magnesium is less *noble* than zinc but tends not to be used as a sacrifice. A highly noble

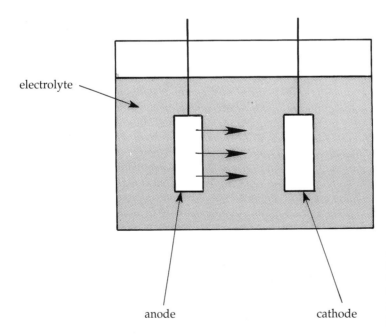

electrolyte

anode

cathode

Fig 47 A basic cell resulting in material loss from the anode, the less noble metal. Connection to the terminals emerging from the electrolyte would produce a potential difference.

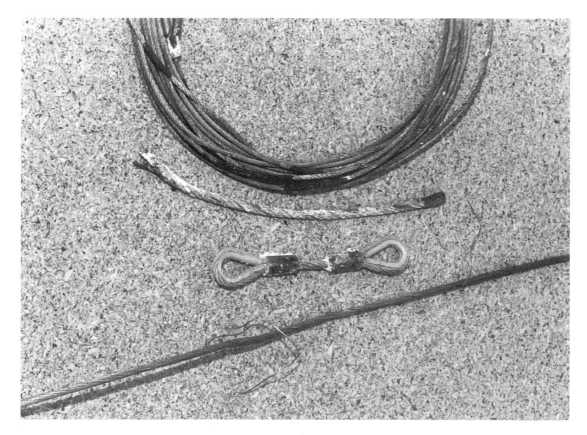

Fig 48 Items of rigging left in a wet locker have corroded because of the different metals involved.

metal indeed is titanium, increasingly used for its combination of corrosion resistance and strength for low weight, although it will still corrode under certain conditions relative to gold. Interestingly, the order of the galvanic series can be electrolyte-specific, and in sea water carbon (though not a metal, of course) is the most noble and causes corrosion in all metals.

Relative scale also comes into it. An example of brass nails holding lead sheet provides a combination that fares reasonably well when immersed because the mass of the lead is much greater than that of the brass, even though normally the lead would be the material that is sacrificed.

In a similar way bimetallic corrosion of a

Supplementary Note

The extent to which bimetallic corrosion occurs depends upon the voltage potential between the two metals. A selection are listed, in what is termed the *galvanic* (electrochemical) *series*. The further apart two metals are in the list, the greater the corrosion is likely to be. The first-listed metal is sacrificed relative to the second: zinc/aluminium/aluminium alloys/steel/cast iron/lead/brasses/copper/bronzes/stainless

sort may occur within an alloy. For example, brass, an alloy of copper and zinc, loses the anodic zinc, leaving porous and weak copper. This is known as *dezincification*.

Aluminium alloy properties

Aluminium alloys that include a relatively high proportion of copper are noted for their high strength and have a place as far as aircraft are concerned – and competition horseshoes. But copper-bearing aluminium alloys are prone to corrosion and therefore are unsuited to marine use. **In practice, only the aluminium alloys that carry magnesium-based or magnesium plus silicon-based alloying elements are used.**

Fig 49 Lots of aluminium alloy. The interior structure is to a slightly different material specification than the hull, but not so that corrosion problems are likely.

These are defined by the 5000 and the 6000 series, respectively, this numbering system being established by the Aluminum Association of America. Specific numbers refer to individual alloys. For example, 5083 aluminium alloy plate can be used for hull construction and, in order to improve its strength, may be strain-hardened, that is strained to the extent that hardening occurs, in a similar fashion to the shaping of a copper bowl by using a wooden mallet which work hardens the copper. Strain hardening is denoted by an H, so the full designatory number might be 5083-H321.

Heat treatable alloys are usually used for *extrusions* such as masts, in which the alloy in semi-molten form is pushed through a die. Subsequent heat treatment significantly elevates the strength of these alloys but welding has a *normalizing* effect in the weld area as for steel. Of course, reheat treatment is feasible. A typical specification for a mast extrusion is 6082-T6.

It is feasible to leave certain grades of

Fig 50 Welding, in this case of aluminium alloy plate, produces significant heat.

Supplementary Note

Although the American system for classifying aluminium alloys has become international, reference is sometimes made to the now-outdated British system. By way of example, 5083 is equivalent to NP8, where N symbolizes non-heat-treatable and P plate; 6082 may be compared with HE30 where H indicates that the alloy is heat-treatable and E that it is produced in extruded form.

aluminium alloy in their natural state without finishing. Although oxidation occurs, which creates powdery deposits, the metal is not affected to any significant depth, unlike steel. Nevertheless, aluminium-alloy hull plating is generally painted and this also gives the opportunity to fair the hull using fillers (normally epoxy-based) to correct any welding-induced distortion. The resulting finish can be the equal of a moulded GRP hull.

Fibre Composites

Development of materials

After an indifferent childhood, GRP has come of age. Other than the issues of biodegradability and health hazards to workers, there is confidence in the material, though some uncertainties remain. *Osmosis*, in which blisters are produced within the laminate, and the structural failure of lightweight cores where fibre–resin composite boats have been built using sandwich techniques, are two examples, although the problems related to both have been largely overcome.

In the 1950s it was speculated by the sceptics of the time that 'fibreglass' boats would not last the fifty-years' life-expectancy of a wood boat. It seems likely that they are going to be proved wrong.

Although there has been considerable development of the materials used all those years ago, glass-fibre reinforcement and polyester resin still provide the staple of the boat building industry. The same principle still applies: large numbers of fine fibres of glass are combined with liquid polyester resin which then hardens by chemical reaction.

SUMMARY: METALLIC MATERIALS

1. The strength of metals may be enhanced by the use of alloying elements; for example, mild steel is stronger than iron by the inclusion of carbon and manganese, but at the expense of corrosion resistance and weldability.

2. A particular composition of steel for hull construction – Cor-Ten – is some 10 per cent stronger than mild steel, but can be welded readily and is slightly more corrosion-resistant than mild steel, particularly in air.

3. The addition of chromium prevents steel rusting, at least 11 per cent being required for full protection, though an alternative lies in metallizing the surface with zinc, which is anodic to steel.

4. Aluminium alloys categorized by the 5000 and the 6000 series, with inclusions of magnesium and magnesium plus silicon respectively, corrode little yet provide a major improvement in strength over pure aluminium.

Bonding glass fibres

We generally think of the resulting composite as glass-fibre-reinforced polyester; but this implies that the resin is the dominant material. **We could alternatively think of the composite as resin-bonded glass fibre, which is perhaps more accurate from a structural point of view.** Obviously the two materials behave synergistically in that the final product is superior to either of the components separately.

The glass fibres used have quite different properties from the panes of glass in our windows. The processes of normal glass production result in myriad cracks in the surface. These defects are not visible without a microscope because the sides of the cracks are so close that there is no disruption to the light path. Failure is likely to be initiated under relatively low levels of stress at one of these cracks.

The process of crack-induced failure was described in Chapter 1 in the section 'Physical Stress', sub-section 'Stress concentration'.

Fibre strength

The process of drawing molten glass of an appropriate composition into filaments about a tenth of the thickness of a human hair leads to relatively defect-free and very strong fibres. The brittleness associated with window glass is not present. For instance, we could tie a single fibre into a bowline, given small enough fingers, except that contact with fingers – even tiny ones – would introduce the imperfections that would weaken it.

If the fineness of the fibres lends strength

> **Supplementary Note**
>
> Although widely known as S-glass, strictly speaking this type of glass fibre is designated R-glass fibre in the United Kingdom, with some difference in composition. The S-glass designation originated in the USA.

> **Supplementary Note**
>
> The composition of E-glass is calcium-alumina borosilicate and S-glass is silica-alumina-magnesia.

then it would seem sensible to produce ultra-fine ones. **Although some research indicates that finer is stronger, more recent study confounds this within the range of diameters common to glass fibres.** Nevertheless, very thick fibres are significantly weaker as they tend towards becoming glass rods.

Change in the composition of the glass does have an effect. The fibres commonly employed in fibre–resin composites are known as *E-glass fibres*. **For boats of a higher specification, the use of *S-glass fibres* of a different composition and drawn to about two-thirds of the diameter of E-glass provides about one-and-a-half times the strength.**

It is feasible to manufacture glass fibres which are stronger than mild steel.

Mat and rovings

Glass fibres are not used in the form in which they are produced. As fibres are drawn they are bundled together to produce strands of effectively unlimited length. **Two hundred or so continuous fibres make up a strand and these form the building blocks of *chopped***

> **Supplementary Note**
>
> An alternative approach to fibre reinforcement examines the use of whiskers of high-strength materials. Although whiskers occur naturally, laboratory-grown varieties of a short but usable length have shown strength many times that of the parent element. As yet the use of whiskers is not a commercial proposition, in part because of the time they take to grow and the bonsai-like forests needed to fabricate a usable product.

strand mat, the most widely used reinforcement material.

Strands are cut to a length of about 40mm and held together randomly by using a binder which is soluble in the resin. In appearance and structure chopped strand mat resembles the breakfast cereal 'Shredded Wheat', except that the mat is prepared in sheets two millimetres or so thick and the fibres are rather more random. The mat can be laminated layer upon layer in order to build up thickness, although commonly it is combined in alternate layers with *woven rovings*.

Woven rovings comprise fibres loosely held together to form *continuous rovings* which are then woven to produce a coarse fabric. Visually there is a similarity between woven rovings and magnified 'Shreddies'.

Glass-fibre cloth

If we look at woven rovings through a reversed telescope, we see something like the appearance of *glass-fibre cloth*, which is of very fine weave. **Cloth is different from woven rovings because the 'threads' consist of twisted rather than parallel strands.** The weave of the *yarns* is usually fairly tight and, together with being similar in weight, makes glass-fibre cloth not unlike the breakfast tablecloth.

Glass-fibre cloths have limited applications in boat building because the heavy duty lay-ups of glass necessary for boats of any size tend to include heavy duty reinforcement. Nevertheless, for performance-oriented dinghies, small catamarans and smaller yachts there may be a weight bonus. Glass-fibre cloth also *drapes* well, that is to say it forms readily around difficult contours.

Directional strength

Both glass-fibre cloth and woven rovings differ fundamentally from chopped strand mat. Because of the multidirectional arrangement of the strands, **the strength of a chopped strand**

mat laminate is more or less the same in all directions. However, both cloth and rovings have specific directional properties, well demonstrated by the table napkin test.

Pull the napkin from two adjacent corners and it does not yield readily, but a tug from opposite corners results in considerable stretch. Although starching the napkin, rather like impregnating the cloth with resin, introduces a resistance to this diagonal or bias distortion, the starch or cured resin fails readily enough, and so strength in this direction is lower than along the threadlines (the *warp* and the *weft*).

Minimizing crimp

The nature of the weaving process for fabrics results in *crimp* in the threads, yarns or rovings as they criss-cross. **This waviness means that the stability of the fabric is lower than it would be without crimp,** because stretch in the fabric occurs as the threads straighten under load, failing the matrix as they go.

Alternative weave patterns limit or avoid this disadvantage. Instead of the over-one-under-one, black-white-black-white style of the plain weave there are others, such as the satin weave which goes over-one-under-three or black-white-white-white-black, and so on. The longer the series of 'whites' the fewer the number of crimps. This results in less stretch and, it is claimed, greater strength. (Denim is over one and under two.)

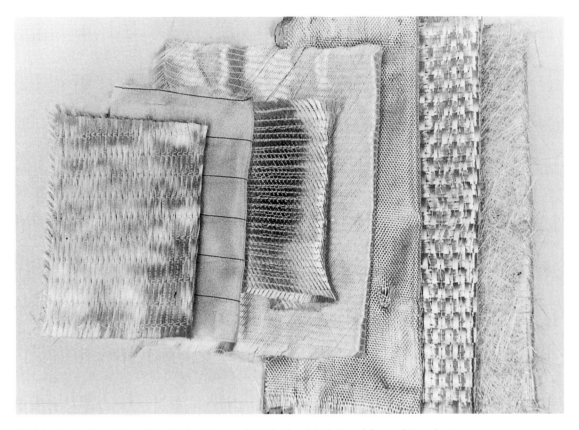

Fig 51 *A selection of glass-fibre fabrics, the sample at the far right being of chopped strand mat.*

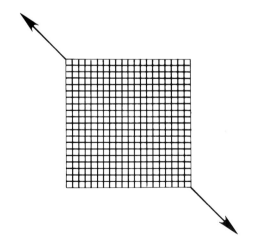

Fig 52 *Bias load on a fabric produces high stretch in this direction.*

Stitched fabrics

It is better to avoid crimp altogether. **Stitching together the rovings running in different directions holds together the fabric without the need for weaving and therefore achieves this objective with significant gains in strength and Young's modulus**. *Stitched fabrics* make possible the *wetting out* of multiple layers in one.

Supplementary Note

Reducing the number of crimps, like reducing the number of weak links in an anchor chain, may bring about only little enhancement of strength.

Fig 53 *Multi-layered, stitched glass-fibre fabric.*

Usually each layer is oriented differently; for example, along the length of the fabric, then at 45 degrees to the edge and then at 45 degrees in the other direction. Fabrics of this kind are described as *multi-axial*, in this case more specifically *tri-axial*. Not mentioned hitherto has been *unidirectional* fabric, comprising rovings in one direction only, also stitched or with light, infrequent, perpendicular yarns to hold together the rovings.

Directional orientation

The use of fabrics with such directional properties is limited to situations in which the stresses are similarly unidirectional. When the stresses are directionally predictable it is tempting to use fibres which are of higher strength than glass, oriented accordingly.

They are, however, more expensive than glass and so there also is a temptation not to use such exotic materials in situations where the fibres, or some of them, are not highly stressed. For this reason they are not available in chopped strand form.

Carbon fibre

Of the exotics carbon fibre is the most talked about. Unidirectional carbon fibre and fabrics look like their counterparts in glass, except for their glossy, burnt-out look, which stems from the fact that the base *polyacrylonitrile* fibres are heated to a sizzlingly high temperature.

Not that carbon-fibre composites are bullet-proof. A relatively minor impact can produce

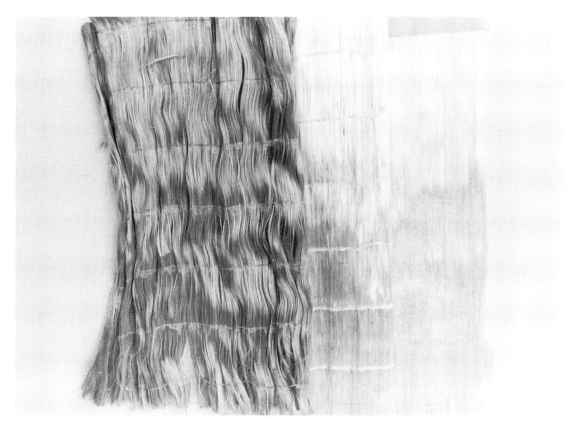

Fig 54 Unidirectional fibres. The sample on the left (which is gold-coloured) is aramid fibre.

fracture, not unlike the manner in which window glass fails. Nevertheless, carbon fibre is available in a variety of grades, but usually the tougher ones are not so strong.

Aramid fibre

Next in line in terms of street credibility is

Supplementary Note

Such is carbon fibre's reputation that all sorts of sports equipment is constructed from this material. Even bottom-of-the-range, low-cost equipment has appeared sporting graphite-coloured fabric patterns to substitute for the real thing.

aramid fibre, best known by its trade name Kevlar (usually 49). Again, its availability is in unidirectional and fabric forms.

The principal virtue of this yellowish fibre is its toughness, which is rather like that of mild steel. Woven aramid fibre really is bullet-proof – a favoured use is for protective vests.

Another virtue is that it is very strong and stiff in tension, but not, unfortunately, in compression. Indeed, this property severely limits its uses in boat building where so many structural elements are subjected to bending, which produces significant compressive stress. Its strength and low stretch under tensile loads reflect its significant use for high-performance ropes such as sheets, halyards and control lines on yachts and dinghies.

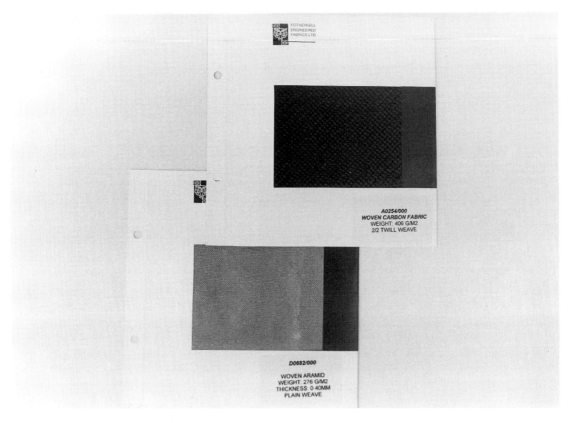

A0254/000
WOVEN CARBON FABRIC
WEIGHT: 406 G/M2
2/2 TWILL WEAVE

D0682/000

WOVEN ARAMID
WEIGHT: 276 G/M2
THICKNESS 0.40MM
PLAIN WEAVE

Fig 55 Carbon and aramid fibre fabrics.

Polyethylene fibre

In competition with aramid for such uses is the high-performance *polyethylene* fibre, known under the trade names of Dyneema and Spectra. It also provides an alternative reinforcement in cloth, possessing high impact strength. One difficulty in the use of the material is that the fibres require a special surface treatment to ensure that the resin employed adheres well, since polyethylene is renowned as a resin release surface.

Demands are also placed on the resin when polyethylene fibre is used. **This fibre is able to stretch rather more than glass fibre before failing and so the resin needs to be able to deform similarly without also failing.** Greater strength in a composite is achieved if the resin matrix is able to stretch at least as far as the fibres so that, ultimately, the fibres fail before the resin.

Strain in resins

Polyester resin, the most common one in use, is able to be strained 2 to 3 per cent to failure, which is about the same as glass fibre. By contrast, epoxy resin will elongate about 5 per cent before failure occurs. This clearly provides a reserve, particularly where higher strain fibres are used. Vinylester resin, the other main resin in use, falls between the two in terms of strain capability.

Resin types

Polyester resins may be subdivided into two types: *orthophthalic* and *isophthalic*, named after their acid-based origins. Isophthalic is the more capable resin. It will extend 0.5 percent more than orthophthalic resin and is deemed to be the more waterproof. Predictably isophthalic resin is the more expensive and therefore tends not to be used for mass-produced boats.

Vinylester resins resemble both polyester and epoxy resins. The styrene used with polyester resin is present in vinylester resin and gives the familiar styrene odour, while, chemically, vinylester is similar to epoxy. **In addition to its superior strain capability in comparison with polyester resin, vinylester has superior water resistance but is more expensive.**

Epoxy resins are more expensive still and in most respects are of correspondingly higher quality. Unlike the *catalyst* added to polyester resin to initiate curing, the *hardener* used with epoxy resin is an integral part of the reaction. While the catalyst may be varied within limits to vary the cure time, particularly as regards the ambient conditions, no such variance is feasible for epoxy resin without an adverse effect on curing.

One drawback with epoxy resin is a tendency to creep at moderately high temperatures, such as arise on a hot Mediterranean day. It is best to avoid dark-coloured, epoxy-based decks as one heads towards the equator. **Epoxies achieve the most satisfactory final cure if the laminate is subjected to elevated temperatures after the initial cure has taken place.** This improves the resin's mechanical properties and also its heat resistance.

Pre-impregnated materials

Post-cure heating sets out to raise the temperature of the epoxy to at least that likely to be met in service, thus minimizing the tendency to creep. Achieving this by using huge ovens further adds to the cost of the product. But having got this far, it makes sense to adopt a cost-no-object approach for a top-flight performance boat, and this leads to *pre-impregnated (pre-preg)* materials. Instead of applying resin to reinforcement by using a wet lay-up, the epoxy resin together with hardener is incorporated at manufacture, requiring only heat to effect a cure.

The major structural benefit of pre-pregs is that the ratio of reinforcement material to resin can be controlled carefully, ensuring maximum strength for the least weight. The major benefit in the construction process is that the pre-preg can be handled easily because it is neither wet nor sticky, and there is no great rush to get it into place before curing begins.

Sandwich construction

The use of such advanced materials goes hand-in-hand with sandwich-type constructions in which a low-density core has a layer of high-strength, fibre–resin composite laminated on each side. Common core materials are significantly thicker than the laminates, known as the *faces* (or *skins*). Each face might be just 1mm thick for a core of perhaps 12mm.

Since the core does not experience such high stresses as do the faces, *rigid foam* proves effective, although there have been cases of core failure. Such difficulties may be overcome by the use of higher density foams, since strength matches density

Foam cores

Polyvinyl chloride (PVC) foam has proved a successful core material and is available in several densities depending upon the degree to which it is blown. Most foams used are *cross-linked*. This structure provides high shear,

Supplementary Note

An ultra-reliable but consequentially high-density core comprises *core mat*, a non-fibre, lightweight mat which is impregnated with resin.

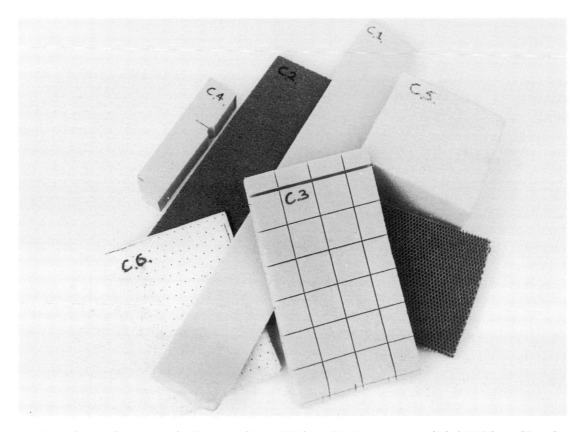

Fig 56 A selection of core materials. C1: Airex – linear PVC foam; C2: Termanto – cross-linked PVC foam; C3: as C1 – cut for easier forming; C4: Divinycell – high-density PVC foam, used instead of plywood pads in decks in the way of fittings; C5: Styrofoam – high-grade polystyrene, not strictly a core material, attached by polystyrene resin; C6: Core mat – lightweight material soaked with resin; unmarked: aramid paper honeycomb.

compressive and impact strength, but such foams tend towards brittleness and are somewhat stiff to contour to the moderate curves typical of yacht hulls. Also available are non-cross-linked *linear foams*, which are more ductile but lack the mechanical properties of the cross-linked forms.

The downside of the PVC foams is that they soften at elevated temperatures, which means that they are not suited to pre-preg materials. Polyurethane foams have better resistance to .heat but inferior mechanical properties to PVC foams at normal temperatures.

Other types of foam are available but some are too weak, some, like polystyrene, dissolve in polyester resin, and others are eminently suitable for sandwich cores for boats but are of aerospace grade and not really affordable. One type of foam of a type worth mentioning consists of tiny, hollow glass or plastic bubbles mixed with resin. This can be brushed or spread as a putty, though its density is about five times higher than that of the more conventional foams.

Balsa cores

A much used alternative to foams is *end-grain balsa*, sawn across the grain to standard core thicknesses so that resin can penetrate readily.

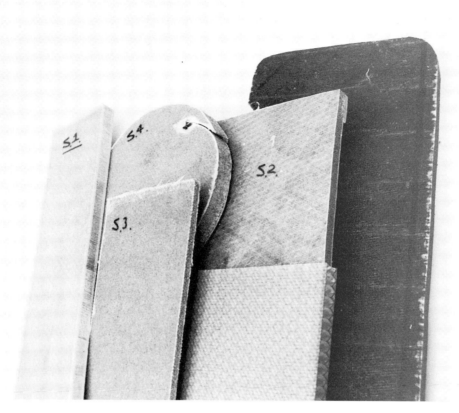

Fig 57 *A selection of sandwich panels. S1: stitched, tri-axial, glass-fibre fabric faces, balsa core; S2: bi-axial glass-fibre faces, PVC foam core – for interior furniture; S3: woven glass-fibre fabric, PVC foam core – for interior work; S4: bi-axial, glass-fibre faces, PVC foam core – for bulkheads and hull; unmarked (front): glass-fibre faced aluminium honeycomb; (rear): carbon-fibre faces, PVC core.*

This provides excellent mechanical adhesion. Panels of this core material take the form of squares of about 50mm by 50mm, held loosely together by an open-weave fabric, rather like sheets of mosaic tiles.

In this configuration the balsa conforms reasonably to typical hull curves, but its favoured application is for decks where the curvature is gentle. **End-grain balsa has superior mechanical properties in terms of shear resistance and adhesion to the faces, but any water that leaks into the core may prove disastrous because of this material's absorbancy.**

Honeycomb cores

For lightweight, specialist applications *honeycomb cores* are available in a variety of

---

Supplementary Note

Filling agents and putties can be created by mixing resin with glass *microspheres* or plastic *micro-balloons*. The density of these bubbles is low, particularly in the case of microspheres which float readily in the air, presenting a potential health hazard unless a mask is worn.

Supplementary Note

Foams are essentially monocellular, which implies no interconnection between cells and therefore little water take-up. But balsa fairly readily becomes waterlogged, a circumstance which raises some doubt about this material, despite its reliability in other respects.

Supplementary Note

One recent, interesting development is a core comprising glass strands which run from one face to the other perpendicularly. Each face comprises bi-axial woven fabric and, when wetted out, the faces and core strands are impregnated with resin. The maximum available thickness of this three-dimensional glass – known as *Parabeam* – is 9.5mm with 0.35mm faces.

materials, such as aluminium, fibre–resin composite or resin-impregnated paper. Such cores may be difficult to form, but they are notable for their use in constructing lightweight bulkheads and cabin soles. The faces may be of fibre–resin composite or aluminium alloy. The boards are premanufactured, which aids consistency and quality.

Guaranteed to lighten the boat, the use of honeycomb panels is also going to lighten the bank balance. But then, if you cannot afford honeycomb you probably cannot afford really high performance.

Mechanical Properties

Strength and stiffness

For many materials it usually happens that there is a correlation between strength and stiffness. This is to say that a strong sample will usually be stiff, but it need not be so. For example, nylon is flexible but strong and uncooked spaghetti is reasonably stiff but weak.

For different varieties of wood there is a reasonable correlation between strength, stiffness and density. If this relationship were invariable then one type of wood of twice the

---

SUMMARY: FIBRE COMPOSITES

1. The staple material used in the current boat-building industry is glass-fibre-reinforced polyester resin, the resin bonding the reinforcement; this is available in a variety of forms, both directionally- and randomly-oriented.

2. Laminate strength and stiffness are achieved by relevant fibre orientation with minimal crimp, stitched fabrics being notable, but significant improvements are given by the so-called exotic reinforcement materials.

3. A high level of deformation in a laminate before failure is sought and ideally the polymer's strain capability should exceed that of the reinforcement, epoxy resin being exceptional in this respect.

4. High-performance constructions are achieved by using a choice of epoxy and vinyl ester resins, pre-pregs, and sandwich constructions employing cross-linked foams and honeycombs.

---

density as another could be expected to be twice as strong and twice as stiff.

Several metals tend to follow the same pattern. But variance occurs where alloying elements are used. In this way the strength may be increased three, four or five times over that of the parent metal. **However, as a rule the stiffness of the metals is changed to a smaller degree despite the transformation in strength.**

Comparing materials

Suppose we compare two masts made from round tube. One is extruded from a typically used, heat-treatable aluminium alloy such as 6061, which is quite strong, while the other is the kind of low grade, low cost, mundane alloy easily obtained from a local steel and aluminium supplier. Under normal sailing conditions both masts perform similarly. Each bends to much the same amount, since the stiffness of the alloys is similar. The only real difference is felt in extreme conditions, perhaps in very strong winds when crashing down a wave.

Both masts are bent to a greater degree as a result of the increased loadings, but when safely back in harbour the mast of low grade alloy does not return fully to its original straightness. The material has exceeded its elastic limit. Thus the search is for both high strength as well as impressive stiffness in mast materials.

Flexural characteristics

The search does not stop there, for it is necessary to examine the properties of materials more closely yet. Traditionally, engineering has focused upon tensile strength with no account being taken of the strength in compression. This is not unreasonable, however, because the strength of metals is more or less equal in both tension and compression. And, because bending is a composite of these two stresses, the bending or

flexural strength will not be wildly different.

This consistency does not apply to wood and reinforced plastics. The tensile and compressive strengths of these materials may vary widely. **Flexural strength is significant because many structural components on boats experience bending.**

The flexural strength of a material may be obtained from published data or experimentally by bending a sample until it fails. Given the load, load conditions, beam length and cross-sectional dimensions, the stress producing failure may be calculated. Failure could be either in tension or compression. Whichever, the stress that produces failure defines the flexural strength of the material.

Material stiffness, assessed by the modulus of elasticity, is also of importance, as has been indicated already. Again, the flexural modulus of elasticity is of particular interest, except for metals which, not surprisingly, possess the same modulus in both tension and compression.

Directional properties

Unless forged to impart directional properties, the strength and the stiffness of metals vary minimally no matter in which direction the properties are tested. **Having the same properties in all directions, metals are described as *isotropic.***

For materials such as wood and reinforced plastics their properties vary depending upon whether they are tested along the grain or in the line of the reinforcement or at an angle.

These directional materials are described as *anisotropic* or *orthotropic*. For example, wood is about thirty times stronger along than across the grain, the relative strengths of unidirectional roving being even more extreme. Further examples of the directional behaviour of reinforcements were discussed earlier.

Supplementary Note

Although bending is rife, the design concern extends beyond flexural strength. This property is of greatest significance for wood and single-skin, fibre-composite laminates, perhaps, but the manner in which the exotic fibres are utilized is largely with direction in mind; for example, in tension or compression in sandwich constructions. Metal components are commonly stressed in bending, tension and in other ways, but their properties vary little with manner of stressing.

The following table of structural properties attempts to reflect these points. The values given are approximate in order to give a flavour. This is not to say that the advanced composites, in particular, vary in their properties, but rather that there are wide-ranging specifications. The following are intended as indicators only. Different values will be found elsewhere; it is best to contact the suppliers or manufacturers for specific advice.

	Flexural strength (MN/m^2)	Flexural modulus (GN/m^2)
Woods		
Western red cedar	65	7.0
Sitka spruce	75	10.5
Agba	80	7.5
African mahogany	85	9.0
Douglas fir	95	12.5
Teak	105	10.0
Metals		
Pure aluminium	80	70
Aluminium alloy (e.g., 5083 or 6061	310	70
Mild steel	460	210
Cor-ten	480	210
Stainles steel type 316	620	210
Titanium	800	120
Composites		
E-glass chopped strand mat + polyester	120	6
E-glass chopped strand mat/woven roving + polyester	180	8

Directional Composites	Ultimate tensile strength (MN/m^2)	Ultimate compressive strength (MN/m^2)	Tensile modulus (GN/m^2)	Compressive modulus (GN/m^2)
E-glass fabric + epoxy	400	440	23	24
E-glass unidirectional + epoxy	1,000	600	45	45
Aramid fibre fabric + epoxy	510	170	30	28
Carbon fibre fabric + epoxy	670	590	60	60
Carbon fibre unidirectional + epoxy	1,500	1,100	135	110

Some properties are peculiar to particular materials or design situations, depending upon vulnerability. For example, *impact strength* is especially pertinent to wood and reinforced plastics, *shear strength* to foam-sandwich cores and to metals subject to torsional stress, while yield strength is also relevant to metals.

Yield strength

It might be thought that yield strength is the same as ultimate tensile strength. However, the characteristic of steel, in particular, is to reach a value of stress at which the metal stretches permanently to a small degree (this value of stress being the yield strength) but then goes on, somewhat remarkably, to withstand a higher stress to failure (the ultimate tensile strength). For a low carbon steel, this may be as much as 50 per cent greater, the difference being much less for higher strength steels.

For most alloys, notably aluminium alloy but also the heat-treatable steels, the yield point cannot be identified readily, elastic merging with plastic behaviour. **In order to provide a criterion for design, the yield strength of such materials is usually based upon the stress producing a permanent set of 0.1 per cent of the original length.** This measure of strength is known as *proof stress*. The same criterion may be applied to reinforced plastics, which have a tendency to permanent deformation when loaded.

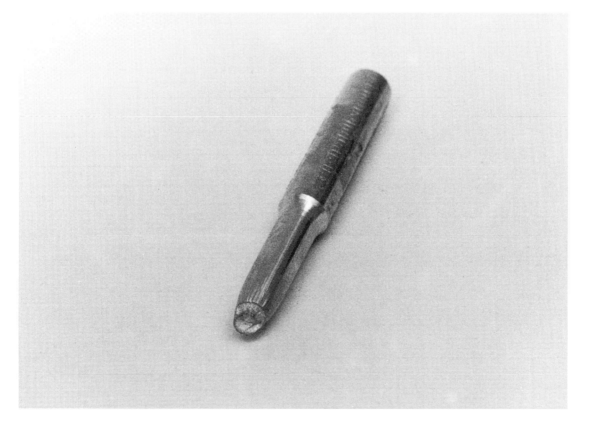

Fig 58 The aluminium sample necks as it yields under tension, the reduced cross-section resulting in prompt failure.

Specific properties

Although structural analysis often rests upon a value of ultimate or yield strength or proof stress, design decisions are not necessarily based upon a the-stronger-the-better approach. **Weight is an important consideration for many components, and so material strength for weight is more significant than just strength alone.**

This is measured by the *specific strength* of the material, defined by the ratio of the material's strength to its density. The particular manner in which a material is stressed when loaded would define the particular specific strength characteristic, such as the specific tensile strength or the specific flexural strength.

Similarly, *specific stiffness*, frequently referred to as the *specific modulus*, expresses the ratio of a material's modulus of elasticity to its density. The specific modulus can be applied flexurally or to some other type of strain as is the case for specific strength.

Under bending

In making choices about structural materials the specific strength and the specific stiffness are very compelling. For tensile and compressive loadings the two measures of structural properties provide the last word. **But in the case of bending it is not necessarily true to say that the material with the highest specific properties will produce the most structurally-efficient beam.**

For equal weight, a beam of low density material has a larger cross-section than one of high density. The effect of the larger cross-section (which is best arranged so that the depth is increased) markedly increases the beam's strength and stiffness.

Thus low density materials are to be

Supplementary Note

A comparison of different materials used to construct a solid beam is illuminating. The depth of beam in each material is varied for equivalent bending strength, and the weight of the beam calculated and expressed as a percentage of the heaviest beam, the mild steel sample. Similarly, the required weight of each sample, again as a percentage of the mild steel sample, is calculated for equivalent stiffness. The samples are listed in order of density.

The lower the number, the more structurally efficient the beam. The fibre–resin composites, notably the exotics, appear unimpressive on account of their high density relative to the woods. A carbon-fibre–resin composite would not be used in this way, the preference being to create sandwich constructions that place the faces in tension or compression and not bending.

Material	Weight for equivalent strength (% of mild steel)	Weight for equivalent stiffness (% of mild steel)
Mild steel	100	100
Aluminium alloy	41	49
Chopped strand mat in resin	38	71
Woven rovings in resin	33	61
Aramid fibre fabric in resin	27	33
Carbon fibre in resin	17	30
African mahogany	15	19
Spruce	14	9
Western red cedar	13	15

favoured for beams of uniform, solid construction. This reminds us that strong and stiff structures can be achieved by using relatively weak and flexible materials, and that strong and stiff materials do not guarantee strong and stiff structures – but they do help!

Supplementary Note

Sandwich constructions follow the route of achieving low overall density but with the added advantage of combining materials having different properties such that a structure superior to a low-density wood results.

Fatigue syndrome

In designing a structure, whether a hull, a rudder, a cooking stove bracket or the clip to hold up a pair of waterproof trousers, consideration needs to be given to the structural properties of the materials to be used for the parts. Although various figures are presented, for example, of strength, these tend to relate to new, out of the box, previously unloaded samples.

No account has been taken of the way in which the material properties, notably the strength, change in service. In particular, it is found that materials become 'tired', that is, suffer from *fatigue*.

This process may be likened to the way in which people become fatigued with exercise. Bench press a bar loaded with weights lots of times and we reach a point when the only way we could continue would be if the weight were reduced. In order to measure our fatigue strength we could load the bar and count the number of times we could press the weights, effectively to the point of collapse. We then could alter the weight and repeat the exercise (with adequate rest between exercises). The results could be plotted, displaying weight against the number of repetitions.

Supplementary Note

The fatiguing process starts with the initiation of tiny cracks which then extend with further fluctuations of stress. For metals, stresses which close the crack are not damaging in the way that stresses which open the crack are. But some materials do suffer as a result of compressive stresses.

Stress reversal

Similarly, if a material experiences a number of consistent loading changes, producing *stress reversals*, eventually the material fails, unless the stress were at a sufficiently low level. Returning to the bench pressing example, we might say that if we reduced the weight to a particular level we could continue to press the weight indefinitely. Of course, this is not true, but there is a feeling when bench pressing that, below a threshold weight, it is very easy.

It is found that mild steel is able to withstand a stress of about half its ultimate tensile strength for an unlimited number of cycles. The testing of mild steel indicates that it can be stressed to about $500MN/m^2$ once, that

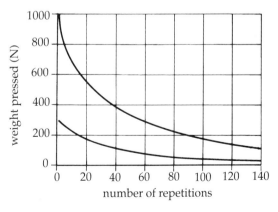

Fig 59 A representation of the supposed weight that can be bench-pressed by a strong and also by a weak person for a particular number of repetitions (constructed without experimental data!)

is, this is its ultimate tensile strength. Subject another sample to a cyclical stress of $400MN/m^2$ and it will last about a hundred cycles. Stress a further sample to $350MN/m^2$ and it will be good for about a thousand cycles.

Bring the stress down to $300MN/m^2$ and it will withstand some 25,000 cycles.

Endurance limit

At a stress level of about $260MN/m^2$ the mild steel sample will last a million and upwards cycles. Provided that the allowable stress in the steel is less than the so-called *endurance limit* or *fatigue limit* of $260MN/m^2$ the material will never fail, regardless of the number of cycles.

Components subject to vibration or high-speed reciprocation, as in an engine, produce multi-million stress reversals in a remarkably short period. Ensuring that the stress remains below the endurance limit is critical in the design.

For such components it would seem preferable to use high-strength materials so that there is a greater reserve. A high-strength chromium molybdenum steel has two to three times the ultimate tensile strength of mild steel, and the tolerable stress, even for a very large number of cycles, remains above that of mild steel.

But the reduction in tolerable stress is greater for the higher strength material, which also has a much less well-defined endurance limit. The maximum stress which chromium molybdenum steel can withstand for 100

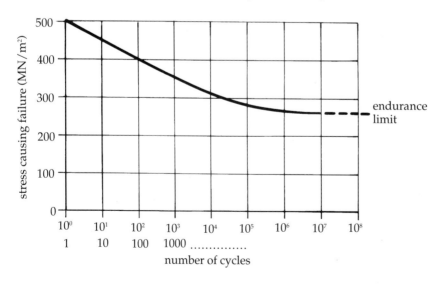

Fig 60 The stress causing failure is shown for mild steel against number of cycles. At a stress level below the endurance limit of about $60MN/m^2$ the material will not fail regardless of the number of cycles. The scale shown is logarithmic.

Supplementary Note

Although fatigue-testing is primarily concerned with stress reversals within the elastic limit, metals in particular can be examined beyond the yield point. This implies permanent deformation such as occurs when a sample of stainless steel, for example, is bent so that it takes a permanent set and is then bent in the opposite direction. This kind of low-cycle fatigue is very demanding and the materials which are resistant to failure when bent to and fro, like lead, usually perform well in terms of high-cycle fatigue. Rest assured that your lead ballast keel will not break because of fatigue.

million cycles is about $700MN/m^2$, some $50MN/m^2$ less than for a million cycles.

High-strength aluminium alloys demonstrate this characteristic to a much greater degree such that there is no actual endurance limit. **The implication is that if a very large number of stress reversals are likely to be experienced by an aluminium-alloy component, the stress level at a maximum needs to be relatively low.**

Fatigue resistance

Similarly, fibre–resin composites display no real endurance limit. Higher fibre fractions result in higher fatigue strength because failure occurs essentially within the polymer matrix, in the vicinity of the bond to the fibres. Interestingly, fibres of high modulus of elasticity, such as carbon fibre, subject the matrix to less stress and therefore are less prone to fatigue.

Although wood has a reputation for being fatigue-resistant, it similarly displays no endurance limit. Realisically, the kind of alternating loads a hull is subjected to over, say thirty years, implies that the design should be on the basis of a flexural strength which is half its initial value. **It follows that, for this period of typical use, wood is likely to fatigue no more than steel.**

Design stress

It would seem that structural design can take account of the fatigue characteristics of the materials of construction by using a somewhat arbitrary factor of safety related to the material's yield or ultimate strength. For example, a factor of safety of about two applied to the ultimate tensile strength of mild steel (about $500MN/m^2$) would ensure that design stress does not exceed the strength of the material at the endurance limit (about $260MN/m^2$).

However, a more accurate model is obtained by considering the number of stress reversals to which the material is likely to be subjected and then to design on the basis of the relevant

Supplementary Note

The S-N curves for different materials may be contrasted. It is to be noted that where the curve for a particular material levels out, as for mild steel, the stress indicated is the least strength the material possesses, regardless of the number of stress reversals. Greater caution is needed, in terms of structural design, where the slope runs down and shows no sign of levelling.

The scale for the N-axis is expressed logarithmically so that the strength values at lower numbers of cycles may be better appreciated. But the effect is to exaggerate the slope at larger numbers. Furthermore, logarithmic scales give the appearance that the larger numbers are larger than in actuality. Some perspective is given by the theoretical calculation that the totality of all particles in the universe amounts to 10^{80}! In other words, the logarithmic scale makes a material look more prone to fatigue than it is in reality.

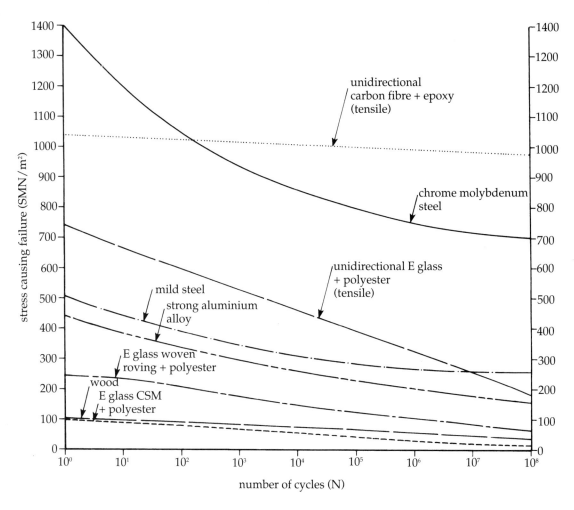

Fig 61 The fatigue characteristics of a number of materials.

Supplementary Note

Fibre–resin composites tend to display two-stage fatigue failure. Initially, and at relatively low stress values, the bond between fibre and resin starts to break down, the resin showing signs of *micro-cracking*. For conventional composites, this occurs at around a quarter of the stress to failure. To make matters worse, composites become weaker when wet, water absorption, like fatigue, being time-dependent.

For design purposes the working stress level this implies needs to be low, probably less than $5MN/m^2$ for a chopped strand mat–reinforced polyester structure. If allowance were also made for some of the design unknowns, by way of a factor of safety, the construction might well need to be substantial in order to keep the stress level down to perhaps one or $2MN/m^2$. This is lower than the stress required to cause failure in a wood sample along the grain, as in a short-grain situation.

fatigue strength. Data relating to fatigue strength are not so readily available as ultimate strength values but do provide a more sound basis for the designer to work from.

SUMMARY: MECHANICAL PROPERTIES

1. For a number of materials, strength, stiffness and density correlate reasonably, but with metal alloys strength can be enhanced over that of the base metal with little change in stiffness or density.

2. The structural design of boats places emphasis on the flexural and directional strength of materials, with due consideration being given to the yield strength or proof stress.

3. Specific strength and stiffness are significant in terms of structural efficiency, although in the case of rectangular-sectioned, solid beams, low-density materials prove the most structurally efficient.

4. For long life, design is better based upon fatigue strength rather than ultimate tensile strength, adequate reserve being allowed for materials demonstrating no obvious endurance limit.

Chapter 4

Constructing Small Craft

Construction Theory

Construction types

Of the many systems of hull construction available most fall within one of three types or may be described by some combination of the three. It is convenient to consider *monocoque* (single, complete shell), *framed* (framework covered with a skin) and *space-framed* (interlinked network of tensile and compressive members), each being a 'pure' form of construction providing a basis for analysis.

Monocoque

Stress continuity

This form of construction is characterized by an unsupported shell, an egg being a good example of the type. The classic party trick in which participants are challenged to break a hen's egg when it is squeezed evenly between thumb and finger produces no winners. As a structure, the egg is successful in terms of its strength relative to its weight.

Provided that the shell remains intact, the forces imposed, in theory, are distributed evenly throughout it. Similarly, any corners or sudden changes in shape will lead to failure at a discontinuity; this type of construction is unsuited for point loadings. (There is usually one clown at the party who breaks the egg by using his fingertips or nails.)

Gentle curvature

At first sight it would seem that the monocoque principle is appropriate for hull construction. Water provides a uniformly distributed load and the hull is usually curved, except, of course, in the case of *chined* craft. The join between topsides and deck does produce a discontinuity although there have been attempts to avoid this.

A good example was the appropriately named *Sea Egg*, notorious because of its extremely small size and the long, single-handed voyages which John Rider made in the boat. However, it has to be said that the strong curve between hull and deck did prevent tripping when the boat was heeled over, in that the round allowed the boat to slide down waves. This hydrodynamic consideration is more significant probably than the structural benefit.

Inevitably the monocoque's structural integrity is lost in way of cockpits and coachroofs where various corners and discontinuities occur. **Gentle, transitional curves and built-in roundedness support the monocoque theory.** The rounded buoyancy tanks fitted to some racing dinghies, popular at one time, required little in the way of additional support because the strong curve was so effective.

Panel buckling

But there is a flaw in the use of curves: they are prone to buckling. Suppose we consider the design of an after deck made from thin plywood which must withstand the weight of the helmsman sitting on it. Suppose too that no deck beams are fitted (although this is not entirely realistic) and that the afterdeck can be either flat, convex or concave. If we surveyed the dinghy-sailing public about which would be the strongest, the vote would probably be for the convex deck.

Yet, this form does not work as well as expected. The convex afterdeck bulges either side of the gluteus maximi and, because of the extreme bend in the plywood, failure is embarrassingly and painfully imminent.

Shell thickness

The foregoing is not meant to condemn convex curves. The Romans were very strong on arches. Long, straight spans using great lumps of stone were bad news because the stone cracked on the underside where it was under tension, but, with an arch, the interlocking nature of each of the stones is such that the material is under compression only, and this is stone's forte.

Comparison between the stone arch and the afterdeck reveals a difference, namely in thickness. Thin plywood in large panels is unsuited to being compressed on edge, and this is the cause of its buckling. A better solution, given the constraints, is a flat or concave deck such that the plywood is under tension, and so behaves basically as a catenary, like the anchor chain described earlier.

Practical considerations

So, monocoque rules okay, provided, in the case of the hull, the shell is sufficiently thick. The use of steel is seen not to align with this thinking because, for an acceptable hull weight, the steel plate needs to be thin. The process of laminating GRP boats would appear to lend itself to a monocoque type construction because of the structural continuity of the material and the ability to vary thickness gradually. But the result is unsatisfactory, the

consequent hull being very flexible and heavy.

The monocoque principles are better effected when thick-cored sandwich construction is used. Even so, those areas of the hull that are reasonably flat subject the hull to local bending. Point loadings, such as from rigging attachments or engine beds, also weigh against the purity of this approach for the construction.

Framed

Skeletal strength

Without doubt, this is the most common approach to boat construction. Both the coracle and canvas canoe demonstrate the principle at its most extreme – **a skeleton provides the strength of the structure** and the animal skins or canvas serve as the means of keeping out the water.

Another form of framed structure is seen in craft of traditional wood construction which use a *backbone* and beam shelves linked by *frames* or *timbers* to form the skeleton of the hull. This form of construction does rely upon the *planking* to complement the framework structurally, in belt and braces style. In this respect, the construction is different from the coracle or canvas canoe.

Framework characteristics

In terms of the bending of the hull from rig or wave loadings, the typical framed structure is not the most efficient. **The framework tends to lozenge just as a garden shed door drops on its hinges if no braces are fitted.** For a boat of traditional construction, the *caulking* between the planks limits their sliding one against the other and this restricts the lozenging effect.

Modern wood construction commonly utilizes a framework which, in the main, is reinforced by the skin. The framework is spaced sufficiently closely that the skin can withstand the water and other loadings. A series of *panels*, circumscribed by elements of the framework, is formed.

For large boats particularly, the framework may be graded in that a large number of frames can be supported by several *longitudinals* and these then can be supported by bulkheads. This system can produce a very lightweight, if costly to build, hull construction. Taken to its extreme, the framework would be very closely spaced and the skin very thin whereupon, as previously discussed, the main disadvantage is poor puncture resistance.

Diagonal reinforcement
It has become common to use the skin as a significant contributor to the overall structure. **Fibre-resin composite construction is fabricated commonly with a proportion of the fibres having a plus and a minus 45º orientation in order to achieve the diagonal reinforcement desirable in the topsides.** Since the reinforcement provides strength and significant resistance to deformation, the mimicking of the trussed beam proves structurally efficient as a means of resisting the shear stresses in the topsides.

Modern wood construction, utilising several layers of *veneer*, each layer being bonded to the next, obtains the same properties by varying the direction of the planks of veneer, and thus the wood grain. **A plus and minus 45º arrangement of the planks of veneer can be likened to that used in fibre-resin composite construction.**

Space-framed

Tensile members
The bicycle wheel is reputed to be one of the most efficient structures ever designed in terms of the weight it can withstand relative to its own weight. A lightweight racing cycle wheel under test is reported to have carried over seven hundred times its own weight, which is about the weight of a small car. The wheel's secret lies in its use of spokes, which are extremely efficient members in tension, and markedly more efficient than those in compression or bending

It often is a target in structural design to employ members which are in tension rather than bending where possible. But there is a downside to the use of tensile members. This is to do with action and reaction. Not all parts in a structure can be in tension (except for inflated structures). **The tension in one member must be opposed in some way, typically by placing another member in bending or in compression.** For the bicycle

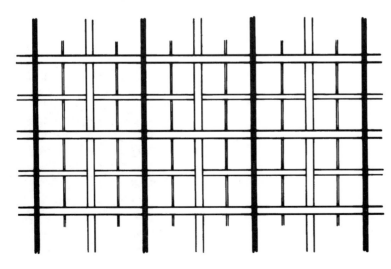

Fig 62 Complex, multiple framework reduces panel size, thus permitting a very thin skin.

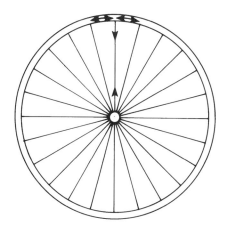

Fig 63 Tension and compression in a bicycle wheel. Under load, the rim would be subject to bending and buckling between the spokes.

wheel, the rim experiences both bending and compression, and therefore needs to be considerably more robust than the spokes.

True space-frames

Strictly speaking, the wheel is not a true space-frame. **By definition, all members should be in either pure tension or pure compression in order to achieve this accolade.** If the wheel rim were straight between each spoke position (which could lead to an uncomfortable ride!), and loadings occurred at these points, often termed *nodes*, the spaceframe requirements would be met.

Another precept of the space-frame is that the structure should be stable, even if all

Fig 64 The strut and tie deal with the mast compression by placing the main beam that links the two hulls of the catamaran in compression.

joints are imagined to be bolted together, or *pinned* loosely so that they could articulate. It follows that this can be achieved only by ensuring that any space within the structure is surrounded by three members. Make it four or more and the structure is seen to be unstable if pinned at its joints.

By locating all loads at the nodes, bending of the members of the space-frame is avoided. Bending is not welcome if the member must also deal with compression, since a bent strut will be bent further by the compressive load and therefore is liable to fail. By contrast, the straight strut more easily remains *in column*, as it is often described.

Integrated system
A boat's rig is an example of a space-framed structure, all the stays and shrouds being under tension and the spreaders and mast itself being compression members. Loadings on the mast resulting from the wind in the sails may lead to some bending in the mast, but this just means that its effectiveness as a compression member is reduced. **If all these rig loadings are linked to a space-framed structure inside the hull, a complete, integrated system results.**

In order to deal with the significant fore and aft hull bending loads, an idealized centreline structure could be employed. This could utilise tubes, perhaps in aluminium alloy for the struts, and rod, wire or flat bar for the tension members, usually termed *ties*. However, this could make for less than comfortable living quarters, notwithstanding the obligatory crash hat; and working conditions in the cockpit would be tailor made for a party of chimpanzees.

It makes more sense to spread the spaceframe around the hull in order to minimize interference with the accommodation. The shrouds need also to be tied in with the space-frame. Restrictions in squeezing past the mast area and in the accommodation forward are likely to

remain, however. *Ring frames* provide a means of overcoming these drawbacks, the space-frame being arranged close to the shell, linking one ring frame to the next.

Compromise solutions
Such adaptations reduce the system's efficiency, however, because the structure ceases to be a true space-frame. But the contribution made by the hull is likely to stabilize the structure sufficiently, and any resultant bending can be minimised by using beams of substantial section. Thus, the use of a space-frame, if only partial, is an effective way of reducing the bending of the hull and enhancing the driving force produced by the sail plan.

Although the space-frame serves as part of the construction of the hull, its purpose is very specific in that it is designed to limit the amount of bend in the hull, thus improving rig stability. While the fitting of a space-frame would add to the strength of the hull, this is incidental to its main function. In general, the hull is strong enough without the benefit of the space-frame. From this perspective, it is reasoned that the space-frame is an addition to the construction, and a heavy one at that.

Space-frame desirability
Racing yacht construction has come round to the concept of resisting hull bending by considered hull reinforcement. The utilization of diagonal type reinforcement in the topsides reflects space-frame technology. Efficiency is not as high as for the space-frame because of the curvature of the hull, but space-frames tend to make the rest of the hull structure redundant in terms of hull bending, and this is wasteful.

Racing dinghies present a case for the use of space-frames, principally because no backstay is used and forestay (or foresail luff) tensioning relies upon the shrouds. These resist the side forces on the mast but, because they are displaced aft, also serve to keep the forestay taut.

The shrouds need to be highly tensioned to be effective in achieving a straight foresail luff, especially if they are little displaced aft, and yet some dinghy hulls are not well braced enough to permit this. A spaceframe connecting the mast base to the shrouds' attachment to the hull, and for good measure to the forestay, provides a route to good rig performance.

Of course, space-frames, or exotic hull construction systems, have no place on cruising yachts, simply because there is little need for achieving the level of rig stability required of racing craft.

Reactive systems
Rig deflections can be reduced to zero if a self-compensating, reactive system is employed. This could work by responding either to load or deflection. **Thus, as the forestay sags, hydraulic rams could serve to increase tension in the forestay, perhaps even beyond the level required to maintain the status quo.** Reactive systems have been tried and could perhaps become commonplace for leading edge racing yachts.

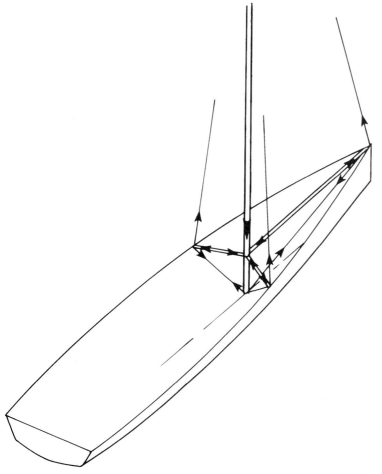

Fig 65 A rig space-frame for a racing dinghy. The tensile and compressive loadings are demonstrated.

Fig 66 The struts are indicative of a space-frame, but there are no tensile members from the base of the mast to lessen the rig loadings on the hull.

Speculative pre-stressing

Another approach would be by pre-stressing all elements of the space-frame. **Thus, ties would be pre-tensioned, which correspondingly would compress the struts.** These stresses would be locked in before racing and would have the effect of lessening the deformation of the system when under load and therefore would improve rig stability.

Speculatively, this concept could be extended to the hull construction, so reducing the need for a space-frame. In theory, this could involve pre-tensioning the carbon fibre or other reinforcement material in a composite, essentially by placing the fibres in tension while the resin matrix cures. Whether the compressive stresses can be dealt with

adequately by the resin or in some other way is a different matter, however. Perhaps the greatest drawback would be that the failure of one strand would result in a massive release of energy, resulting in the ejection of bits in all directions, with cries not so much of 'man overboard' as 'boat exploded'!

Traditional Wood

Joining materials

Except for some non-reinforced-plastic boats and wood dug-outs, all boats are built from materials joined together. Two obvious categories are created. Fibre–resin composites

SUMMARY: CONSTRUCTION THEORY

1. The monocoque principle implies a thick hull skin, unsupported by frames, with gentle curves and uniform loadings, though the model is corrupted by the need for rigging and other highly loaded attachments to the hull.

2. The skeleton of a framed construction hull provides global strength and stiffness, compromised by a tendency to lozenge under bending, though corrected by plus and minus 45º reinforcement orientation in the topsides.

3. Space-framed structures are fitted to racing yacht hulls in order to enhance rig stability by lessening hull bending, though the contribution of the hull becomes redundant because of its relatively high flexibility.

4. The concept of reactive systems, leading to minimal, zero, or even negative hull bending, results in ultimate rig stability, a half way measure being achieved with pre-stressed systems.

Fig 67 Riveting planks using copper fastenings.

and welded constructions produce, with successful joining, a continuous structure, effectively without joints. By contrast, traditional wood construction, comprising joints which are fastened together, is much more divisible.

Although few boats are built commercially in the traditional way these days, the principles of construction are informative. Without resin adhesives to bond together the components, joints rely for success upon their fit, their design, and mechanical fastenings (with a smear of *bedding compound* maybe).

Backbone jointing

The backbone of the traditional wood sailing or motor yacht serves as the main structural part of the hull, as its name implies. Several lengths of wood suitably joined enable the backbone to follow the line at the stem and to cut upwards at the stern. The *stem* to *wood keel* joint relies upon *tenons* to prevent lateral movement and bolts to hold the joint together. A minor refinement is the *snape* in which the wood keel is shaped so that a vulnerable *feather edge* is avoided, although this does not contribute to the integrity of the joint.

The stem, if not constructed from one piece of timber, is joined using a *scarph joint*. The wood keel employs a *hooked scarph joint* if built from two lengths of wood. This joint is locked together by the hook, enhanced by the wedge effect produced by the angles of the scarph.

Scarphing principles

For continuity of strength from one section to the other, scarph joints need to be of respectable length. **For major structural items the length of the scarph should be at least six times the depth of the wood being joined.**

Unlike the behaviour of a glued joint, movement between sections cannot be eradicated totally and therefore scarphs are generally *lipped* (like the snape used on the stem to wood keel joint), to avoid feather edges. These lips do lessen the strength of the joint because the cross-section is reduced.

wood keel

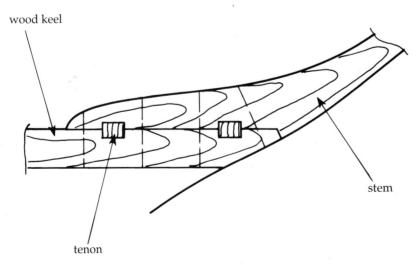

stem

tenon

Fig 68 A stem to wood keel joint.

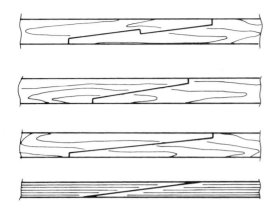

Fig 69 Top to bottom: hooked scarph; lipped 4:1 scarph; lipped 6:1 scarph for main construction; plain 8:1 scarph for plywood.

However, traditional wood construction is not known for flimsiness, the wood members being of substantial dimensions at the outset.

Curved members
The need for scarphed joints in traditional construction comes about because wood of the required section and species is unavailable in sufficient length for straight or, in particular, curved members such as the stem. **For greatest strength, the grain of the wood must follow the curve fairly closely, otherwise a weakness will occur where the grain runs across the curve.**

Supplementary Note

Boat builders using wood have a respect for their material. They like continuous lengths and they like to make the most of their stock. One well-known builder would vary the length of his boats (of about 6m) according to the length of wood available for the wood keel, rather than to scarph it.

This *short grain*, as it is known, is avoided by using *grown wood*. This is not wood which is bent into shape, bonsai-like, to train it into a curve. Grown wood comes from trees (both trunks and branches) which naturally grow crookedly, and the curved portions are matched to a suitable pattern for the formation of a stem or other construction member.

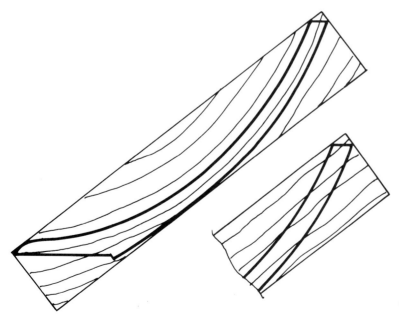

Fig 70 Stem marked out on a board of grown wood (top). Short grain would produce weakness in the stem (bottom).

Skeleton integrity

An important principle of traditional construction is that the skeleton of the boat should be jointed so that, as an entity, it is structurally sound. Thus the backbone, comprising stem, wood keel, *stern post* and *horn timber* are jointed in the manner described. The frames are notched into the wood keel and fastened to the beam shelf.

Not only must the deck beams support the deck, but they need to prevent the topsides from spreading or closing. (The deck planks, being laid fore and aft or swept parallel to the beam shelf, do not assist in linking the beam shelf from one side to the other of the boat.) These requirements result in a complex joint between the beam and the beam shelf, particularly as the structural integrity of the beam shelf is compromised the more the cross-section is reduced by way of the joints. The solution developed is the *skewed dovetail*, a joint which reduces the cross-section (known as the *score*) of the beam shelf by only about 10 per cent.

Knees and floors

Joints frequently need further reinforcement by the use of brackets, called *knees*, to support adjoining members of the framework and provide a 'fixed-ended beam' effect. **Thus knees are fastened between the deck beams**

Fig 72 Knees strengthen and stiffen the thwart and hull joint area.

and frames in way of the mast; between deck beams and the beam shelf; and between the two beam shelves and the transom. Knees which lie vertically are termed *hanging knees* and those which reinforce horizontally as *lodging knees*.

In order to minimize the space occupied and for extended continuity, *strap knees* are used. For example, where a hanging knee links frames to deck beams, to *carling* (an inner

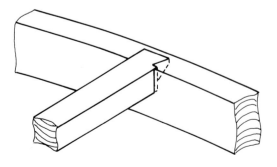

Fig 71 Skewed dovetail joint between deck beam and beam shelf.

Supplementary Note

A knee of a sort is used to reinforce the stern post to a wood keel joint on a traditional yacht (and called a *deadwood*).

Fig 73

beam shelf), and to coachroof sides and top in way of the mast, a strap knee would be constructed from galvanized steel of reasonably substantial section, fastened through each of the wood members.

Similar knees are used to link the frames on one side of the yacht to the wood keel and then to the frames on the other side. These are termed *strap floors*. An alternative is the use of what are called *wood floors* in which these joints are achieved by using substantial sections of wood.

In terms of fixed-endedness, wood floors or knees are more effective than strap floors or knees, which may bend in the corner. However, it has to be said that traditional wood construction tends toward a belt-and-braces philosophy and it seems unlikely that a frame, for example, would deflect sufficiently to bend a strap floor. Nevertheless, a wood floor would be the stronger, in theory anyway.

Bilge stringer

In some measure, the *bilge stringer*, which is fastened to the inside of the frames and runs the length of the hull, reduces the bending load on the frames, though not to a substantial degree since the force required to bend a long length of wood, even of substantial section, is not great.

From this point of view, the frame is more resistant to bending than the bilge stringer. **But the bilge stringer does link one frame to the next so that the force bending one frame is transferred to the next.** The planking has a similar effect and adds to the structural integrity of the skeleton.

Butt straps

In contrast with the sophisticated jointing of the skeleton, the manner in which planking is joined to extend its length appears crude. The relative thinness of the planking, which creates

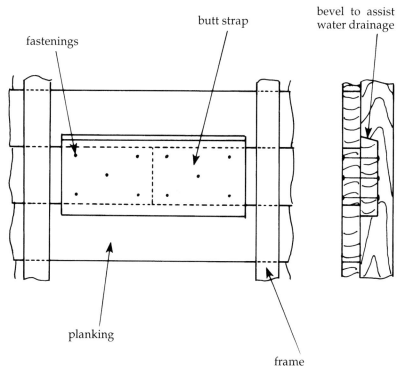

fastenings

butt strap

bevel to assist water drainage

planking

frame

Fig 74 Butt strap used where hull planking is butted.

difficulties in producing adequately strong lipped scarphs, makes the use of butt joints common. The two ends of the planks are butted together and then backed by a *butt strap* of the same thickness as the planking. An array of through fastenings holds the butt strap to each plank end.

For the greatest strength, the butt straps need to be as long as possible, although they are not attached to the frames. The butts are arranged so that coincidence is avoided, being staggered throughout the length of the hull. This reminds us that the planks of a traditional *carvel*-planked yacht contribute significantly to the total strength.

Fig 75 A carvel-planked dinghy under construction.

Monocoque principle

It is incorrect to describe the wood hull as a framed structure with a thin skin since the hull deforms under a loading over a large area, the framework deflecting relatively readily. The absence of solid bulkheads, combined with thick planking and frequent non-substantial frames and longitudinals, results in a yielding structure lacking significant *hard spots*.

Hard spots, as would be produced by a deep sectioned bilge stringer, may lead to frame breakage. A more forgiving and longer-lasting structure results where the bilge stringer is shallow and wide. **This heads towards traditional construction, being of the monocoque principle and not a framed structure at all.**

The planking clearly contributes to the strength of the hull and, although each plank is separate, the shell is cohesive. In order to ensure watertightness the *seams* between planks are *caulked* and this locks the planks together, as mentioned previously. Caulking involves driving *caulking cotton* into the seams with a *caulking iron*. When water is taken up and the wood and the caulking cotton swell, considerable compressive and therefore frictional forces between planks result. A plank does not move readily relative to the adjacent plank.

Alternative systems

Other planking systems demonstrate cohesiveness. *Double diagonal* utilizes two layers of thinner planks laid at 90 degrees to each other and at about 45 degrees to the longitudinal axis. A calico membrane separates the two skins which then are through-fastened extensively. The result is a unitary construction.

Clinker planking, in which planks overlap and are through-fastened along the overlap, produces the same result. This system uses *steam-bent* timbers, which are typically of smaller cross-section than a grown frame and

Fig 76 A clinker-planked dinghy under repair.

at a smaller spacing. This implies a hull construction which tends further towards the monocoque than even carvel construction (though timbers can be used with carvel planking), and one which is structurally very sound.

Modern Wood

Defining characteristics

The introduction of synthetic resin adhesives in the early 1940s revolutionized wood boat construction. Before then the lack of waterproof glues perpetuated traditional construction with its multitudinous fastenings and magic-brew bedding compounds. In fact, all three traditional constructions described can be produced in a similar form using resin adhesives instead of fastenings.

One significant difference between modern and traditional wood construction, already referred to, is that the former utilizes smaller sections of wood which, when laminated together, help to resist the movement resulting from changes in moisture content. Furthermore,

---

SUMMARY: TRADITIONAL WOOD

1. Traditional wood construction is based upon jointed members, with fastenings to hold the joints together and provide face-to-face friction, reinforced where necessary by knees and floors.

2. The systems of jointing in traditional construction have evolved so that joints lock or are tenoned together and provide continuity of strength, while making provision for movement in terms of vulnerability and watertightness.

3. Without the benefit of resin adhesives, curved members are built from grown wood in order to minimize short grain, joined if necessary for adequate length and satisfactory grain direction.

4. The flexibility of frames or timbers and bilge stringer, coupled with substantial planking, indicates a construction that is closer to a monocoque than a framed structure because of the hull's yielding characteristic.

in contrast with traditional construction, which experiences significant moisture-content changes because of water absorption and loss, modern wood construction sets out to stabilize the moisture content by sealing the surface.

Strip planking

In contrast with the wide planks associated with carvel construction, **movement is better controlled if the planks are narrower, glued together and sealed.** This system of construction is known as *strip planking*. Using narrow strips enables one strip to be fastened to the next by nailing from one edge through to the adjacent strip, along with gluing, of course. Not only does this make building much easier, but the nails do reinforce the planking from splitting while in service.

Another bonus in using narrow strips is that there is no need to shape each one individually, whereas carvel construction requires that each plank is *spiled*, meaning that its outline is defined so that it will fit the adjoining plank. The edges must also be bevelled to fit and the face of the plank requires shaping to the curve of the frame.

All this may be avoided with strip planking. Strips can remain parallel and therefore no outline shaping is needed and their narrowness invites no face shaping. The only hitch remaining relates to the bevelling of the edges, which may be overcome by the use of constantly convex and concave edges which then fit together. An alternative is given by tongue and groove systems which provide better locational characteristics than the convex-/concave- edge approach, but require joints that are tolerant so that planking around curves is feasible.

Laminated frames

In modern wood construction, instead of using grown frames, laminations of glued wood are built up to the required curve. Overall strength is likely to be marginally better for the

Fig 77 Convex and concave strip planks.

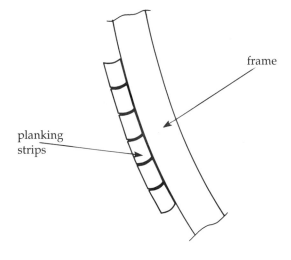

frame

planking strips

Fig 78 Assembled strip planking.

laminated frame, not as a result of gluing as such, but any defects are likely to be only a single lamination deep and the grain direction is likely to follow the curvature of the frame more consistently than is feasible for a grown frame.

Moulded construction

The modern wood construction version of double diagonal planking is achieved by moulding the hull using wood veneers. These are thinner than the planking used for double diagonal. For dinghies, 3mm veneers may be used and up to 6mm (or more) for larger craft, emphasis being given to the ease of bending the veneers.

Several layers to the required thickness are employed, normally running at 45 degrees to the fore and aft line of the hull, in both directions, crossing at 90 degrees. Fore and aft and sometimes vertical veneers are also employed, **the aim being to provide a balanced construction resulting from veneers running in different directions.** The resultant composite provides strength in different directions, depending upon the grain direction, and a relative freedom from splitting.

Bonding veneers

Each layer is glued to the previous layer of veneer, and each plank is glued to the adjacent plank. The gap-filling properties of resin adhesives are used to good effect as the very close fitting of veneers is not feasible. **The**

Fig 79 Two layers of 3mm veneer are used to construct a small, cold-moulded praam dinghy.

amount of glue required is surprisingly high, perhaps as much as 20 per cent by weight of the wood veneers used.

One difficulty lies in ensuring that each plank lies in close contact with the previous layer. For each plank to lie flat it is necessary to spile each so that it fits the adjacent plank without distortion. Another difficulty is that there is a practical limit to the number of staples that may be used to secure the planks, and so hold-down pressure is limited.

Vacuum bagging

An alternative is vacuum *bagging*. In this process, a membrane is placed over the layers of veneers already wet-glued into position and stapled at infrequent intervals, and then a vacuum pump is applied. **The air is removed from between the membrane and the veneers, resulting in the membrane's pressing on the surface, at atmospheric pressure if the seal is perfect.** (The same technique is used for vacuum-packing food, for the purpose of air exclusion and a reduction of the oxidation of the contents.)

The difficulties associated with vacuum bagging mean that it is not used universally for wood moulding. It is desirable that prefitted planks are used for the process. A layer or part layer must be laid quickly, even with a slow-curing adhesive that sets at room temperature.

Fig 80 A Fairey Swordfish, over four decades old and showing its age a little through the varnish.

With the vacuum-bagging process, there is a human tendency to use an excess of glue in order to lessen the chance of voids. Seeing glue squeezing out of a joint as one progresses with each plank in the conventional way is reassuring but not possible with vacuum bagging.

Moulded versus plywood

Early techniques of moulding boats in wood were pioneered by Fairey Marine and known as *hot moulding* because the adhesives available required that the construction was placed in ovens to provide a cure. The development of adhesives which set at room temperature led to the description of *cold moulding*. Both systems have a good reputation for producing hulls that are structurally sound and strong for their weight.

The construction of *plywood* is much the same as for moulded wood. Each ply or layer of veneer is oriented at 90 degrees to the adjacent layer in order to produce a multi-laminate sheet. However, it is possible to control the manufacturing process more carefully, a press being used to provide high pressure between the veneers, thus requiring a minimal amount of adhesive.

Glued clinker

This is an example of a system of construction using plywood in the form of planks glued at their overlaps. The system has been used successfully for class dinghies where the class rules specify that clinker construction must be used.

A number of small yachts have also been built in this way, the laps performing structurally like *stringers*. This makes for a lightweight, frameless construction, although there is a hydrodynamic disadvantage as water flows across the planks.

Sheet materials

By approximating the common, round-bilged form to a chined form (*single* or *double chine*

being the most common), a reasonable form can be produced with only moderate disruption to the water flow. Indeed, for planing craft the chined form is desirable. Construction employing a single chine involves the use of two panels, appropriately bent and twisted, for each side of the hull. Double chine demands three panels on each side.

Many *sheet materials* may be used to form the panels, including steel, aluminium alloy and even glass-reinforced plastic if laminated in flat sheets; **but plywood lends itself very well, particularly for smaller craft because of its structural efficiency.** A large number of dinghies and some yachts have been built in this way from the 1940s onwards, declining in the 1960s as moulded GRP construction took hold.

Plywood construction

The major objections to plywood construction have rested upon aesthetics and longevity, a potential lifespan of only ten years being popularized at one time. However, plywood boats are quick and easy to build and lightweight.

Typically, a *hog*, a lightweight version of a wood keel, runs along the middle of the boat. Stringers are used at the chines, in which case they are called *chines* or *chine logs*, and at the top of the topsides where they are described as *gunwales*. These stringers provide a peripheral surface to which the panels can be glued.

While the construction may be unitary, the plywood playing a significant role in the construction, the structure is enhanced by jointing the members of the skeleton. To make this point we could consider the hog, chines and gunwales of a dinghy to be just butted to the transom and glued into position. Although the plywood would reinforce the joints, the loading on the hog from a dinghy trailer chock would put the plywood at the inner edge of the transom in shear, with little resistance by the hog.

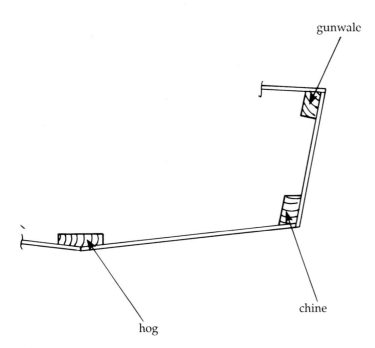

gunwale

Fig 81 Plywood, single-chine construction.

chine

hog

Jointing the hog into the transom would eliminate this tendency. A knee between hog and transom would enhance bending strength, although it might not be necessary because a more effective constraint is provided by the gunwales.

Stitch and glue

A minor revolution occurred in plywood dinghy construction with the introduction of the *glass-fibre taping* of the joins between panels. The technique is known commonly as *stitch and glue*, the best known British example being the Mirror dinghy.

Supplementary Note

One of the golden rules in boat building is never to glue end-grain wood. The reasoning behind this relates to the weakness of the glue itself. Glue a couple of lengths of wood together so that they butt end-to-end and it would be a fair guess that failure would occur at the glue joint under a tensile or bending load.

Nevertheless, an end-grain-glued joint is stronger than the conventional long-grain joint because of better glue penetration and greater resistance to the wood's tearing. Gluing the end-grain hog to the long-grain transom, and then lightly bending one relative to the other probably results in a splitting of the transom. The wisdom of not gluing end-grain rests upon the high strength of the wood in this direction, which makes the glue look weak (the ratio of strengths is about 25:1).

Glue end-grain by all means, but do not expect the joint to be much stronger than wood along the grain, and in this direction it is relatively weak. It is best to use joints.

The stitching relates to the wiring together of the panels. A common arrangement involves threading short lengths of copper wire through pairs of matched holes at the edges of the panels to be joined and then twisting the ends together on the outside to close the seams. Then comes the somewhat inappropriately-termed gluing operation. **Glass-fibre tape (essentially glass-fibre cloth woven in narrow widths, 50mm being typical) is applied to the inside of the seam and impregnated with resin.**

When the system was first introduced polyester resin was generally available and mostly used, but the superior adhesion of epoxy resin makes this preferable. **When the resin is cured, the wires are trimmed down to the surface of the plywood whereupon the outside of the seam is similarly taped over.** Taping both sides makes the joint much stronger, effectively producing a sandwich.

Structural considerations

The corners produced by chines lend global stiffness rather as corrugations enhance plastic roof sheeting. Unlike corrugated sheeting, chined hulls usually comprise large, nearly flat panels which contrast with the chines in terms of flexibility. **The consequential hard spots produced by the chines may result in local fractures under dynamic loadings.** An improvement to the joint at the chines could be effected by using more glass-fibre tape which extends into both panels, the strength gradually diminishing with distance from the corner.

A preferable solution involves a reduction in the flexibility of the panel. Commonly, the bottom panel for a sailing dinghy is reinforced by using longitudinal strips of wood glued to the plywood. The side *buoyancy tank*, if fitted, further stiffens the bottom panel, although it has to be said that yet another hard spot is created.

Using the same glass-fibre taping technique, the vertical panel of the side buoyancy tank is bonded into position. The tape is applied on both the inside and the outside corner of the vertical panel in order to fix it to the hull bottom, the same approach being used for the bulkheads.

Stiffening vertical panels improves the strength of the joints because bending is reduced. A side loading on the bulkhead, such as might arise from water filling the hull on one side of the bulkhead or from impact, results in shearing in the corner, which is more easily dealt with than the stress resulting from bending.

Egg-box construction

Where loadings from bending are low the use of *fillets* of resin (normally epoxy) mixed with a lightweight filling agent permits a fast and easy-to-build system for plywood construction. Better than using wire to join butted panels, systems involving tabs and slots simplify assembly. The fillet is then run round all internal panel corners (without the use of glass-fibre tape).

Supplementary Note

Filling agents and putties can be created by mixing resin with glass microspheres or plastic micro-balloons. The density of these bubbles is low, particularly in the case of microspheres which float readily in the air, presenting a potential health hazard unless a mask is worn.

This system has particular merit where the panels are *laser-cut* using *numerical control* techniques. The process starts with a computer-based design of the hull and interior panels leading to the *development* (the outline of the actual shape) of the panels.

The information is filed in the form of *offsets*, which specify distances from a baseline to an edge in order to define the outline. Panels

Supplementary Note

The shape of the fillet has a bearing upon the strength of the joint. If the fillet were square-sectioned (left) failure would be likely in the plywood at one of the edges of the fillet. Extending the fillet further into each panel grades the stiffness provided (right). However, a shaped fillet extending no further than the square-sectioned fillet would most likely be weaker (centre).

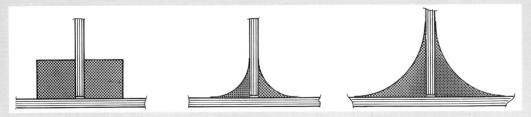

Fig 82 The extended fillet is the most successful.

are then cut out from the numerical data without the need to draw out the shape. Tabs, slots for the tabs and even slots for wedges so that the panels can be pulled together and held tightly, may be incorporated. The cut produced by the laser shows an element of charring on the edge of the plywood but its extent is minimal.

The technique is fast, reproducible and accurate to one millimetre or so. Its only real disadvantage is the initial equipment and software cost, which obviously has to be reflected in the cost of the kit of panels. The ease of assembly and filleting enable the main structure to be constructed surprisingly quickly.

The structural form produced is *egg-box* like. As already reasoned, panel deflection of hull, bulkheads, and all other surfaces for that matter, needs to be minimized in order that the joints will last. Although glass-fibre taping the joint over the fillet would enhance strength, the provision of *stiffeners*, in plywood or otherwise, at reasonably close spacing, on all panels reduces the vulnerability of the joints.

SUMMARY: MODERN WOOD

1. The distinctive feature of modern wood construction is that resin adhesives are employed and these lend themselves to the construction of curved laminations and the use of small sections of wood.

2. Strip planking requires no individual fitting of the strips; moulded construction produces a hull skin which has more or less equal strength in all directions; while glued clinker construction involves shaped plywood planks.

3. To ensure a good bond between layers of veneer for moulded construction, an excessive amount of adhesive may be used; this is not entirely overcome when vacuum bagging is employed if good veneer contact is to be assured.

4. Plywood permits lightweight construction taking the form of a panelled skeleton or panels held together with glass-fibre tape or with resin-based fillets, in all cases using panel stiffeners or an egg-box type of construction in order to minimize panel deflection.

Fabricated Metal

Panelling and welding

Boats built from steel or aluminium are the product of fabricated sheet materials. **Chined construction usually enables the plates to be** *sprung* **into position** (within the elastic limit) in the same way that plywood panels are pulled together. **For round-bilged craft, however, the construction is much more complex, the hull being divided into panels small enough that they can be rolled and shaped to fit.**

The system for joining the plates and just about everything else that forms the construction, is by *welding*. For low carbon steel, the common *electric-arc* welding process is used. Cor-Ten, with its different composition, requires an *argon-arc* process in which the inert gas argon is used to surround the weld as it is formed in order to prevent oxidation.

The welding of aluminium alloy also demands an inert gas method. *MIG (metal inert gas)* welding, in which filler metal is fed automatically into the weld, proves most satisfactory because distortion is minimized. *Weld distortion* is particularly problematical for construction involving aluminium alloy which has a coefficient of linear expansion several times greater than that of steel. At the same time, the problem cannot be ignored for steel.

Welding techniques

The technique for welding, particularly where panels are relatively flat and unsupported, is to use *tack welds*. Short lengths of weld are completed at widely spaced intervals, which then hold together the panels. Welding continues between the tack welds, limited so as to avoid heat build-up in the panels.

Adequate *weld penetration* is achieved with thick plate by bevelling its edges, thus providing a V-shaped trench which is effectively filled with weld metal. The weld usually is made from both sides, such that both welds meet. Welding produces watertight interconnections with almost continuous strength.

Fig 83 A flat plate stiffener about to be tack-welded to a hull panel

Supplementary Note

Welds may suffer from many potential defects, despite the sophistication of the technology. Fortunately, the operations used for boat building seem to be reliable.

One system used for joining steel to aluminium alloy, for instance where the hull is of one of these two materials and the superstructure the other, is by using an explosive technique.

Fig 84

Hull reinforcing

Metal hulls are reinforced in much the same way as wood hulls. Frames, longitudinals and bulkheads are employed. Bulkheads comprise flat plate, appropriately stiffened.

Watertight bulkheads need to be strong enough to withstand the weight of water which would fill the hull on one side of the bulkhead, and this is not vastly different from the strength requirement of the hull panels.

Frames are usually built from flat plate on edge, or from angle- or T-section. The last is the most structurally efficient because under a water load there is significant material displaced from the neutral axis to withstand bending effectively. By contrast, the inner edge of a flat plate frame is highly stressed. The angle frame is welded in such a way that, like the T, the flange is opposite rather than against the hull panel but, because of its asymmetry, there is a tendency for the angle frame to distort when the hull panel is loaded.

Longitudinals, as subsidiary strength members, are frequently of flat plate welded

Fig 85 Bulkheads of flat plate aluminium alloy. Stiffeners have yet to be added.

on edge. **Chines are often fabricated from tube,** which lends strength and provides an external radiused form. **Tube is commonly used for the stem also,** although there is a possibility with steel of internal corrosion occurring. The resulting structure comprises a framework which provides comprehensive strength in terms of water and rig loadings, the skin contributing to this and, of course, providing local strength.

Ferro-cement

Building boats by using steel and *mortar* has been a popular choice for amateur construction because of its low cost and relative ease. This method is generally referred to as *ferro-cement* construction.

However, the method has lost an element of credibility due to the 'unfinished project' syndrome. The problem lies with the fact that the proportionate cost of the hull is small compared with that of the completed boat, and so the total savings in using ferro-cement

Fig 86 Left to right: flat plate, angle and T-sectioned stiffeners.

Supplementary Note

Although the term 'concrete' is used, sometimes disparagingly, to describe ferro-cement construction, the term is not accurate and greatly upsets the owners of these boats.

construction are relatively small. Nevertheless, if recycled wood (church pews proving a popular choice) and second-hand equipment are used, **large ferro-cement boats may be completed within a remarkably low budget.**

The structure of ferro-cement boats is based upon the high tensile strength of steel and the high compressive strength of mortar. Frames of steel tube are linked with multitudinous steel rods arranged longitudinally. Diagonals may be incorporated in order to help in resisting hull-bending loads.

Welded mesh is then added to the framework to provide a ground for the mortar and make a further contribution to the strength. The mortar, filling all spaces in the framework, adds to its cohesion. The mortar enhances the compressive strength of the structure, not only because it is naturally strong under

compression but because buckling of the panels is limited. The shell of a ferro-cement boat is relatively thick and the steel rods are constrained by the mortar, thus giving good compressive strength.

The resulting hull is robust, if heavy for boats below about 15m, withstands impact well and has the potential for long life, despite the sceptics' fears about corrosion.

Reinforced Plastic

Glass laminates

GRP construction resembles ferro-cement in that a reinforcement material (glass rather than steel) is held within a cured matrix (resin rather than mortar). Directional strength is obtained by using directional glass fibres, like the steel rods used in ferro-cement boats, although random mat is commonly employed in conjunction with directional fibres. The conventional constructional method for boats larger than dinghies is to use alternate layers of chopped strand mat and woven roving, wetted out with polyester resin.

Although the chopped strand mat fills the

SUMMARY: FABRICATED METAL

1. Sheet metal hulls generally are constructed either by springing plates into position (for chined hulls) or by rolling small panels to shape (for round-bilged hulls).

2. Joining the plates is achieved by welding – electric-arc for mild steel, argon-arc for Cor-Ten, and MIG for aluminium alloy, the last in order to minimize the distortion that results from the high thermal expansion of this material.

3. Usually, frames, longitudinals and bulkheads in plate, flat, T or angle are used, the chines and stem often being fabricated from round tube.

4. Ferro-cement benefits from the tensile strength of steel and the compressive strength of mortar, the steel framework comprising tubed frames, longitudinal rods and welded mesh filled with mortar.

undulations of the woven roving fairly well, there is no fibre interconnection, and therefore *interlaminar strength* depends upon the bond produced by the resin. Provided that the previous layer is *green* (a term indicating that the resin in the laminate is not fully cured) when the next layer is applied, adhesion proves adequate and interlaminar stresses in the cured lay-up are unlikely to produce failure, although it has to be said that the composite is considerably weaker in the direction perpendicular to a laminate.

Moulding process

For production boats as opposed to one-offs, *female moulds* are produced from a *plug* so that the hull, deck, coachroof and other mouldings may be *moulded* (or laminated) using the mould as a surface. The inside surface of the mould for the hull needs to be highly finished so that the outer surface of the hull will be so too. A thick layer of unreinforced resin, the gel coat, provides the outer, relatively waterproof surface of the hull.

It is convenient to mould hulls of some size in halves because of the physical difficulties of moulding in one or because of poor access for laminating. **The two halves are then bonded together while still green, using a butted joint with layers of glass and resin providing the butt strap.** Obviously the bond is critical. The result is a fairly homogenous structure.

Fig 87 The deck mould for a dinghy, showing reflections picked up by the high gloss finish.

Supplementary Note

An up-and-coming system for mass-producing smaller boats involves *rotational moulding*. This process utilizes a complete mould to which plastic material is introduced. The mould and contained plastic are heated in an oven and rotated continuously about the horizontal and the vertical axes in order to distribute the plastic evenly; this is then allowed to cool. Both thermoplastic and thermosetting materials may be used and it is feasible to incorporate reinforcement fibres.

The Laser Centre has developed the Dart 16 using this technique. The plastic compound produces a sandwich having an inner, cellular structure of closed-cell type.

Hull stiffening

Stiffening in the form of bulkheads, frames and longitudinals is used to provide support for the relatively flexible laminate and to lend global stiffness to the hull. The flexibility of the laminate gives the advantage of shock absorption, but also the disadvantage of a proneness to cracking in way of stiffeners, particularly on the outer, non-reinforced, gel-coat surface. Where a non-flexible stiffener, such as a bulkhead, is attached to the laminate a hard

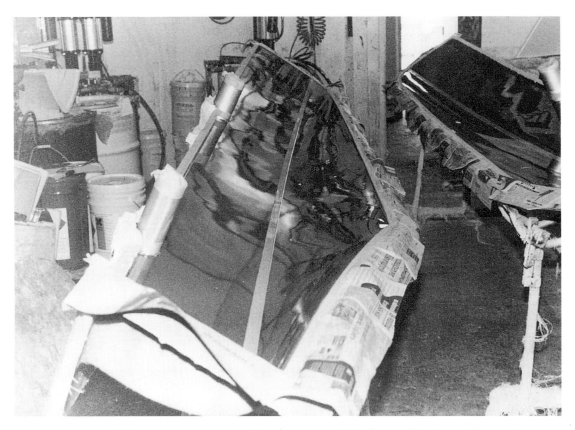

Fig 88 The split mould for a catamaran. Because of the narrowness of the hulls, moulding in one is less satisfactory.

Fig 89 A complex of plywood bulkheads to be glassed to a dinghy hull of advanced fibre-resin composite construction. The aim is to distribute mast loads in the hull.

spot is produced, bending the laminate around the bulkhead on either side when loaded.

The solution is to lessen the degree of local stiffness. This involves modulating the flexibility of the skin from virtually zero at the stiffener, a bulkhead providing the best example, to full flexibility at as great a distance as is feasible from the hard spot. One approach is to laminate into the corners between the bulkhead and the hull, using progressively wider strips of glass-fibre material so that the thickness is reduced gradually. Another is to use glass in the corner, then a fillet of lightweight filler plus resin, followed by further layers of glass fibre.

Better still is a bulkhead to hull skin interconnection which has in-built flexibility.

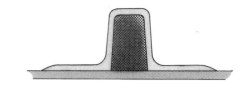

Supplementary Note

A common procedure when glassing-in plywood bulkheads is to bore holes of large diameter around the perimeter so that laminating into the holes results in a 'rivetted' effect.

This may be achieved by assembling the bulkhead clear of the skin and then glassing over a former so that the hull skin can still flex. Similarly, the local stiffness produced by frames and longitudinals may be lessened by ensuring that the size of the section is not too great, compensated for by using a smaller spacing between frames or longitudinals. Flexibility may also be incorporated along the same lines as for the bulkhead.

Top hat stiffeners, as they are called, are constructed by laminating over a foam former.

Fig 91 The classic 'top hat' stiffener results in local stiffness, lessened for the flattened stiffener.

Increasing the angle of the sides of the former produces a more forgiving 'sombrero' stiffener.

Structural joinery

Interior joinery such as berth fronts and tops, compartment divisions, cupboards, lockers,

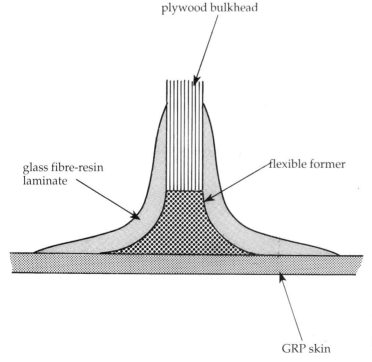

plywood bulkhead

glass fibre-resin laminate

flexible former

GRP skin

Fig 90 Flexibility is achieved by a contoured laminate over a flexible former, thus lessening the hardspot produced by the bulkhead.

shelving and worktops provide ready-made stiffeners for the hull and need to be taken into account in the design of the structure. As with bulkheads, hard spots are to be guarded against and the techniques described to achieve flexibility are worthy of consideration. Discontinuity of stiffeners also occurs where items of joinery end. For structural elegance some way of gradually reducing the degree of rigidity needs to be sought.

In order to meet global strength and stiffness requirements it is necessary to consider whether there are structural gaps. For instance, the hull could run unsupported between a berth top glassed to the hull and a built-in locker. This is like reinforcing a length of wood at both ends but not in the middle. As a result the wood under bending is no stronger than if it were not reinforced (in fact, it may be weaker

because the degree of flexibility is reduced). **As far as the hull is concerned the solution is to provide structural continuity between items of joinery, supplemented with additional stiffeners where necessary.**

Deck attachment

The deck contributes significantly to the structural integrity of the yacht's hull and, because it is usually moulded separately, needs to be joined to the hull. Many different systems have been and are used. Most rely upon lapping the deck and hull mouldings, and then applying layers of glass fibre and resin in order to reinforce the joint. For production boats, polyester resin and glass fibre are commonly used for reinforcing the joint. Care has to be taken to ensure a sound bond. Curing progresses as the mouldings age,

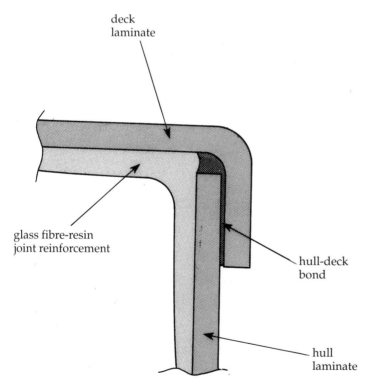

deck
laminate

glass fibre-resin
joint reinforcement

hull-deck
bond

hull
laminate

Fig 92 Typical hull to deck joint, using a 'butt strap' of glass-fibre-resin reinforcement. Alternatively and more neatly, the hull laminate may be extended to form the deck surround, the lap joint on the deck being covered by a foot rail, inset from the deck edge.

making chemical cross-linking with the surface more difficult.

If the hull and deck mouldings are joined when each is in an advanced stage of cure it becomes necessary to abrade the surface mechanically, although excellent results are obtained by 'conditioning' the surface with *acetone* (a solvent used for cleaning tools and brushes coated in uncured resin and also used for removing nail polish). Tests have shown that preparation with acetone (or alternatively *trichloroethane*) is the equal of thorough mechanical abrasion of the surface.

One-off glass

Boats of moulded construction are by far the most common. For one-off construction, the expense of producing a mould is hard to justify. **One system, known as *C-flex*, utilizes manufactured glass composite rods running the length of the hull and bent round temporary frames.** (In wood construction these are also termed moulds, an obvious source of confusion.)

Supplementary Note

The glass rods used in the C-flex system comprise unidirectional glass-fibre rovings in resin and resemble long fishing rods.

The rods adjoin each other, providing a surface which is glassed over. The removal of the temporary frames permits the laminating of the inside of the shell. A similarity with ferro-cement construction will be evident.

In structural terms the glass composite rods provide good longitudinal strength and, because they are bonded together when glassed, produce good bending strength. The arrangement of glass-fibre fabric so that the reinforcement runs at about 45 degrees to the longitudinal axis in both directions enhances the overall bending strength and stiffness, provided that local deformation of the hull skin can be limited.

One-off sandwich

Another system of one-off construction involves the use of foam, usually *polyvinyl chloride (PVC)*, to form a sandwich, with layers of glass-fibre cloth on each face. The technique starts with the production of a temporary framework, usually of wood. Panels of foam are mounted on the framework and then glassed over. When cured, the shell is removed from the framework and glassed on the inside.

Historically, the boat builders Kelsall's have been a major protagonist of sandwich construction. Recently, the company has developed an alternative approach in which flat sheets of foam are glassed on only one side initially to form panels of the hull. When the resin is part-cured the panels are pulled together in much the same way that plywood boats are built.

Since the panels are bent while the resin is in a green condition, some permanent distortion is possible, as is equally true for steel or aluminium construction. The similarity does not stop there. *Darts* and local shaping are feasible so that the desired shape can be achieved. Finally, the shell is glassed on the inside as for the framework-based system.

The benefits of using foam-sandwich construction are well established. Reduced noise transmission, thermal insulation and the reduction or absence of internal stiffening result in a more comfortable interior. **Structural efficiency is achieved because panels are thick but of low density, enabling particularly lightweight hulls and decks to be produced with good panel stiffness.**

Moulded sandwich

Even when the hull is built by using a conventional resin and glass lay-up, decks are

Fig 93 A carbon fibre/fibreglass PVC foam sandwich, approximately equivalent in strength and stiffness to the much heavier, chopped strand mat and woven roving solid laminate.

frequently of sandwich construction to reduce springiness. **For multiple production it is necessary that a good surface can be obtained readily by using moulds, although this does create difficulties in attaching the core to the deck's outer face because this face is laminated first.**

It has been common practice in constructing decks to use a core consisting of panels of end-grain balsa bonded to the cured outer face with a lightweight filling agent and resin to form a putty. Typically the balsa is held in contact by the use of sandbags or weights until the resin in the putty has cured. The sandwich is, of course, completed by laminating the deck's inner face to the core and then, when it has cured, releasing it from the mould.

Due to the manner of laminating the inner face directly on to the core, voids and attachment failures are unlikely. **Unfortunately, because the core is bonded in place, the same is not true of the outer face, separation over a fair percentage of the area of the deck being not uncommon.** Another problem arising in service is that balsa is prone to absorbing water, and it is all too easy for water to penetrate the faces through fastener holes, joins, edges or face damage.

These two problems are less serious for decks than for hulls and are largely overcome by the use of vacuum bagging techniques and foam cores. The use of a bonding agent which is able to withstand higher levels of strain, such as *urethane acrylate*, reduces the chance of failure between the

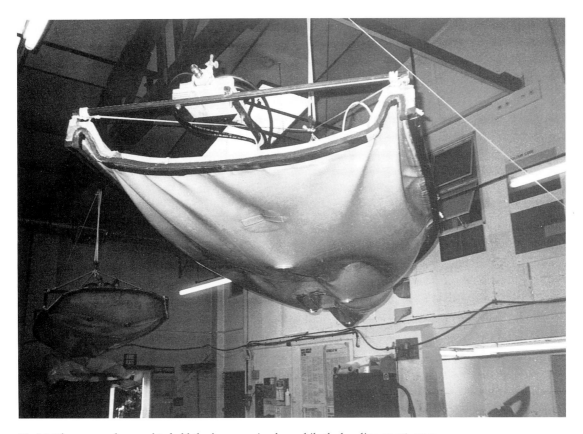

Fig 94 The vacuum bag used to hold the foam core in place while the bonding agent cures.

Fig 95 Job done. The foam has been bonded to the outer face and is being readied for laminating the inner face.

> ## Supplementary Note
>
> Low-pressure vacuum bagging, operating at about half an atmosphere pressure, normally proves adequate.

outer face and the core. **Such failure is a major concern with sandwich construction because, unless the two faces remain interconnected by the foam, the strength is reduced virtually to that given by the faces alone.**

Interlinking faces

Tying together the faces may be achieved by laminating over spaced strips of foam, infilling with further strips of foam and then laminating the inner face. This makes for a robust and reliable sandwich construction, but one which is significantly heavier than the more simple core plus two faces, though it is lighter than a typical single skin with stiffeners.

The use of polyester resin reinforced with E-glass in chopped strand mat and woven rovings is common for small cruisers. To use a sandwich construction, perhaps with unidirectional glass fibre where the loadings are predictable, takes a step towards the lightweight but is more costly. The use of vinylester resin adds further to cost but with some improvement in reliability.

Exotic construction

More exotic structures incorporating carbon fibre, in particular, fall within the province of leading-edge racing yachts, dinghies and sailboards and have little place in cruising yachts. The principal reason for this is cost; but it has to be said that the high strength and stiffness of carbon fibre reduce the amount of

material needed and therefore the time, and cost, of applying it. As the cost of carbon fibre falls its use could become much more widespread, although a carbon and epoxy-hulled fishing boat does seem far-fetched.

Weight reduction when glass is replaced by carbon fibre is substantial. Aramid fibre is often used in conjunction with carbon fibre. Aramid lends toughness to the laminate, although as tougher carbon fibre becomes available the need to incorporate aramid fibre, with its doubtful characteristics in compression, lessens. **Cored panels are characteristic of the exotic reinforcements** and, in the extreme, include the honeycombs of aluminium and, as a next step, those constructed from aramid paper coated with phenolic resin. **At this level of sophistication pre-pregs would be expected.**

Weight comparison

In order to give an idea of the scale of weight reduction conferred by the use of increasingly exotic construction, the weight of several systems for building the hull and deck of a

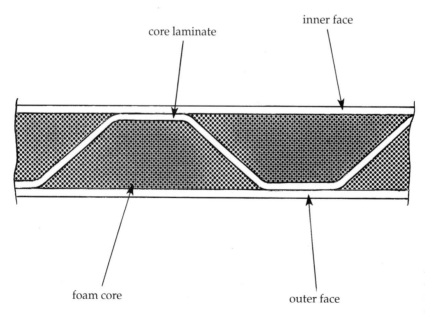

core laminate

inner face

foam core

outer face

Fig 96 Sandwich construction having interlinked faces. Heavy but reliable.

12m yacht may be compared: a single skin, chopped strand mat and woven roving construction with stiffeners would weigh about 18kN (1.8 tons or 4,000lb). A balsa-cored sandwich with chopped strand mat and woven roving faces would tip the scales at around 12kN (1.2 tons or 2,700lb). The benefit of epoxy resin-impregnated carbon fibre and aramid fibre, together with a PVC foam-core shaves down the weight to about 8kN (0.8 tons or 1,800lb). Exchanging the core for an aramid-based honeycomb, pares a further 1kN (0.1 ton or 225lb) or 2kN (0.2 ton or 450lb) from the hull and deck weight.

To put this into perspective, the several steps reduce the weight (as a percentage of the glass-fibre, single-skin hull construction) by **about 30 per cent (balsa core plus glass fibre); by a further 20 per cent (foam core plus carbon/aramid fibre); and by a final 10 per cent (honeycomb core plus carbon/aramid fibre).** The effect is seen to be fairly dramatic, although the law of diminishing returns is an inevitability.

Cost follows a predictable inverse relationship, half the weight relating to twice the cost, except for the more extreme exotics when cost accelerates faster than weight reduction occurs.

Glamour materials

The glamour associated with the exotic materials gives them more than their fair share of media coverage. This presents a disproportionate impression of the number of boats built with these materials. As new materials make their appearance, such as super-strength polyethylene fibre, the implication is created that these constructional materials are more common than perhaps they are. Maybe the same could be said of wood.

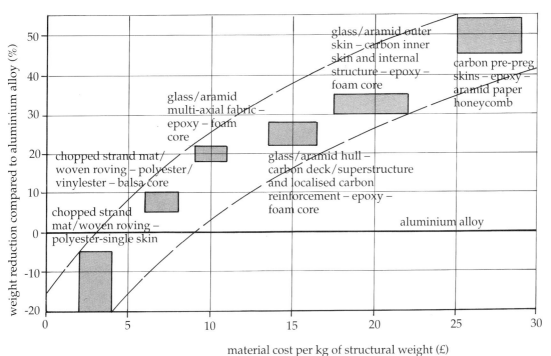

Fig 97 A graphical representation of the hull weight reduction achievable by using different fibre-resin composites in comparison with aluminium alloy. Representative costs are also depicted. (Courtesy of ABS)

SUMMARY: REINFORCED PLASTIC

1. Commonly, yachts are constructed with polyester resin and glass fibre (in chopped strand mat and woven roving form) made up from several sections, including the deck, and butt-strapped together with further laminates.

2. Bulkheads, frames, longitudinals and interior joinery may be used for stiffening the hull, care being taken to minimize hard spots, either by using graded reinforcement or by creating flexibility in the stiffeners.

3. One-off systems of construction are feasible, such as by building the hull from glass- fibre rods or foam and then laminating on both sides, the foam sandwich in particular conferring structural efficiency.

4. So-called exotic materials, notably carbon fibre, combined with advanced core materials, permit major reductions in weight in contrast with conventional GRP construction, 18kN to 7kN for a 12m yacht hull being feasible.

Panelled Construction

Sheet materials

As with any other production process, the faster a boat can be built, the lower the cost will be. Although moulded GRP lends itself to speedy construction, the production of a plug and mould adds considerably to the time to completion and therefore to the cost. One-off or small run production demands simpler systems.

Sheet material in suitably shaped panels can be bent to form the hull, deck and superstructure. **However, an important limitation of sheet material is that it cannot be bent to form local curvature in more than one direction,** whereas the hull of a round-bilged boat is of compound curvature.

Cylindrical projection

In terms of design a simple hull form can be based upon panels of sheet material, bent as if part of a large cylinder. Although this seems to imply that boats designed in this way would be suitable only in novelty events, in fact reasonably shaped hull forms can be produced.

Supplementary Note

Steel and aluminium sheet may adopt a small amount of compound curvature due to their yielding nature. This results in a degree of permanent bend, unlike plywood which shows signs of buckling when bent in two directions.

Cylindrical projection provides scope because the diameter of the cylinder used to generate the panel curvature may be varied. In other words the panel may be bent more or less tightly. The panel can also remain flat in part, in which case it could be said that the cylinder diameter is infinitely great.

Flat-bottomed boats are of cylindrical design, varying curvature being built into the panel in the fore and aft sense. Provided that the panel is not representatively wrapped around the cylinder at an angle, there would be no twist. **Thus, for all intents and purposes, sections (that is, transverse cutting planes) used to design the hull form would be parallel at any position along the panel.**

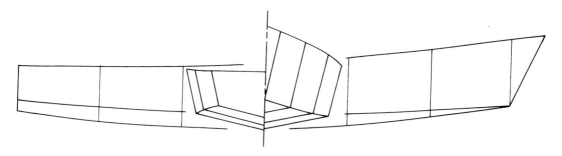

Fig 98 A single chine dinghy based upon cylindrical projection. No twist occurs in the panels, demonstrated by the parallel sections throughout the length.

Limitations of form

If the topsides are to be of a single panel each side and again of the cylindrical form described, the design can be developed by ensuring that the sections are again parallel. An angle of *deadrise*, in which the bottom is formed from two canted panels, provides further opportunity for shape enhancement as does a multi-chined approach.

Although the panels can be easily bent into position, provided that the curvature is not too great, there are limitations in the form it is possible to produce. Praam dinghies can be designed with a reasonable shape. **But the bow profile of stem dinghies is determined by the flare of the panels and therefore may not be as the designer would choose.**

Conical projection

A more sophisticated system for design involves basing the form of each of the panels on a cone and positioning the imaginary panel so that twist is introduced. It may seem that this indicates compound curvature, but it is to be noted that a sheet of plywood may be twisted successfully without its buckling. The panels may be imagined drawn on the surface of a cone.

Given that the cone may be of any height and base diameter and that the panel may be drawn anywhere on it, there is much design scope. Reasonably curved, non-chined forms are feasible, especially for narrow hull forms such as multihulls, although the use of chines remains a norm.

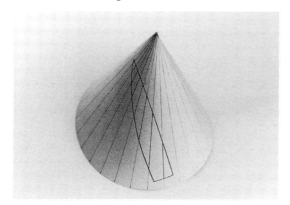

Fig 99 The hull bottom panel drawn on the cone is photographed to show a view as in the half-breadth plan …

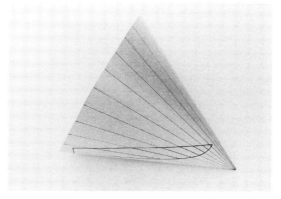

Fig 100 … and to show a profile view.

The practicality of *conical projection* usually does not involve the use of cones in the way described, though the principles are fundamental. Straight lines may be drawn on the cone from the apex to the base, and these are called *generators* or *ruling lines*.

Drafting techniques

When drawing the design the panel and the generators are constructed progressively in both a side view, known as the *profile plan* (plan meaning drawing), and a bird's eye view, called the *half-breadth plan*, on a *lines plan*. The apex of the cone, at which all generators focus, must correlate between the views. Similarly, the intersections of the generators with chines, *sheerline* or *keel line*, depending upon the panel, must correspond in each view.

A vertical cutting plane parallel to the centreline, known as a *bow line* forward of amidships and a *buttock line* aft, produces intersections in the same way that the keel line cuts the generators in different views. Bow and buttock lines permit the development of the sections of the boat in the *body plan*. **The sections demonstrate definite curvature, the extent depending upon the placement of the cone apex.**

Design possibilities

There is considerable scope for cone apex positioning, and this permits the geometrical generation of the topside and all the other panels for single or *multi-chined* construction.

The possibilities may be widened further by utilizing alternative cones, for example, a cone with an elliptical base. **Also, provided that one generator is common, a *multi-conical* approach is feasible.** This involves the selection of different cones by merging one with the next. It is also feasible to merge cylinders with cones, the cylinder having parallel generators.

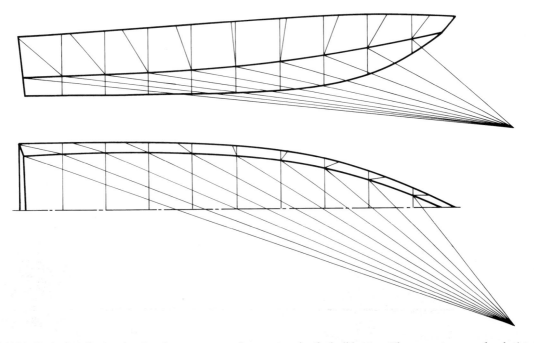

Fig 101 Conical projection showing the cone apex and generators for the hull bottom. The generators are also depicted for the topside projection, but are not followed through to the apex in each view, for reasons of clarity. The body plan may be constructed using the information shown.

Despite the range of possibilities presented, in reality the final shape of the panels, dealt with individually, is quite restricted. The process is one of trial and error in that a cone apex is tried and the panel form developed using the generators, perhaps merging to a second, then a third cone or cylinder to make minor adjustments, as one works along the panel.

The opportunity for error in terms of cone apex selection is such that the full potential of the system cannot be explored if working by hand.

Computer drafting

The use of dedicated computer software does overcome this, at least in part. Lines for the keel, chines and sheer can be developed on the screen and then the computer is set to work to attempt to establish the generators for each of the panels.

Any generators that cross indicate that the panels are not of multi-conical form, and therefore changes to the keel line, sheer line or chine lines need to be made. Some software possesses a function in which the degree of distortion in the panels is demonstrated by different colours.

This approach helps one to make a judgement about whether sheet materials will bend to the form designed. The generators alone do not provide this information with assurance.

Consideration needs to be given to the choice of sheet material to be employed. Since

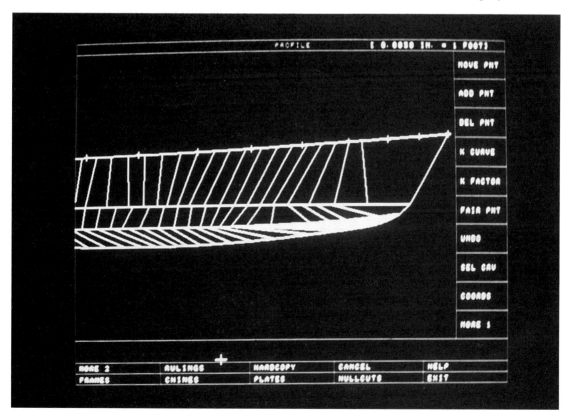

Fig 102 The bow of a computer-generated double-chined craft demonstrating generators based upon multiple cones. The extension of the generators demonstrates the way in which the apex changes.

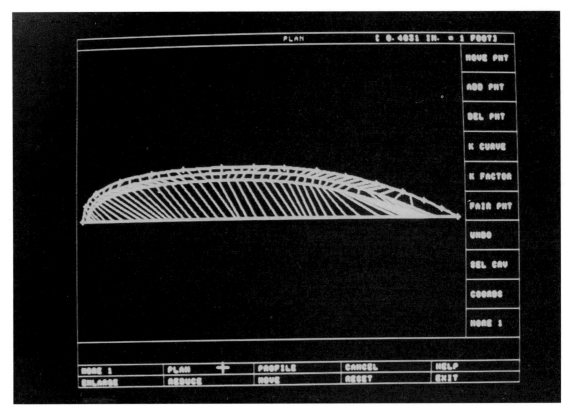

Fig 103 Multi-conic projection is also shown in the half-breadth plan.

plywood is intolerant of compound curvature, while steel and aluminium-alloy plate can adopt a permanent set when bent into position, a more relaxed approach may be adopted where metals are intended for the construction. The occasional dart in a panel overcomes minor difficulties where the plate will not conform.

Panel development

In order to take the step from the completed lines plan to the hull construction, it is helpful to establish the development of each panel.

The approach involves subdividing the panels into elements, each being bounded by two *stations* (which denote the position of the sections) and the keel line, chine lines or sheer line, depending upon the panel to be developed. The elements then need to be further divided by

diagonals to form triangles and are established on both profile and half-breadth plans.

The next step involves finding the *true length* of all lines which run between every intersection of station, diagonal, keel line, chine lines and sheerline, as relevant, since the profile and half-breadth plans do not display the true lengths of these lines any more than a photograph taken at an angle to the transom accurately represents its width. Using the true lengths between intersections, the development of the panel may be drawn, one element at a time and is usually undertaken from one end of the hull to the other.

It has to be said that the scope for error is large, making computer-generated panel development much favoured. Once the hull design is completed by using a computer and

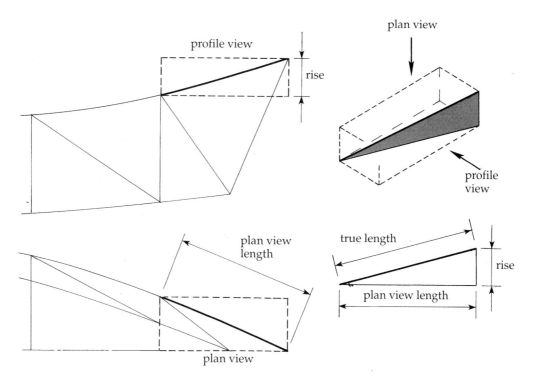

Fig 104 *The method of manually constructing the true length of the sheerline between the bow and the first station. It is best to consider the straight line distance between points. When the true lengths of all lines between intersections are established, they may be pieced together to provide the development. A continuous line is used to connect the intersections of the sheerline, keel line and chines.*

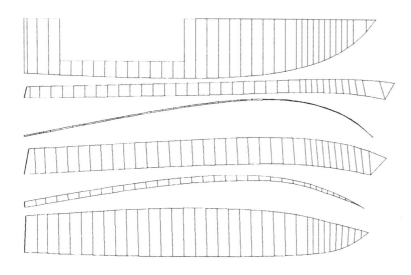

Fig 105 *A computer-generated development of the panels of a powered craft. The panels shown are, from the top: deck; topside; knuckle; intermediate; knuckle; and bottom.*

software package, the development of the panels is the press of a computer key away.

Coachroof design

Coachroofs are not unlike inverted hulls and lend themselves to construction in sheet materials. The limitations of form which apply to chined hulls are extended to panelled coachroofs. Nevertheless, it is so convenient to build in plywood that it is tempting to design the coachroofs of fibre–resin composite boats in this way, thus minimizing the cost of the initial plug.

The tops of coachroofs, and decks for that matter, require careful design. If compound curvature is avoided and the top and the deck have conventional camber the coachroof profile and deck line at centre would need to be straight. Even with plywood some degree of curvature in both directions is feasible, but, if taken too far, buckling will occur.

Tortured plywood

A successful means of distorting plywood is with the so-called *tortured plywood method*. Most suited to multihulls because of their fine hulls, each is built from two panels. These are wired and glassed, using epoxy resin, along the centreline join at a defined angle of deadrise, with the panels spread, the bow portion not being joined. **When the resin is cured the panels are pulled towards each other at the top and the panels closed at the bow, distorting the plywood into a moderately round-bilged form.**

Combining systems

Cold-moulded construction may be combined with sheet plywood panels to improve the appearance and efficiency of chined hull forms and boxy superstructures. For instance, the bottom of the hull could be built by cold-moulded construction, perhaps using the constant camber system for speed, and the topsides could be in plywood.

Similarly, boats built in metal having some panels sprung into position, blending with other panels rolled to shape, possess an improved overall hull form. But for working craft, corners, simplicity and the functionalism of chined construction do present a certain chunky, 'get-the-job-done' appeal.

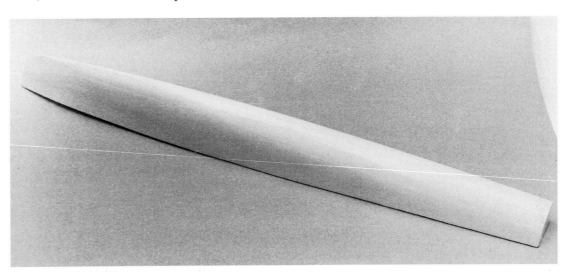

Fig 106 A scale model of one hull of a Tornado catamaran, built using the stressed plywood method.

Supplementary Note

Another novel system for construction design originated with the American Jim Brown and is primarily suited to multihull construction. Although it is not a method aimed at sheet materials, it has the benefit of fast construction. The system is known as *constant camber*, so describing the shape of each half of a hull.

The starting point is a mould having an asymmetrical, constant camber throughout its length. The mould is curved to the arc of a circle of large radius along its length. From this single mould the two cold-moulded halves of a hull can be produced, one half having the bow to the right and the other the bow to the left. What is more, a variety of hull forms is achievable from the same mould by choosing the positioning of the half hull, rather like selecting a position for a sheet panel on a cone.

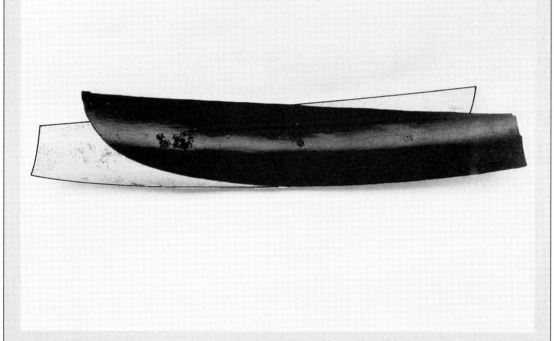

Fig 107 The surfaces at the two halves of the hull fit together, demonstrating that they have come from the same mould (GRP was used for convenience).

The time-saving feature arises because of the constant camber. Just as cold-moulded construction requires that the edges of planks are spiled so that each fits the adjacent plank to account for the compound curvature, so the constant camber requires that planks are shaped. But because the mould is of regular form (of constant camber) all planks can have the same shape. As a result, all planks may be produced in a batch, in fact, to fit any hull from the particular mould. Each half is laid in usual cold-

Fig 108 The complete hull.

moulded style, but with no individual spiling of planks and with minimal stapling because the layers of planks can be consolidated by vacuum bagging. When the glue is cured (slow-setting epoxy being the most suitable), the other half of the hull is laid on the mould. The construction proceeds by joining the two halves and adding reinforcement as for normal cold-moulded construction.

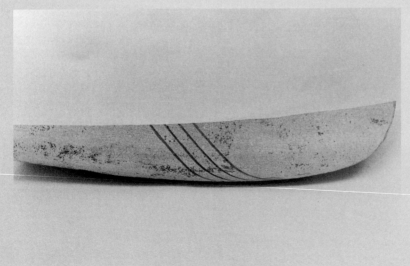

Fig 109 Planks drawn on the hull all have the same shape.

SUMMARY: PANELLED CONSTRUCTION

1. The use of sheet material provides a fast means of building hulls, usually of chined construction, with the important limitation that compound curvature is not feasible, although metal panels are more forgiving than plywood.

2. Cylindrical design presents serious limitations of form, the sections being parallel and the degree of flare defining the bow profile, while conical design offers greater variability, the sections possessing an element of curvature.

3. Computer-based systems permit a more extensive exploration of form, particularly for multi-conical design, and provide an accurate means of determining the development of the panels for ease of construction.

4. The tortured plywood method presents a way of achieving a reasonable round-bilged form, though for fast, cold-moulded construction, the constant camber system has merit.

Chapter 5

Scrutinizing Case Studies

Keel Bolts

Keel attachment

The most common arrangement for attaching the ballast keel to a yacht is to use a series of bolts. These may be threaded into the keel, in which case they project from the root of the keel through the hull and are retained by nuts.

This arrangement is similar to the method commonly used to hold engineering components together, such as the cylinder head to the block of an engine. In engineering parlance these would be termed *studs* rather than bolts, although it is convenient to refer to the fastenings generally as bolts rather than to differentiate between them.

Alternatively, the keel bolts may be inserted from inside the hull and threaded into the keel or into nuts tucked away in *galleries* in the keel. The traditional arrangement is one in which long bolts pass right through the keel from underneath and are secured inside the boat on to floors using nuts.

Keel-bolt stress

When the yacht is afloat and upright, the keel hangs by the bolts, which therefore are clearly in tension. When the yacht heels it is easy to think that the principal stress on the keel bolts is one of bending but, if this really were the case, it would prove difficult to make the keel bolts sufficiently substantial. In actuality only if there were a gap between the root of the keel and the bottom of the hull or slack in the bolts

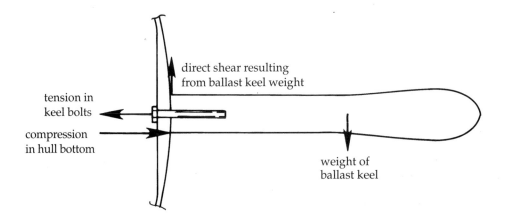

tension in keel bolts

direct shear resulting from ballast keel weight

compression in hull bottom

weight of ballast keel

Fig 110 The opposing couples are numerically equal.

would they be liable to bend.

Because of the nature of the loadings, the keel bolts are subject to tensile stress, even when the yacht is heeled. The greatest stress occurs when at 90-degrees heel, that is with the keel parallel to the water. In this situation the weight of the keel produces leverage by pulling on the keel bolts and pushing on the hull about the lower edge of the keel. These forces are equal in magnitude but opposite in direction, and form what is termed a *couple*, measured by the product of one of these forces and the distance that separates them.

The couple acting to wrench off the keel comprises the keel weight acting downwards and an upward shearing force at the keel's contact with the hull, the two forces being separated by the distance between the centre of gravity of the keel and the hull. The keel is held in position by the opposing and equal couple resulting from the tension in the keel bolts, compression on the hull and the distance between the keel bolts and the lower edge of the keel.

Calculation of diameter

Different keel bolt arrangements are feasible. Theoretically, the tension in the bolts could be dealt with by one keel bolt of large diameter, more realistically by several bolts of moderate diameter or, of course, a multitude of bolts of small diameter. Although the tension in each keel bolt is likely to vary, for a normal multi-bolt fixing a reasonable estimate of the tension in each bolt is given by dividing the total tensile force by the number of bolts.

Suppose the weight of a ballast keel is 10kN, centred 0.6m below the hull (when upright), and the distance of the centreline keel bolts from the edge of the keel (regarding the maximum distance) is 50mm. The total tensile force exerted by all keel bolts for a keel of 10kN is calculated to be 120kN.

Allowing a factor of safety of seven, the

Supplementary Calculation

The total tensile force supplied by the keel bolts, in total, may be found given: weight of ballast keel: 10kN; distance between hull and ballast keel centre of gravity (CG): 0.6m; distance between keel bolts (on the centreline) and the edge of the keel root (maximum distance assumed): 0.05m.

Couple holding keel in position $\quad = \quad \left(\begin{array}{c}\text{total bolt}\\\text{tension}\end{array}\right) \times \left(\begin{array}{c}\text{distance from}\\\text{edge to bolts}\end{array}\right)$

$$= \left(\begin{array}{c}\text{total bolt}\\\text{tension}\end{array}\right) \times 0.05$$

Couple tending to wrench $\quad = \quad \left(\begin{array}{c}\text{weight of}\\\text{keel}\end{array}\right) \times \left(\begin{array}{c}\text{distance between}\\\text{CG and hull}\end{array}\right)$
off keel

$$= (10 \times 10^3) \times 0.6$$

$$= 6 \times 10^3$$

Equating couples,
(total bolt tension) $\times$ 0.05 $\quad = \quad 6 \times 10^3$

$\Rightarrow$ total bolt tension $\quad = \quad \dfrac{6 \times 10^3}{0.05}$

$$= 120 \times 10^3 \text{N}$$

The total tensile force in the keel bolts is 120kN (12 tons).

---

design load, as it is described, would be 840kN. Suppose twelve keel bolts are employed, their material having a yield strength of 230MN/m², the required diameter of the bolts, measured to the bottom of the threads, would be 19.7mm.

Factor of safety

The need for a healthy factor of safety springs from the possibility of additional loadings on the keel, such as would occur if a large wave were dumped on the keel when the yacht was heeled to an extreme. Who knows but the situation could be exacerbated by a hefty whale caught up in the wave!

Keel bolts are inconspicuous in an expansive bilge and their out-of-sight, out-of-mind nature tempts designers to add a little extra, particularly as any additional weight is unlikely to be detrimental. That the yield strength and not the ultimate tensile strength has been used in the example to calculate the keel-bolt diameter implies a further reserve. If the calculation were based upon ultimate tensile strength, a factor of safety of ten to fifteen would be appropriate.

It does, however, make sense to base the design of the bolts upon yield strength because, beyond this point of extension, pre-tension is lost and this compromises the

Supplementary Calculation

The required diameter of a set of keel bolts, all placed on the centreline of the keel, may be found using the following data: total tensile force for all keel bolts: 120kN; yield strength of keel bolt material: 230MN/m²; factor of safety: 7; number of bolts employed: 12.

total design load	=	(total tensile force) × (factor of safety)
	=	$(120 \times 10^3) \times 7$
	=	840×10^3N

This design load is shared, assumed equally, between all bolts

Thus,

design load per bolt	=	$\dfrac{\text{total design load}}{\text{number of bolts}}$
	=	$\dfrac{840 \times 10^3}{12}$
	=	70×10^3N

Now,
for a tensile member, considering a single bolt

	stress	=	$\dfrac{\text{load}}{\text{cross-sectional area}}$
⇒	230×10^6	=	$\dfrac{70 \times 10^3}{\text{cross sectional area}}$
⇒	cross sectional area	=	304.3×10^{-6}m²

Now,
the diameter of the circular cross-section is given by:

	cross-sectional area	=	$\dfrac{\pi \times (\text{bolt diameter})^2}{4}$
⇒	304.3×10^{-6}	=	$\dfrac{\pi \times (\text{bolt diameter})^2}{4}$
⇒	bolt diameter	=	19.7×10^{-3}m

The required diameter of each keel bolt is 19.7mm to the bottom of the threads.

integrity of the keel joint.

Individual stressing

Making the assumption that all keel bolts are loaded equally may not be accurate. The stress in each bolt is a function of how much it is strained and this will vary with the flexibility of the keel and the hull. Strain in the bolts will be lower if the keel and the hull deform more readily.

For the purposes of analysis it is most simple to assume the same diameter for all, ensuring that the bolts experiencing the greatest stress are adequately catered for. The factor of safety would deal with this.

Regarding the keel as inflexible supports the argument for giving the keel bolts equality. **The keel could be seen to hinge about its lowest point, assuming extreme heel as before, and therefore all bolts are stretched equally.** But this holds only where the keel bolts are on the centreline.

Offset keel bolts

An alternative and more common arrangement of keel bolts is to offset them from the centreline, usually staggered but otherwise in pairs, and of variable distance from the centreline. This layout may appear superior because the offset upper bolts provide a greater distance to the lower keel edge (with the yacht heeled). However, for every bolt working to advantage there is one which is correspondingly close to the lower keel edge and contributing little. These bolts are little strained and therefore of low effectiveness.

The conclusion is that the resulting total cross-sectional area required by offset bolts is more or less the same as for bolts placed on the centreline.

However, there are advantages in offset bolts. A better distribution of load is provided and the arrangement is helpful where a keel has flanges at its root. A further consideration is that offset bolts result in less compression on the hull than centreline bolts.

Pre-tensioning

Significant pre-tension needs to be given to the bolts by applying torque to the nuts. This ensures that the keel remains in contact with the hull, even for the 90-degree heel, worst case. Although it may appear that pre-tension would require bolts of higher strength and that the compression between keel and hull would be elevated, this is not appreciably so provided that excessive pre-tension is not used.

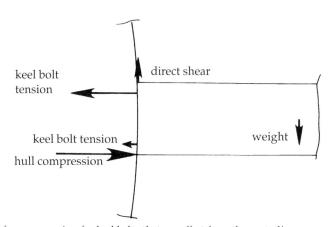

keel bolt tension

direct shear

keel bolt tension

weight

hull compression

Fig 111   The forces occurring for keel bolts that are offset from the centreline.

Supplementary Calculation

The diameter of offset keel bolts may be calculated from the following data: weight of ballast keel: 10kN; distance between hull and ballast keel CG: 0.6m; distance between keel bolts and edge of keel: 0.02m; thickness of keel: 0.10m; yield strength of keel bolt material: 230MN/m²; factor of safety: 7; number of bolts employed: 12.

With the yacht heeled 90 degrees the upper keel bolts will be strained to a greater degree than the lower ones in proportion to their distances from the lower edge. Since the keel bolt material and the diameter are consistent for all bolts, the stress in the bolts, and therefore the tension, will be proportional to the strain and therefore to the distance from the lower edge.

$$\frac{\text{tension in upper bolts}}{\text{tension in lower bolts}} = \frac{\text{distance from edge to upper bolts}}{\text{distance from edge to lower bolts}}$$

$$= \frac{0.08}{0.02}$$

$$= 4$$

and,

$$\text{couple tending to wrench off keel} = \left(\begin{array}{c}\text{weight of}\\\text{keel}\end{array}\right) \times \left(\begin{array}{c}\text{distance between}\\\text{CG and hull}\end{array}\right)$$

$$= (10 \times 10^3) \times 0.6$$

$$= 6 \times 10^3 \text{ Nm}$$

The couple holding the keel in position is given by the sum of the moments of the total tension in both the upper and the lower keel bolts from the lower edge of the keel.

$$\Rightarrow \text{couple holding keel in position} = \left(\begin{array}{c}\text{tension in} \times 0.08\\\text{upper bolts}\end{array}\right) + \left(\begin{array}{c}\text{tension in} \times 0.02\\\text{lower bolts}\end{array}\right)$$

Since this couple is equal to the couple tending to wrench off the keel,

$$\Rightarrow \quad 6 \times 10^3 \quad = \left(\begin{array}{c}\text{tension in} \times 0.08\\\text{upper bolts}\end{array}\right) + \frac{\left(\begin{array}{c}\text{tension in} \times 0.02\\\text{upper bolts}\end{array}\right)}{4}$$

$$= 0.085 \times (\text{tension in upper bolts})$$

$$\Rightarrow \quad \text{tension in upper bolts} = 70.59 \times 10^3 \text{N}$$

Only the upper bolts need to be considered since they are under the greater stress and therefore liable to failure. Since there are six upper bolts,

$$\text{tension per bolt} = \frac{70.59 \times 10^3}{6}$$

$$= 11.76 \times 10^3 \text{N}$$

and,

$$\text{design load per bolt} = \text{tension} \times (\text{factor of safety})$$

$$= (11.76 \times 10^3) \times 7$$

$$= 82.35 \times 10^3 \text{N}$$

Because,

$$\text{tensile stress} = \frac{\text{tensile load}}{\text{cross-sectional area}}$$

$$\Rightarrow \quad 230 \times 10^6 = \frac{82.35 \times 10^3}{\text{cross-sectional area}}$$

$$\Rightarrow \quad \text{cross-sectional area} = \frac{82.35 \times 10^3}{230 \times 10^6}$$

$$= 358.0 \times 10^{-6} \text{ m}^2$$

and, as before,

$$\text{cross sectional area} = \frac{\pi \times (\text{bolt diameter})^2}{4}$$

$$\Rightarrow \quad \text{bolt diameter} = 21.35 \times 10^{-3} \text{m}$$

It is to be noted that the bolt diameter, at 21.35mm to the bottom of the threads, is similar to the diameter required for the same number of bolts placed on the centreline.

Supplementary Note

The clamping effect of pre-tensioning the keel bolts is like stretching elastic inside a vertical tube and fixing it at the top and the bottom of the tube. The tension in the elastic must be equal to the compression in the tube. Now hang a weight on the elastic and the tension is increased and the compression reduced. The stretch of the elastic is much less than without pre-tension. For this reason the root of the keel remains in contact with the hull even when the keel bolts are placed under a high load.

Compression of the hull is unlikely to be problematical, unless the keel to hull mating area and the keel root width are particularly small. It is unlikely that compressive stress in the hull bottom could lower the factor of safety to single figures.

This does make the assumption, however, that normal materials are used for the hull in this area. Woods of very low density could suffer crushing while foam sandwich definitely would. The solution for boats of this construction is to employ solid glass-reinforced plastic in the way of the keel bolts, and this material has more than adequate compressive strength.

Lloyd's Rules' approach

A rather different and more extensive approach is given by *Lloyd's Register Rules and Regulations* for the calculation of the size of keel bolts. Instead of adopting an approach in

Fig 112 A ballast keel of small footprint need not exaggerate the stress in the keel bolts if the weight is correspondingly low.

Supplementary Calculation

The compressive stress on the hull (and the keel) may be estimated by assuming the compression to be equal to the total loading on the keel bolts which would cause them to yield. Based upon the earlier example, we could assume this load to be 840kN. If we assume a keel root area of $0.12m^2$ and the compressive stress is assumed constant,

$$\text{compressive stress} = \frac{\text{compressive load}}{\text{cross-sectional area}}$$

$$= \frac{840 \times 10^3}{0.12}$$

$$= 7.0 \times 10^6 N/m^2$$

The resulting compressive stress in the hull and keel is $7MN/m^2$. Even if all the compression is assumed to occur over just 20 per cent of the mating area, the compressive stress would be $35MN/m^2$, which provides an adequate reserve for all but the more crushable hull materials.

which the ballast keel and the hull in the vicinity are assumed inflexible, Lloyd's Rules regard the keel as separated into vertical portions, each independent of the next, thus implying flexibility in the extreme.

The diameter of each keel bolt is related to the portion of the keel the bolt is seen to support, calculated by equating couples as previously.

A further deviation from the earlier approach is the use of the ultimate tensile strength and not the yield strength. Although the ratio of the two varies for some keel bolt materials, the factor of safety used would depend upon which measure of strength the calculations are based on and therefore would have a corrective effect.

The evolutionary as well as the analytical basis of Lloyd's and other classification societies' rules provide an inbuilt factor of safety (which becomes less arbitrary with time). This does mean that relatively unusual occurrences or those outside the normal design parameters are catered for indirectly.

Major impact

An example of an unusual occurrence is seriously running aground (although this may not be so unusual for some). **It would be a difficult exercise to account for this in the design, principally because it is hard to assess what the loadings are likely to be.**

Running aground in soft mud or gently sloping sand when sailing in light winds and therefore travelling slowly may be unnoticeable. There are no structural problems here, except when a swell is running and the sand is hard. Coming in to land feels sickeningly solid and potentially damaging although, it has to be said, to the hull rather than the keel bolts.

Hitting large, submerged rocks is worse. Under this load the keel bolts are placed in shear, although the clamping effect of the bolts results in a high level of friction between the mating faces and it is this that resists the shear rather than the bolts as such. The increased tension in the forward bolts may be fairly significant as the hull trips over the keel.

Running aground in this way can easily damage the hull, usually around the aft end of the keel as it pushes upwards from the impact. The crew may not be as healthy afterwards either. The effect is to throw them forwards, and all without seat belts or air bags.

Supplementary Calculation

In order to give a feel for the approach presented by Lloyd's Rules, the basic data from a previous example are used so that solutions may be compared: weight of ballast keel: 10kN; distance between hull and ballast keel CG: 0.6m. We may suppose that twelve keel bolts are used and their material has an ultimate tensile strength of 600MN/m². For simplicity, we may assume that the centre of gravity of each portion of the keel is equidistant from the hull and that the weight of each portion is the same. In reality, the foil shape of the keel requires that the centre of gravity and the weight of each portion are determined individually so that the diameter of each keel bolt may be calculated separately.

The Lloyd's Rules formula for the keel bolt diameter is:

$$d_K = 0.71 \times \sqrt{\left(\frac{K_b \times w \times d_{cg}}{b_K}\right)}$$

$$= 0.71 \times \sqrt{\left(\frac{1.5 \times 84.95 \times 600}{100}\right)}$$

$$= 19.6mm$$

where w = the portion of the weight of the ballast keel supported by the bolts in kg (=84.95kg)

d_{cg} = vertical distance of the centre of gravity of weight w below the top of ballast keel in way of bolt in mm (= 600mm) (yacht upright)

b_K = breadth of top of keel in way of bolt in mm (= 100mm)

σ_u = ultimate tensile strength of the bolt material in N/mm² (= 600N/mm²)

$K_b = \dfrac{\sigma_u}{400}$

The required keel bolt diameter (to the outside of the threads) is 19.6mm.

Since this diameter is measured to the outside of the threads the specification is slightly lower than that calculated earlier (19.7mm to the bottom of the threads where the bolts are on the centreline, and just over 21.3mm where offset) but the figures are not far apart.

As a point of note, Lloyd's Rules do specify that the keel bolts should be fitted so that they are alternately on opposite sides of the centreline.

SUMMARY: KEEL BOLTS

1. A yacht's ballast keel bolts experience tensile stress principally, even when the yacht is heeled, as a result of the keel's weight hinging about its edge at the root, producing couples generated by the bolts and the keel weight.

2. Although stress in the keel bolts varies with the flexibility of the keel and the hull, a simple approach is to assume that the total tensile force is shared equally among all bolts (if they are located on the keel's centreline).

3. The diameter required of offset keel bolts is similar to that of centreline bolts, assuming the same number are used, but hull compression is significantly lower; pre-tension is a necessity for either arrangement.

4. A more exacting approach, in which the diameter of each bolt is calculated by regarding the keel in individual, vertical portions, is adopted by Lloyd's Rules, developed evolutionarily to accommodate varied loadings.

To analyse the yacht's deceleration in order to estimate the forces exerted upon it would involve a fair number of assumptions, including the buoyancy take up in the bow and the inertia of the hull and rig, not to mention the solidity of the rock. Perhaps it is best to keep the analysis simple after all.

Hull Panel

Shell distortion

As a structural concept the hull may be viewed as a tube having a very thin wall, although this comparison is more true of a ship, for which the form may be likened to a box construction of rectangular section.

In action, for instance, when the hull is supported by waves at bow and stern, the thin shell is liable to distortion. Such instability in the walls of the tube is likely to precipitate failure. Sagging of the hull results in compression in the deck, which is then likely to buckle. In turn this reduces the compressive loading the deck is able to withstand.

Beam representation

Until the panels of the hull begin to distort it is reasonable to suppose that beam theory may be used with validity to determine the hull's structural characteristics by regarding it as a beam. In order to apply beam theory there is a need to calculate the second moment of area of the cross-section of the hull with deck or coachroof. This can be found, in principle, by splitting the cross-section into elements, finding the second moment of area of each about the neutral axis and then adding these together to obtain the total second moment of area.

The difficulty lies not in the calculation of second moment of area, but in the validity of the assumption that the section retains its form. Structural analysis which makes

allowance for these distortions lies outside the scope of this book, but an appreciation of the problem goes far in finding design solutions.

Analysis is simplified if constructional components are regarded independently. The hull, deck and other panels may be regarded as locally loaded and supported by a framework, which in turn may be thought to withstand the global loadings. Some allowance for the complementary contribution made by the panels in terms of the global loadings needs to be made, although neglecting this does provide a reserve. Much would depend upon whether the structure is designed to follow monocoque, framed or space-framed structural principles.

Sea water head

Water loadings are perhaps most intensive in large wave conditions. For displacement craft we may reasonably suppose a head of water of perhaps two or three times the hull depth, such figures being arrived at largely by experience in terms of what boats generally can withstand and by reviewing structural failures. The required thickness of the hull shell can then be determined based upon the loading this implies.

It is convenient to consider areas of the hull shell as flat and subdivided by fairly closely spaced frames (or longitudinals) of unlimited length. The requirement then is that each panel, bordered by the frames or longitudinals, should be able to withstand the chosen head of sea water.

Under this loading the panels are bent in a wavy fashion. **Consideration of a single panel indicates bending which may be likened to a fixed-ended beam with uniformly distributed load.** For the purposes of determining the thickness required of the panel, it helps to think of a strip of, say, 10mm width running from frame to frame (or longitudinal to longitudinal). We may then imagine this strip to be loaded by a column of water in the same

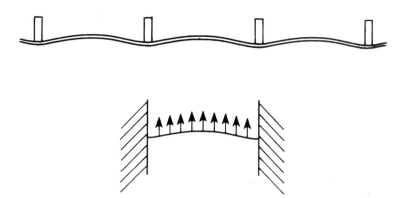

Fig 113 *The hull panel between frames may be modelled as a fixed-ended beam with uniformly distributed load.*

way that we might line up weights along the strip. Although the head of water produces an upward force on the strip this can be equated to a column of water bearing down on it.

Panel calculation

So the procedure required to find the panel thickness is first to determine the weight of the column of water imagined above the strip of the panel and then to apply beam theory, regarding the strip as a uniformly loaded, fixed-ended beam. The maximum bending moment arises where the strip, representing the panel, meets a frame (or longitudinal) and this indicates where failure ultimately would occur.

As an example of the calculation of the bottom panel thickness for a working yacht

of 19.3m we may start with the depth of hull (2.47m), the frame spacing (1.00m) and the material (aluminium alloy). This frame spacing is unusually large and results in thick plating, but this makes for ease of construction for a chined vessel and proves very robust and resistant to puncture.

For a metal hull it makes sense to design the panels on the basis of the yield strength of the material rather than on the ultimate tensile strength. Depending upon the material, the yield strength may be as little as half the ultimate tensile strength. However, the use of the latter permits a more universal approach covering a range of materials, including fibre–resin composites and wood. The consideration of the ultimate tensile strength of the material does imply the use of a lower

Supplementary Note

Of interest, the bending moment in the middle of the hull panel strip may be shown to be half the value of that at the frame or longitudinal. Additionally, where the curvature of the strip changes from concave to convex, the curvature and therefore the bending moment is zero. Two such *double inflections* occur in the strip and therefore in the panel, indicating an area of low stress.

For the real weight fanatic this might provide something of a guide about detailed weight pruning. Thus the panel would need to be of the greatest strength and therefore thickness in the vicinity of the stiffeners and then vary in thickness across the panel, producing a pattern of: thick, thin, moderately thin, thin, and then thick again. Not for the faint-hearted.

Supplementary Calculation

The aluminium-alloy hull bottom-panel thickness may be derived for a head of sea water of 2.5 times hull depth and given: hull depth: 2.47m; frame spacing: 1.00m; ultimate flexural strength: $275MN/m^2$. A sample 10mm wide strip, of length equal to the frame spacing, must support the weight of a column of sea water, the depth of which is equal to the required head.

$$\text{head of sea water} = 2.5 \times \text{hull depth}$$
$$= 2.5 \times 2.47$$
$$= 6.175m$$

$$\text{weight of column} = \text{head} \times (\text{frame spacing}) \times (\text{strip width}) \times (\text{sea water density}) \times \begin{pmatrix} \text{gravitational} \\ \text{acceleration} \end{pmatrix}$$
$$= 620.9N$$

The strip may be described as a uniformly-distributed, fixed-ended beam

and,
$$\text{maximum bending moment} = \frac{(\text{weight of column}) \times (\text{strip length})}{12}$$
$$= \frac{620.9 \times 1.00}{12}$$
$$= 51.74\,Nm$$

Now,
$$\text{maximum stress} = \frac{(\text{bending moment}) \times (\text{distance from neutral axis to outer surface})}{\text{second moment of area}}$$

and,
$$\text{second moment of area} = \frac{(\text{strip width}) \times (\text{thickness of panel})^3}{12}$$

The stress under consideration is the stress which would cause the aluminium alloy to fail, that is, its ultimate flexural strength.

$$\Rightarrow \quad 275 \times 10^6 = \frac{51.74 \times (\text{thickness of panel})/2}{0.01 \times (\text{thickness of panel})^3/12}$$

$$\Rightarrow \quad \text{thickness of panel} = 10.6 \times 10^{-3}m$$

The hull panel thickness required is 10.6mm.

factor of safety or, in this case, a greater head of water than would be employed if the yield strength formed the basis of the calculation.

An appropriate figure for the head of water which the bottom should withstand can be arrived at only derivatively. Variables, such as the conditions in which the boat is designed to operate, will also affect the chosen head. Given a head of sea water 2.5 times a hull depth of 2.47m (that is, 6.175m), the thickness of the hull bottom is calculated to be 10.6mm based upon the ultimate tensile strength of the aluminium alloy planned. No one could put his sea boot through this.

Panel variation

It is evident that more closely-spaced framing results in a thinner skin requirement. For example, a frame spacing of 0.5m warrants a skin thickness of 5.3mm, in the same material.

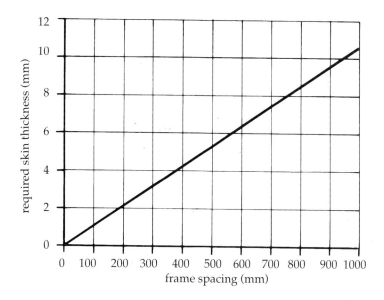

Fig 114 The required thickness of a solid-skin panel increases linearly with frame (or other stiffener) spacing. The specific figures relate to the example in the text in which aluminium alloy plate is involved.

Given constancy of all the variables except for the frame spacing, the calculated panel thickness produces a straight-line graph, demonstrating a linear relationship.

It could be argued that the topsides can be of thinner plate than the bottom because they experience a smaller head of water. Targeting a position just above the waterline for the example considered, the head would be about 5.0m. This reduction in loading for the same frame spacing implies a reduction in panel thickness of 1mm to bring it down to 9.6mm.

In the event the built hull comprises 12mm aluminium alloy plate below the waterline and 11mm above. This results in a mass increase of about 300kg over 11mm and 10mm plate, respectively, but for a go-anywhere, 19.3m vessel the extra strength is justified and provides reassurance.

Modelling deficiences

This approach to determining panel thickness is a fairly simple one and the calculations could be simplified further by making approximations, a not unreasonable approach given the imprecision presented by assuming (or guessing at) an approximate head. A more advanced mathematical model is likely to produce better results.

The decision about the scale of the head of sea water is somewhat arbitrary and no account is taken of the length or the displacement of the vessel. Additionally the panel is assumed to be flat (before being loaded) and yet curvature improves its strength. **Perhaps the most significant assumption made is that the frames are of unlimited length and therefore, when loaded, the panel bends in one plane only.**

If we suppose the bottom of the boat to comprise frames as before, but with occasional longitudinals, it is seen that the longitudinals contribute to the support of the panel. For closely spaced frames and widely spaced longitudinals the level of support by the longitudinals is low, but, as the framework becomes closer to square, so the longitudinals play a greater part. Although we could

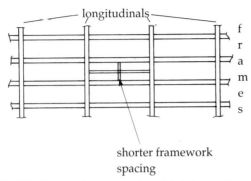

Fig 115 *Greater stress occurs in a strip between the shorter framework spacing. Since both strips are deflected equally by a water load, the shorter strip is bent to a greater degree.*

consider the lesser of the two spacings either between frames or longitudinals and then neglect the contribution being made by the member at the greater spacing, this would result in excessive panel thickness.

Framework design

Consideration of the sectional dimensions of the framework presents similar limitations in adopting this simplified approach. The framework can be designed to withstand the water loadings as if the hull skin were transferring these loadings direct to the framework. For example, a frame would be designed to cope with water up to half the frame spacing to either side of the frame.

The assumption is that the skin merely

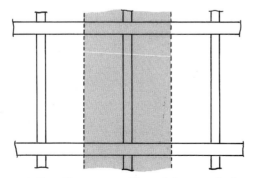

Fig 116 *The stiffener must withstand the water load over the area shaded.*

relays the loading but does not contribute to withstanding it. This could be seen to provide an element of reserve, but the approach is relatively unsophisticated.

Improved modelling

More advanced models attempt to take these factors into account. The rules produced by the classification societies tend to be more expansive and adopt a not dissimilar approach. The *American Bureau of Shipping (ABS)* which, despite its title, also concerns itself with small craft, provides an example. The rules relating to hull plating make allowance for the combination of skin and stiffeners and build in several correction factors. In general, however, the approach is not vastly dissimilar to that used previously.

Water head is based upon both hull draught and *classification length* rather than just hull depth, although the latter does provide an alternative condition. Regarding the skin or plate calculation, the *aspect ratio* of the plate, defined by the framework's greater spacing divided by its lesser spacing, is taken into account. Finally, a correction for the curvature in the plate is made.

By way of comparison the calculated plate thickness for the aluminium-alloy-hulled yacht considered already, assuming a flat panel and frames of unlimited length, is much the same, that is 10.6mm, despite the use of different starting parameters. **However, when an element of panel curvature is introduced (30mm over 1m) and longitudinals are built in (at a spacing of 1.5m) the required panel thickness becomes 10.0mm.**

The difference is small enough that the simpler model dealt with previously appears tolerable, at least as a first approximation. One final condition, as a fall-back in the ABS rules, is that the plate thickness is to be not less than one-hundredth of the frame or longitudinal spacing. As it happens this is calculated to be 10.0mm, the same thickness derived already using a more involved set of parameters, which might cause the reader to think that the one-hundredth rule would provide the simplest model of all!

Allowance also needs to be made for the variation of loading fore and aft. For example, additional strength is called for in way of the ballast keel and the *slamming area* forward.

Planing craft

Assessing the *dynamical loadings* produced by slamming or when planing suggests the need for a different approach involving a consideration of factors such as hull deceleration on impact. It follows that to base the design of a planing craft's bottom panelling on a sea water head which relates to the hull depth is unlikely to be sufficiently accurate.

A better modelling of the situation is achieved if the underwater form, mass and particularly speed are taken into account. The ease with which the hull penetrates the water when driven hard over and through waves is reflected in the hull form; *deep V hulls* notably produce a softer ride and are therefore usually

chosen for high-speed, powered craft. *Momentum* increases with *mass* and therefore a boat of large mass will experience high water loadings during conditions when high impact is likely – falling from wave crests into troughs, for example. Speed is the other component of a boat's momentum and therefore this aspect needs to be included in modelling the loadings on the hull panels.

Dynamic pressure

The ABS rules relating to planing craft take these factors, and more, into account. Pressure of the water on the bottom is calculated under dynamic circumstances. Since pressure is given by force acting over a unit of area – which in the SI system is $1m^2$ – the force applied can be calculated over a given area. Therefore we can determine the total force acting on a strip of hull panel which spans two stiffeners.

In the previous example the weight of water from a given head was shown to produce a uniformly-distributed load on a 10mm-wide strip of the hull panel running from frame to frame. Pressure therefore may be related to the

---

Supplementary Calculation

The rules of the American Bureau of Shipping for calculating the pressure for semi-planing and planing craft hulls require the information which follows. Some data were used previously and some are newly introduced, each being expressed in the units employed by the ABS rules (many of which are non-SI).

Constants

hull depth (D): 2.47 m
frame spacing: 100 cm
longitudinal spacing: 150 cm
mass (Δ): 40,000 kg
stationary length waterline (Lw): 18.1m
maximum beam (B): 4.9 m
running trim (τ): 5°
deadrise at LCG (β): 15°
maximum calm water design speed (V): 20 knots
stationary hull draught (d): 1.1m

$N = 1.0$ (describes the service dynamic factor)
$N_1 = 0.1$
$N_2 = 0.0046$
$K_1 = 9.8$
$Fv_1 = 1.0$ } for maximum
$Fv_2 = 1.0$ } pressure on bottom

contd.

The 'design area' of the plating is given by:

$$A_D = \text{frame spacing} \times \text{longitudinal spacing}$$
$$= 15,000 \text{ cm}^2$$

The 'reference area' is given by:

$$A_R = \frac{6.95 \times \Delta}{d}$$
$$= 252,727 \text{ cm}^2$$

The 'design area factor', F_D, is found using the accompanying graph, produced by ABS.

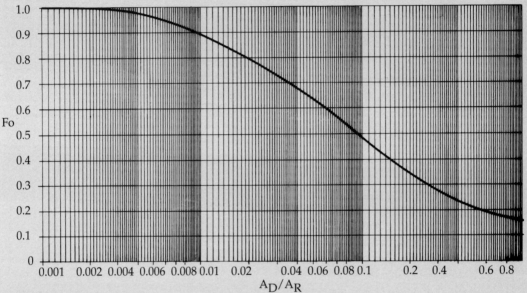

Fig 117 (Courtesy of ABS)

The ratio of A_D and A_R equals 0.0594, which indicates a value of F_D of 0.95.

Now, the ABS rules specify that the greatest resulting pressure from the following three expressions should be used to calculate hull panel thickness. (This would be the predicted greatest pressure experienced by the hull bottom.)

$$P_b = N_1 \times \frac{\Delta}{(L_w \times B)} \times (1+n) \times F_D \times F_{V_1}$$

where $\quad n = N_2 \times \frac{(L_w + 1.008)}{B} \times \tau \times (50\text{-}\beta) \times \frac{(V^2 \times B^2)}{\Delta}$

$$P_1 = 7.5 \times K_1 \times N \times d \times F_D \times F_{V_2}$$
$$P_D = 9.8 \times (D + 1.22)$$

From which we find that:

$$P_b = 81.78 \text{ kN/m}^2$$
$$P_1 = 76.81 \text{ kN/m}^2$$
$$P_D = 36.16 \text{ kN/m}^2$$

The design pressure is assumed to be the largest of the three, that is, 81.78 kN/m^2.

weight of sea water bearing on such a strip and therefore to the head.

Design calculation

Using as an example the 19.3m aluminium-alloy yacht considered previously, but assuming that it is of planing form and capable of 10m/s (assume 20 knots) in calm water, the water pressure for design calculation is 81.78 kN/m². By comparison, the design loading given by a head of sea water 2.5 times the hull depth (used previously as a basis for panel thickness calculation), implies a static water pressure of 62.09kN/m². It can be deduced that 10m/s planing performance results in a design pressure some 32 per cent greater than if the displacement performance were assumed.

The resulting aluminium alloy panel thickness would be 12.2mm compared to 10.6mm. Despite the constructional merits of the system using thick plate with widely spaced stiffeners, a narrower stiffener spacing would be appropriate.

Sandwich equivalence

Alternatively, sandwich-type construction permits wider stiffener spacings because of the inherent strength and stiffness achieved, but without the weight penalty that results from the use of a solid, thick skin. A simple analysis for calculating the thickness of the faces of the sandwich could be made by equating with the solid panel, assuming the same material. **The bending strength of the core may be neglected, in which case the panel may be regarded in terms of the two faces, effectively separated, but by a non-existent core.**

For 0.75mm-thick aluminium alloy faces the required thickness of the sandwich is about 27mm, and this would have a strength comparable with that of the 10.6mm-thick solid skin.

However, because the sandwich is more vulnerable when deflected than the solid skin, it would make sense to apply a slightly greater factor of safety. This may be achieved either by increasing the sea water head or by using a value of allowable stress that is less than the ultimate strength. **If allowable stress is set at two-thirds of the ultimate strength, faces 1.0mm thick and a sandwich just over 30mm thick would meet the requirement.**

Supplementary Note

For a sandwich panel, equivalence under bending is given when the section modulus of the two separated faces is the same as the section modulus of the solid skin. The section modulus is given by the ratio of the second moment of area to the distance from the neutral axis to the outer surface, conveniently obtained by considering a strip of the panel.

For the sandwich, the second moment of area is found by subtracting the second moment of area of the space (the core) from that of the full section, assumed solid, thus deriving the second moment of area of the faces only.

The calculation is a little involved numerically, although a reasonable approximation can be made so that the face thickness can be found directly. Consideration also needs to be given to the strength of the core in order to avoid failure by shearing.

A sandwich construction comprising fibre-composite faces with a foam core is most commonly employed. **For equivalence with the aluminium alloy panel described, a sandwich comprising a GRP-faced foam core would need to be 31mm thick with 2.0mm faces.**

Assessing flexibility

Flexibility tends to be low for sandwich panels because of the effect of their thickness. Solid GRP composite panels are relatively thin and a check should be made that excessive deflection

Supplementary Calculation

The required face and core thicknesses for a GRP and foam sandwich may be found from the seawater head and the consequential pressure used for previous calculations: design pressure: $62.09 \text{kN}/\text{m}^2$; frame spacing: 1.0m; allowable tensile/compressive stress in faces: $80 \times 10^6 \text{ MN}/\text{m}^2$; allowable shear stress in core: $1.0 \text{MN}/\text{m}^2$.

Approximately,

$$\text{core thickness} = \frac{(\text{design pressure}) \times (\text{frame spacing})}{2 \times (\text{allowable core shear stress})}$$

$$= \frac{(62.09 \times 10^3) \times 1.0}{2 \times (1.0 \times 10^6)}$$

$$= 31.0 \times 10^{-3} \text{m}$$

and,

$$\text{face thickness} = \frac{(\text{design pressure}) \times (\text{frame spacing})^2}{12 \times (\text{core thickness}) \times (\text{allowable face stress})}$$

$$= \frac{(62.09 \times 10^3) \times 1.0^2}{12 \times 0.031 \times (80 \times 10^6)}$$

$$= 2.09 \times 10^{-3} \text{m}$$

The core thickness required is 31.0mm and the thickness of each face 2.09mm.

The choice of the allowable stresses in the core and the faces is somewhat arbitrary and figures rather smaller than the ultimate strength values have been selected. Yet these arbitrary values of strength have a significant effect on thickness. For greater confidence in designing the sandwich it is preferable to rely upon authority prescription. Based upon ABS rules the core thickness is calculated at about 30mm and each face thickness at 2mm.

is not likely to occur. This is particularly true for homogeneous constructions, notably where chopped strand mat reinforcement is used. The higher stiffness of rovings, especially where used at a distance from the skin's neutral axis, lessens panel deflection.

Although strength remains the ultimate consideration, flexibility in the hull panels is a concern in terms of performance and user acceptability. To judge the deflection occurring when the panel is on the point of failure is less useful than when it is under working conditions.

Deflection criterion

One criterion that may be applied is that the deflection in the middle of a hull panel between two stiffeners should be no more than 1 per cent of the stiffener spacing under maximum working load conditions. This could be represented by a head of sea water equal to the hull depth.

Although 1 per cent of the stiffener spacing might seem to represent a relatively small deflection, for a frame spacing of 1.0m this does imply acceptability when the deflection is 10mm. For the aluminium-alloy hull panel having a thickness of 10.6mm, the deflection under this head of sea water, using a typical value for Young's modulus for the alloy, is calculated to be 9.3mm, thus falling within the criterion. **For an alternately-layered, woven roving and chopped strand mat laminate 14.8mm thick (equivalent in strength to the aluminium-alloy panel), deflection amounts to 31.5mm, which definitely lies outside the 1 per cent criterion.**

Waterline loadings

In order to provide another approach, we may consider the panel deflection when the vessel is floating at its waterline. Because deflection

Supplementary Calculation

The deflection of a 10.6mm thick aluminium-alloy panel based upon the specification presented previously under a working head of sea water equal to the hull depth may be found using the following information: hull panel (strip) thickness: 10.6mm; Young's modulus of elasticity of aluminium alloy: $70GN/m^2$; hull depth: 2.47m; frame spacing (strip length): 1.0m. For a strip of aluminium alloy of nominal 10mm width and 1.0m length, subject to a uniformly distributed sea-water load, as before:

$$\text{weight of column} = \text{(frame spacing)} \times \text{(strip width)} \times \text{(head)} \times \text{(sea water density)} \times \binom{\text{gravitational}}{\text{acceleration}}$$

$$= 1.0 \times 0.01 \times 2.47 \times 1025 \times 9.81$$
$$= 248.4 \text{ N}$$

Regarding the section of the strip,

$$\text{second moment of area} = \frac{\text{(strip width)} \times \text{(strip depth)}^3}{12}$$
$$= \frac{0.01 \times 0.0106^3}{12}$$
$$= 992.5 \times 10^{-12} \text{ m}^4$$

For a fixed-ended beam (strip) subject to a uniformly distributed load (the weight of the column of sea water):

$$\text{deflection} = \frac{\text{(weight of column)} \times \text{(strip length)}^3}{384 \times \text{(modulus of elasticity)} \times \text{(second moment of area)}}$$
$$= \frac{248.4 \times 1.00^3}{384 \times (70 \times 10^9) \times (992.5 \times 10^{-12})}$$
$$= 9.3 \times 10^{-3} \text{m}$$

The resulting deflection of the panel is 9.3mm.

relates directly to load, the deflection with a head equal to the hull draught (1.1m) will correspond to the deflection with a head equal to the hull depth (2.47m). Thus deflection would be 4.1mm for the aluminium- alloy panel considered. For the GRP panel the deflection would be 14.0mm in the middle of the panel.

Supplementary Note

Deflection of a 14.8mm thick fibre–resin composite panel of alternate layers of woven rovings and chopped strand is calculated in the same way as for the aluminium alloy, the only variance being Young's modulus of elasticity: $7.6GN/m^2$; it follows that

$$\text{second moment of area} = 2.701 \times 10^{-9} \text{ m}^4$$
and,
$$\text{deflection} = 31.5 \times 10^{-3} \text{m}$$

The deflection of the fibre–resin composite panel is 31.5mm.

That the hull panel is bowing between frames to this extent when the hull is at its normal waterline may seem somewhat alarming, particularly with regard to its effect on water flow. Reducing the frame spacing would reduce the deflection significantly, but the result would be a series of ripples, although of much lesser magnitude than the longer waves associated with the greater frame spacing.

Deflection relationship

However, the nature of the formula for deflection indicates that if frame spacing is halved, the deflection is reduced by a factor of one-eighth. If deflection is expressed as a percentage of span, the halving of the frame spacing reduces the percentage deflection by one-quarter. The effect of reducing the stiffener spacing is therefore considerable.

Although the use of a thicker skin achieves a reduction in deflection, strength (and weight) are greater than necessary. This is true especially for the solid GRP panel. **Nevertheless, with increased skin thickness the reduction in deflection is greater than the increase in strength and weight.** Doubling the panel thickness has the effect of increasing strength by four times while at the same time reducing deflection by eight times. In conclusion, deflection is best dealt with by using thicker panels of low density, ideally of sandwich-type construction.

Rig Analysis

Rig failure

Rig demise must be listed among the relatively common major structural failures. One reason for this is that relatively low factors of safety are used in order to minimize weight aloft. Another is that the stayed rig is a complex structure with a large number of interlinked components and the failure of any one can have a knock-on effect resulting in the whole rig's tumbling down.

At the same time, it is not feasible to design the mast so that it will stand if a shroud

---

SUMMARY: HULL PANEL

1. The thickness of the hull skin may be determined by regarding a panel, assumed flat, spanning frames (or longitudinals) under a bending load given by a head of sea water some two to three times the hull depth.

2. An improved model is given by accounting for curvature in the panel, by assuming the panel is surrounded by both frames and longitudinals and by considering the effect of displacement, according to the rules of the classification societies.

3. Hull skin thickness for planing craft is defined by dynamic pressure, calculated by considering hull form, mass and speed, although dynamic pressure can be expressed in terms of an equivalent static sea water head.

4. A sandwich panel can be designed for equivalence with a solid panel, the sandwich producing substantially less deflection under the same loading, solid GRP panels tending to deflect more than a 1 per cent criterion, unless closely-framed.

bottlescrew breaks or unwinds. By contrast, unstayed masts offer a high level of structural security due to the simplicity conferred.

Maximum loadings

Recognizing the circumstance which produces the greatest loading on the stayed mast is not straightforward. **Common practice is to design the mast on the basis of the maximum *transverse stability* of the yacht.** It is logical that the greater the stability the better the yacht will stand up to the wind, and therefore the higher will be the loadings in the rig, but this takes no account of downwind sailing.

When sailing before the wind there is no automatic way in which the force in the sail plan can be limited, as happens by heeling when sailing upwind. One solution would be to consider the downwind condition on the basis of the *longitudinal stability* of the hull in the same way that transverse stability is featured for the upwind case.

The difficulty is that longitudinal stability is comparatively high owing to hull length and increases as the yacht travels faster through the water because dynamic forces lift the bow and hold down the stern. Unsatisfactory though it may seem, to a large extent the solution to the avoidance of rig failure when sailing downwind lies in good seamanship. In terms of the decision about the required mast section it is simplest to base this upon maximum transverse stability and apply an adequate factor of safety to allow for downwind sailing.

Design loading

Transverse stability is measured by the *righting couple*. For the yacht alone (that is without crew) this is the product of the yacht's weight and its leverage from the centre of *buoyancy* (known as the *righting lever*), shifted outboard as the yacht heels. However, where the crew assist stability by sitting on the weather deck or where movable water ballast is employed an additional righting couple, measured in the same way, results. The total righting couple is the sum of these two elements.

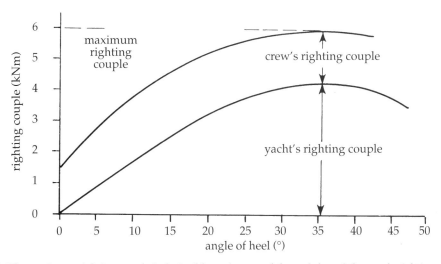

Fig 118 *The maximum righting couple is derived from the sum of the yacht's and the crew's righting couples. For a larger, more heavily ballasted yacht, its maximum righting couple would be at a larger angle of heel – about 55° or 60°.*

Supplementary Calculation

The contribution made to the total righting couple by the yacht and the crew varies with the angle of heel. An estimate of the total maximum righting couple may be made by assuming (for best angle of heel): yacht weight: 10kN; horizontal distance from yacht's CG to CB: 0.45m; crew weight: 1.5kN; horizontal distance from crew's CG to yacht's CB: 1.0m. It follows that:

total righting couple = (yacht weight × yacht CG to CB) + (crew weight × crew CG to CB)
        = $(10 \times 10^3 \times 0.45) + (1.5 \times 10^3 \times 1.0)$
        = $6.0 \times 10^3 \text{Nm}$

Total righting couple is 6.0kNm.

For accuracy, a curve of the total righting couple against the angle of heel needs to be considered, from which the maximum righting couple may be determined. Suppose that at this angle of heel, the yacht's righting couple is 4.5kNm and that the crew contribute a further 1.5kNm, the total righting couple is therefore 6.0kNm.

Since the *heeling couple* must be equal to the righting couple, assuming equilibrium in which the yacht remains at a constant angle of heel, the force applied to the rig by the wind may be found, given also the *heeling lever*. It follows that the the maximum force occurs when the righting couple is at a maximum.

The heeling lever is the vertical distance, measured from the *centre of effort* of the sails to either the *centre of lateral resistance* for equilibrium or to the instantaneous *roll centre* at the yacht's centre of gravity if non-steady state gusty conditions apply. The latter normally presents the worse case.

An alternative, simpler approach assumes that the yacht is heeled by a force acting perpendicularly to the *hounds* (the highest point of attachment of the shrouds). The heeling lever in this case is from the hounds to the chainplate, measured perpendicularly to the heeling force.

This last model is applied to the case study. If the heeling lever measured from the chainplate to the hounds as described is 6m, it follows that the heeling force must be 1kN in

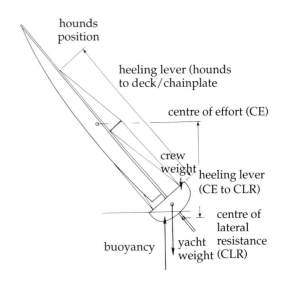

Fig 119 The forces produce equilibrium. Although the heeling lever between the centre of effort and the centre of lateral resistance or centre of gravity are a more realistic representation, it is convenient to consider a single perpendicular force at the hounds, the heeling lever then being defined by the distance along the mast from the hounds to the deck (or chainplate, more precisely).

order that the heeling couple equates with the righting couple, which it has already been specified equals 6.0kNm.

Space-frame modelling
Given the magnitude of the force at the hounds

Supplementary Calculation

The force at the hounds acting perpendicularly to the mast may be found by equating the righting and heeling couples, given: total righting couple: 6.0kNm; distance from hounds to deck: 6.0m.

Now,

heeling couple = (force at hounds) × (distance from hounds to deck)

and, for steady state heel,

heeling couple = righting couple

which implies from the above two expressions that:

force at hounds × 6.0 = 6.0×10^3

⇒ force at hounds = 1×10^3N

The force at the hounds is 1kN.

---

the rig may be analysed progressively as a space-frame. This makes the assumption that all intersections or nodes between members of the mast, shrouds and *spreaders* are pinned, that is, the members are able to rotate freely at each node.

It seems reasonable to assume freedom of movement between shroud and spreader as if linked both above and below the spreader. Similarly, the spreader is taken to be pinned to the mast rather than fixed. **More difficult to appreciate is that the mast is regarded as pinned from one section (known also as a panel) to the next, for the purposes of analysis.**

Yet another requirement for space-frame analysis is that each member, running from one node to another, is under either tension or compression. If each node is regarded as being pinned; if members of the spaceframe form triangles; and if the loadings are applied at the nodes only, then bending is avoided and, indeed, either tension or compression is assumed.

Vector representation

For those architects involved with the structural design of trussed roofs, a system named *Bow's notation* provides a pre-computer age means of determining the nature of the loading in each member and its magnitude. The system notates each member and space in order to build a diagram that represents the forces in all the members by using vectors. For each a line is drawn in the same orientation as the force acts and of a length equal to the force, by way of a suitable scale.

It is not intended that Bow's notation in all its glory should be applied to the analysis of a rig because the procedure itself is reasonably complex. Instead, it is planned that each node is analysed in terms of separate *vector diagrams*. This approach lacks the unifying quality of Bow's notation but does provide an acceptable alternative.

The system rests upon working from the known towards an unknown. In the case of the

---

Supplementary Note

The need for a small shroud angle comes about either because the shroud chainplate cannot be placed beyond the beam of the boat or because an overlapping foresail is carried, in which case it is frequently necessary to locate the shroud inboard of the deck edge so that the sail is sufficiently close-sheeted.

---

rig we start from the force applied at the **hounds.** Applied perpendicularly to the mast, this force produces tension in the main shroud. The amount of tension will vary with the angle of the shroud to the mast: the smaller the angle, the greater the tension.

In resisting the side force, the shroud pulls downwards and this is opposed by the mast pushing upwards, that is, by placing the mast in compression. The angle of the shroud also affects the compression in the mast. Again, the smaller the shroud angle the greater the compression.

Vector diagram

The vector diagram which represents the three forces contributed by the external force and the shroud and mast loadings at the hounds is best developed first. The actual construction of the diagram starts with the external load which is of known magnitude and direction. The lengths of the shroud and mast vectors are not known, but their directions may be obtained from the rig layout and this enables the diagram to be constructed.

Because the vector diagram is representative of the system of forces in equilibrium at the

Supplementary Calculation

For a side force of 1kN the tension in a shroud without spreader may be plotted for different shroud angles. The very noticeable increase at small shroud angles is apparent.
The shroud tension is given by:

$$\sin (\text{shroud angle}) = \frac{\text{side force}}{\text{shroud tension}}$$

$$\Rightarrow \quad \text{shroud tension} = \frac{1000}{\sin (\text{shroud angle})}$$

Similarly,

$$\text{mast compression} = \frac{1000}{\tan (\text{shroud angle})}$$

The compression in the mast is similar in magnitude to the shroud tension at normal shroud angles. Compression and tension are tabulated for various shroud angles (some hypothetical) and values of shroud tension used to construct the graph.

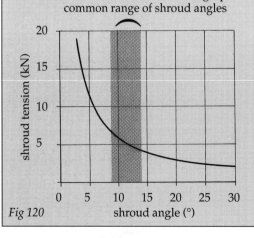

Shroud angle (°)	Mast compression (kN)	Shroud tension (kN)
2	28.64	28.65
3	19.08	19.11
4	14.30	14.34
5	11.43	11.47
10	5.67	5.76
15	3.73	3.86
20	2.75	2.92
25	2.14	2.37
30	1.73	2.00
90	0.00	1.00

Fig 120

hounds, **the direction of the external force (wind) vector, denoted by an arrow, tracks round the other two vectors, indicating the directions of the forces applied by the shroud and the mast at the hounds.** Although perhaps easy to deduce in this case, the vectors provide an indication of tension and compression, respectively. It should be mentioned that where the layout becomes more complex, the nature of the loadings is less obvious.

Tension is indicated by an arrow which points towards the centre of the member, and compression by an arrow pointing towards the node, and the magnitude of the force is given by the length of the vector representation.

Determining loadings

In this way, the rig is analysed progressively. The procedure for evaluating the loadings in each member follows the order shown by the accompanying figure.

Given the side force of 1,000N at the hounds, the tension in the upper main shroud is approximately 5,241N and the compression in the upper panel of the mast is about 5,145N. It is to be noted that these loadings are not wildly dissimilar from each other and are about five times greater than the side force, a factor defined by the shroud angle which in this case is 11 degrees.

Although the loadings may be calculated by applying trigonometry to the vector diagram, it is quite satisfactory to draw the diagram accurately to a suitable scale and then to measure each vector in order to obtain the loadings. Since the loading along the upper shroud acts in a downward manner from the hounds, it follows that the loading will be in an upward manner at the other end of the shroud, that is, where it links with the spreader.

Analysis progression

When considering the node at the spreader end, we start with a known loading – 5,241N – in the upper shroud. The next step is to

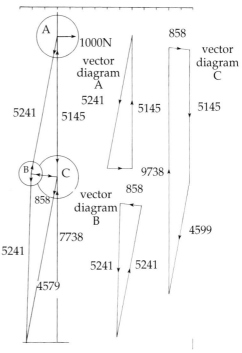

Fig 121 With a wind load of 1,000N, the consequential loadings in the mast and the rigging on one side of the yacht are analysed. Vector diagrams are constructed to represent the loading at node A (hounds), node B (spreader outer) and node C (spreader inner). By measuring the length of the vectors, the loadings in each member of the rig may be deduced.

construct a vector diagram, another triangle since three forces are involved. Since the spreader bisects the angle the shroud makes at the spreader end, the triangle of vectors is isosceles in form. **Thus the force in the lower part of the main shroud is equal to that in the upper part, that is 5,241N. By measurement we obtain the loading in the spreader, which is 860N, indicative of compression.**

Finally, we analyse the node at the inboard end of the spreader. Here four forces act at a point and therefore the vector diagram will be quadrilateral in form. **Again, by measurement, we obtain the loadings in the** lower shroud at 4,579N and in the lower panel of the mast at 9,738N, the loadings in the spreader and in the upper mast panel providing the starting information.

Although separate vector diagrams have been depicted in order to represent each node, they can be assembled to produce a global vector diagram describing all the forces in the system. Bow's notation makes this possible, but for the kinds of problem likely to be encountered by rig analysis it is easier to deal with each vector diagram separately.

Reviewing the loadings

As far as the figures are concerned, the sum of the tensions in both shrouds at 9,820N is similar in magnitude to the compression in the lower panel of the mast, which is 9,738N. This is to be expected because the compression arises due to the shrouds' downward force on the mast, which is more or less equal to the upward force of the shrouds on the hull.

Supplementary Note

More accurately, the vertical component of the tension in each shroud can be considered. For the main shroud, the component is 5,239N and for the lower shroud it is 4,499N. Their sum equates exactly to the compression in the mast, as might be expected for a state of equilibrium. It is also to be noted that the couple produced by the vertical component of the shrouds, the mast compression and the distance of separation (0.6162m – the shroud base) is 6.0kNm, which is equal to the couple produced by the force at the hounds and the distance to the deck. Both expressions of heeling couple equate to the righting couple.

It is also noticed that the lower mast panel experiences a compressive load almost twice that of the upper panel. The unfortunate lower panel not only has to bear the force created by the lower spreader which tensions the lower shroud but also the force of the upper panel bearing down.

Sometimes the bottom panels of masts are *sleeved*, or a *spinnaker pole track* is used for reinforcement, but the spreader height affects the length of the panels and therefore the load to cause buckling in each. Lower the spreaders and the bottom panel is able to withstand a higher compressive loading.

Mast fixity

More significantly, the mast step arrangement has a major effect on the buckling load of the bottom panel. If the mast is stepped on the deck it behaves as a strut which is pin-ended. A snug *tabernacle* could provide an element of support and therefore fixity, but is not to be regarded as contributory. However, the effect of stepping the mast on the keel, and wedging at deck or coachroof level, very effectively fixes the bottom of the mast.

It could be argued (mistakenly) that the lower panel is also fixed at the spreader position because, in reality, the upper and the lower panel are not pinned together but are continuous. However, when loaded in the extreme the mast bends into an S-shape, indicating that no real constraint is being applied at the spreader position. **In terms of analysis we may therefore model the upper panel as double pin-ended and the lower panel as pin-ended at the top and fixed-ended at the bottom, if the mast is keel-stepped.** Strut length for calculation is taken from the position at which the mast is wedged at deck or coachroof level and not at the keel since the amount of mast bury does not significantly affect the fixity.

Sectional properties

Assuming the mast to be keel-stepped; the height from the deck to the hounds to be 6m; and the lower panel to upper panel split to be 54 per cent, the requirement of the mast sectional

Supplementary Calculation

The size of section required for the mast, expressed in terms of the second moment of area, may be found for: the upper mast panel and the lower mast panel; assuming the modulus of elasticity for aluminium alloy is $70GN/m^2$ and a universal factor of safety of four is applied.

For the upper mast panel: compressive load: 5,145N; strut length: 2.75m. This panel may be regarded as double pin-ended, in which case,

$$\text{design load} = \frac{\pi^2 \times (\text{modulus of elasticity}) \times (\text{second moment of area})}{(\text{strut length})^2}$$

$$\Rightarrow \quad 4 \times 5,145 = \frac{\pi^2 \times (70 \times 10^9) \times (\text{second moment of area})}{2.75^2}$$

$$\Rightarrow \quad \text{second moment of area} = 225.3 \times 10^{-9} m^4$$

For the lower mast panel: compressive load: 9,738N; strut length: 3.25m. Because the bottom of the mast may be regarded as fixed,

$$\text{design load} = \frac{2 \times \pi^2 \times (\text{modulus of elasticity}) \times (\text{second moment of area})}{(\text{strut length})^2}$$

$$\Rightarrow \quad 4 \times 9,738 = \frac{2 \times \pi^2 \times (70 \times 10^9) \times (\text{second moment of area})}{3.25^2}$$

$$\Rightarrow \quad \text{second moment of area} = 297.8 \times 10^{-9} m^4$$

Values of second moment of area required for the upper and the lower mast panels are at least $225.3 \times 10^{-9} m^4$ and $297.8 \times 10^{-9} m^4$, respectively.

property for each panel can be established. The second moment of area needs to be 297.8×10^{-9} m^4 for the lower panel, and $225.3 \times 10^{-9} m^4$ for the upper panel. These figures are based upon a mast material of aluminium alloy and a factor of safety of four, which is probably rather generous. The aluminium-alloy extrusion chosen would therefore be based upon the larger second moment of area.

The analysis is rather limited because only transverse loadings are considered. It is reasonable to suppose that the leeward shrouds become slack under strenuous sailing conditions, therefore ruling out the effects of pre-tension and an increase in the compression in the mast. However, tension in the forestay and standing backstay or running backstays adds to the mast compression. Generally the factor of safety takes this into account.

Some consideration needs to be given to the mast column in the fore and aft plane. If the spreaders and shrouds are placed athwartships, rather than being swept aft, only limited fore and aft control will be given to the middle of the mast. **Therefore column length needs to be considered from the hounds to the deck.** To decide upon a suitable imposed load is not straightforward since there is a variation in the compression in the upper and the lower mast panel. Since there are fairly considerable bending loads from the head of the mainsail at the masthead and from the boom above the deck, one approach would be to assume the higher load which, **given no spreader support fore and aft and a factor of safety of four, indicates a fore and aft second moment of area requirement of $1.01 \times 10^{-6} m^4$.**

Section choice

Aluminium-alloy masts are produced

Supplementary Note

Regarding the most as being unsupported fore and aft between the hounds and deck, and keel-stepped, the formula for the lower mast panel applies where: compressive load: 9,738N; strut length: 6.0m, from which it can be calculated, as before, that: second moment of area = 1.01 x 10^{-6} m^4. This requirement of second moment of area is about 3.4 times greater than the transverse second moment of area for the lower panel already derived.

Supplementary Note

In order to place the values of second moment of area in perspective, examples of round tubes of 2mm wall thickness but of varying diameter are listed, together with the second moment of area for each:

diameter (mm)	second moment of area (x10^{-9}) m^4
70	247
80	373
90	536
100	740
110	990
120	1,290

invariably with a second moment of area which is greater fore and aft than transversely, which in this case satisfies the requirements. Reference to mast sections points to the possibility of using a mast such as the extrusion offered by Proctor Spars (now Seldén Masts Ltd) that measures 102mm by 71mm and has values for the second moment of area in each respective plane of 830×10^{-9}m^4 and 380×10^{-9}m^4.

It is apparent that this section would meet the strut requirement in the transverse plane

since a second moment of area of 297.8×10^{-9}m^4 is needed. But the fore and aft requirement is not met. **Rather than use an extrusion of larger section, a preferable solution is to provide support to the middle of the mast.** This is best effected by attaching the main and lower shrouds to the deck aft of the mast position and sweeping back the spreaders and lower shrouds to suit. The lower shrouds

SUMMARY

1. The stayed rig for a yacht may be analysed by considering the yacht's transverse stability, allowing for the righting couple produced by the crew, and by considering the heeling force to be acting perpendicularly at the hounds.

2. Space-frame principles are applied, and so all intersections, including those between mast panels, are regarded as pinned and the loadings in each member are deemed to be either tensile or compressive, resolved by using vector diagrams.

3. For a single spreader rig the compression in the mast upper panel is similar in magnitude to the tension in the main shroud, while the lower panel compression corresponds to the sum of tensions in both shrouds, keel-stepping compensating for the elevated compression.

4. The mast section is determined by the compression in the mast panels and the effective strut length, taking account of the spreader arangement and applying a nominal factor of safety.

Supplementary Note

Given the desire for a lightweight and low windage mast, a smaller section begs consideration. The next section down Proctor's range measures 91mm by 74mm with second moment of area values of $530 \times 10^{-9}m^4$ and $350 \times 10^{-9}m^4$, representing a weight saving approaching 30N. Tempting, but concern about the adequacy of mid-height fore and aft support and the loadings from extra crew on the weather deck is not easily dispelled.

therefore restrict the forward bowing of the mast, while the spreaders restrain the mast from bending aft, provided that they are of fixed rather than swinging type. Although there is some interference with the setting of the mainsail downwind, the result is a sound structural design.

Chapter 6

Adopting Design Procedures

Design originality

The procedure for the design of the construction of boats and their components is not dissimilar to other, related design processes. Design of the hull form, defined by hydrostatic and hydrodynamic criteria, is based upon calculation and reasoning, alongside accumulated personal and general experience. Less analytical design, such as is involved in contriving a comfortable, ergonomic interior for a cruiser, does not disrupt this model, the weighing up of possibilities providing a counterpoint to common practice.

A reasonable start is to apply analysis first and then to refer to previous design as a check or confirmation, and this gives a sense of order (with which not everyone would agree!). Adopting this approach does lessen the chance of missing a novel design solution. By contrast, if the designer looks directly at derivative designs, there can be a mind set tendency.

Building to rules

A variation in this approach may apply where a boat is to be built to class, that is, to the rules of one of the classification societies, such as American Bureau of Shipping, Lloyd's, or Bureau Veritas, in which case it can make sense to define scantlings at the outset to the formulae presented. However, the societies do suggest that their rules are not intended to serve as a design tool, as such, and they do give consideration for approval to constructional design which lies outside the literal prescription of the rules.

The implication is that one should attempt a structural design based upon judged loads first, and then check that the selected classification society's rules are met or exceeded. From a purist's point of view, this approach has much merit. But it is very tempting just to go ahead and derive the scantlings as the first (and last?) step, and arguably this presents the most sensible approach.

Although the classification societies' rules concentrate primarily on items of the main construction, namely the hull, deck, ballast, keel and rudder, some consideration is given to other aspects of the structure.

Regulations relating to masts, rigging machinery, fire protection and the majority of other equipment are also provided, but to varying levels depending upon the classification society.

Construction Standards

As a means of regulating the safety of manufactured boats and their equipment, the European Union has established a set of regulations known as the *Recreational Craft Directive*. This directive impinges upon the construiction, design and use of pleseure craft up to 24m in length and of a beam greater that 1.1m, with exception being granted for certian types, including those for racing.

One of the directive's mandates is the development of applicable standards and the *International Organisation for Standardization (ISO)* as tasked to develop specifications relating to aspects such as stability and construction. Underpinning the standards

Supplementary Note

The ISO working group (WG18) examining construction has produced to date a published third-stage draft of standards relating to resins and glass fibre reinforcer elements, whilst working drafts, as yet unpublished, have been prepared concerning: core materials for sandwich construction; steel, wood and other construction materials; design pressures, allowable stresses and scantling determination; details of design and construction; and strongpoints for anchoring, mooring and towing. The prefix ISO is used with the associated number when a standard is finalized.

developed by the working group examining hull construction are the regulations of the classification societies and various regulatory agencies world-wide, such as the US Coast Guard.

Although the standards are not yet finalized, design consideration needs to be given to their prescription, though it is to be noted that, in the EU, literal adherence to the ISO standards is not required. It is, however, necessary that a boat should be built and outfitted to comply with the Recreational Craft Directive, and this could be demonstrated by observance of the rules of one of the classification societies, or by showing that the boat meets the 'essential safelly requirements', or even by evidence of past satisfactory service.

Design spiral

Despite the legislative nature of these requirements, it is suggested that the basics of the structural design should be sorted out first. **At any event, most design is best progressed using a *design spiral* approach in which the entire procedure is dealt with in a preliminary way and then revisited, more than once if necessary.**

It helps to hold in mind the need to ensure that the construction is sufficiently strong and in other ways resistant to failure, together with being adequately stiff and therefore resistant to deformation (or, indeed, deliberately flexible). These objectives have to be placed in the context of weight; material choice; feasibility of manufacture; general form; and design quality.

Defining a procedure

An invariable order for the design of the construction, or for any other aspect of boat design, appears inappropriate, although a series of steps can be defined:

Step 1: A first step in the structural design of a component or element of a boat is to consider general form, perhaps using sketches, with reference to purpose. Constructional thoughts are set out. At this stage, it is compelling to review previous designs, but it is suggested that this is resisted.

Step 2: In very general terms, the various ways in which the structure may fail are appraised against the initial sketches. Possibilities include bending, tension, compression, shear, torsion and buckling. Material fatigue and possible imperfections represent further routes to failure, as does any deficiency in the manufacturing process. Such appraisal would be preliminary and circumspect.

Step 3: The loads likely to occur from external sources and the way these are transmitted through the structure are examined. Such loads arise from wind; waves; people; weights on board; impact; grounding; laying up; and so on, and take the form of local and global loadings in the structure.

Step 4: Suitable modelling of the loadings and the stresses they are likely to produce are defined with a view to applying relevant structural theory, such as beam; tensile/

compressive; shearing; torsional; strut; or catenary theory. Dynamic loads as well as static loads are appraised, leading to the use of further engineering (and science) theory. Both working loads and worst case scenarios are evaluated.

Step 5: The significance of stiffness in the structure or its elements is reviewed. This can take the form of setting criteria relating to maximum deflection, elongation, or twist (for example, respectively, 1% relative to length, 0.1% also relative to length, and 1° over a length twenty times the diameter). Such criteria are set in the context of a predicted working load.

Step 6: The relative importance of stiffness and strength is considered. It may well be that a high level of stiffness is required and that this will lead to excessive strength in the structure. The need for flexibility is appraised, perhaps in the context of strain energy.

Step 7: Strength criteria, based upon maximum loads, are examined. Suitable factors of safety or levels of allowable stress for components are tentatively established.

Step 8: The properties of the possible materials of construction are researched as relevant to the types of stress predicted. In particular, ultimate strength; Young's modulus; yield strength; proof stress; specific strength; and specific modulus of elasticity all bear consideration. The testing of samples may be called for if published data appear unreliable, are unavailable, or if new ground is being trodden.

Step 9: Potential weaknesses in the structure and limitations in the planned materials are explored. Possible defects in welding, jointing, bonding and also imperfect fibre orientation are weighed. Deterioration in service from corrosion, rot, water absorption, wear and so

on are taken into account, together with the effectiveness of possible systems of protection. The manufacturing process and the quality of workmanship also have a bearing which, like the other factors mentioned, may lead to a revision of the factor of safety.

Step 10: The structural form or layout is refined. Potential weight reduction is appraised, for example by tapering or cutting holes. Possible cross-sections for the members are sketched, and the sectional properties, especially the section modulus, calculated.

Step 11: Relevant structural theory, based upon the sketched cross-sections and simplified if necessary, is applied. The resultant stress and deformation is calculated. Comparison is made with the structural requirements, and the cross-sections are adapted as necessary.

Step 12: Pre-existing structural design or construction is reviewed for comparison. Differences in layout and cross-section are scrutinized in order to check that the loads have been realistically judged and that none of the possible modes of failure has been missed.

Step 13: Other practical considerations are taken into account. Constructional aspects are appraised in order to seek assurance that the design can be built without excessive difficulty – manufacturing processes requiring special skills may lead to unreliability in the construction.

Step 14: Design work involving the hull, rudder, ballast keel or other constructional elements (for sea-going craft) can be checked against the rules of one or more of the classification societies for comparative purposes. If the craft is to be certified by a classification society, the minimum requirements specified are observed, or alternative design proposals submitted to the society. Compliance with the requirements of the ISO Technical Committee on small craft hull construction scantlings and any other regulatory authority is confirmed.

Design practice

The presentation of a set of procedures in the form of a list appears linear and more restrictive than the design spiral implies. **Given an iterative approach, the question of whether external reference is made finally as a check, or initially as a starting point, becomes less of an issue.** Original design would seem to demand an approach that starts from the principles.

At the same time, a part of the process of design is about getting the job done, and it seems sensible to use the experience, expertise and advice of manufacturers and suppliers of mast, rigging, fittings and materials. Boat and equipment designers, surveyors, builders and repairers all have something useful to say about the constructional design of boats and their components. To understand them, you need to be able to talk the language – and perhaps to do a calculation or two.

SUMMARY: DESIGN PROCEDURES

1. Structural design can reasonably start with analysis followed by reference to pre-existing, successful design, which may then modify the original, tentative solution.

2. Although it is logical to proceed with structural design of sea-going craft by calculating scantlings using the rules of the classification societies or the ISO standards (when developed and as applicable), arguably, such prescription should not be used as a design tool.

3. The principal objectives of structural design to be borne in mind are to ensure sufficient strength and adequate stiffness (or flexibility) in the context of weight, material choice, manufacture, form and design effectiveness.

4. A possible design procedure is to: produce initial sketches; appraise failure; examine loadings; define relevant structural theory; review stiffness; consider stiffness relative to strength; examine strength criteria; explore potential weakness; refine structural form; apply pertinent structural theory; consider practicalities; refer to regulatory authority rules.

Appendix: Conversion Factors

Numbers substituted into the formulae in this book must be in SI units (*Système International d'Unités*). These units are: metres (m); seconds (s); kilograms (kg); newtons (N); watts (W).

Measured	Measured in	... is equivalent to ...	Approximate equivalent
Distance and length	metres (m) SI	1m . . . . 3.28ft 1m . . . . 39.4in 1m . . . . 1.09yd 1ft 0.305m	Multiply by three and a bit Multiply by forty About equal A bit less than one third
	millimetres (mm)	1mm . . . . 39.4thou 1in . . . . 25.4mm 1m 1000mm	Multiply by forty Multiply by twenty five Multiply by one thousand (exact)
Area	metres squared or square metres (m^2) SI	$1m^2$ . . . . $10.76ft^2$ $1ft^2$ . . . . $0.093m^2$	Nearly eleven times One tenth or one eleventh
Volume	metres cubed or cubic metres (m^3) SI	$1m^3$ . . . . $35.31ft^3$	Multiply by thirty five
Velocity (or speed) (The change in distance with time)	metres per second (m/s) SI	1m/s . . . . 1.94 knots 1m/s . . . . 2.23mph 1 knot 0.515m/s	Double Multiply by two and a bit Halve
Acceleration (The change in velocity with time)	metres per second per second (m/s^2) SI	$1m/s^2$ . . . . $3.28ft/s^2$	Multiply by three and a bit
Mass	kilograms (kg) SI	1kg 2.205lb	Double and add on one tenth of the result (e.g. 15kg → 15×2 → 30 → 30 → +$\frac{30}{10}$ → 33lb)
	tonnes	1kg . . . . 35.3oz 1lb . . . . 0.456kg 1 tonne . . . . 1000kg 1 tonne . . . . 0.984 ton	Multiply by thirty five Just under one half Multiply by one thousand (exact) About equal
Density (The mass per unit volume)	kilograms per metre cubed (kg/m^3) SI	$1kg/m^3$ . . . . $0.624lb/ft^3$ $1lb/ft^3$ . . . . $16.02kg/m^3$ $1 tonne/m^3$ . . . . $1000kg/m^3$	Don't bother trying! Multiply by sixteen Multiply by one thousand (exact)

Measured	Measured in	. . . is equivalent to . . .	Approximate equivalent
Force and Weight (The product of mass and acceleration due to gravity)	newtons (N) SI kilonewton (kN)	1N . . . . 0.225lb 1N . . . . 3.6oz 1lb . . . . 4.45N 1kg . . . . 9.81N 1kN . . . . 1000N 1 ton 9.97kN	Slightly less than one quarter Multiply by three or four Multiply by four and a half Multiply by ten Multiply by one thousand (exact) Multiply by ten
Stress and Pressure (The loading or force per unit area)	newtons per metre squared (often termed pascals (Pa)) (N/m^2) SI	$1lb/in^2$ . . . . $6895N/m^2$ $1MN/m^2$ . . . . $14516/in^2$ $101300N/m^2$ . . . . . 1atmosphere $1MN/m^2$ . . . . N/mm^2 $1kN/m^2$ . . . . $1 \times 10^3 N/m^2$ $1MN/m^2$ . . . . $1 \times 10^6 N/m^2$ $1GN/m^2$ . . . . $1 \times 10^9 N/m^2$	Multiply by seven thousand Multiply by one hundred and fifty Multiply by one hundred thousand Exact Exact Exact Exact
Power (The product of force and velocity)	watts (W) SI kilowatts (kW)	746W . . . . 1HP 1kW . . . . 1000W 1HP . . . . 0.746kW 1kW 1.34HP	Divide by seven or eight hundred Multiply by one thousand (exact) About three quarters Multiply by one and a third

Further Reading

Many of the out of print books listed could be obtained second-hand. The classification society rules are available only from the society itself (but they're expensive).

American Bureau of Shipping, *Guide for Building and Classing Motor Pleasure Yachts* (1990)

American Bureau of Shipping, *Guide for Building and Classing Offshore Racing Yachts* (1994)

Birmingham, R. *Boat Building Techniques Illustrated* (Adlard Coles Nautical, republished 1992)

Case, J., L. Chilver and C.T.F. Ross, *Strength of Materials and Structures* (Edward Arnold, 3rd edn, 1992)

Colvin, T.E., *Steel Boat Building: From Plans to Bare Hull* (Adlard Coles Nautical, republished 1996)

du Plessis, H. *Fibreglass Boats* (Adlard Coles Nautical, 1996)

Gibbs and Cox, Inc., *Marine Design Manual for Fibreglass Reinforced Plastics* (McGraw-Hill Book Co., 1960: out of print)

Higgins, R.A., *Materials for the Engineering Technician* (Edward Arnold, 3rd edn, 1987)

Gordon, J.E., *Structures or Why Things Don't Fall Down* (Penguin Books, 2nd edn, 1988)

Gordon, J.E., *The New Science of Strong Materials, or Why You Don't Fall through the Floor* (Penguin Books, 2nd edn, 1988)

Gougeon Bros., *The Gougeon Brothers on Boat Construction* (Gougeon Bros., Inc., 1985)

Kinney, F.S., *Skene's Elements of Yacht Design* (A. & C. Black, 3rd edn, 1981: out of print)

Larsson, L. and R.E. Eliasson, *Principles of Yacht Design* (Adlard Coles Nautical, 1994)

Lloyd's Register of Shipping, *Rules and Regulations for the Classification of Special Service Craft* (1996)

Matthews, F.L. and R.D. Rawlings, *Composite Materials: Engineering and Science* (Chapman & Hall, 1994)

Nicolson, I., *Boat Data Book* (Adlard Coles Nautical, 3rd edn, 1994)

Norwood, J., *High Speed Sailing Design Factors* (Adlard Coles Nautical, 1987: out of print)

Parkyn, B. (ed.), *Glass Reinforced Plastics* (Butterworth, 1970: out of print)

Pollard, S.F., *Boatbuilding with Aluminium* (International Marine, 1993)

Ship and Boat Builders' National Federation, *Construction of Small Craft* (2nd edn, 1974: out of print; the Federation no longer exists)

Sims, E.H., *Aluminium Boatbuilding* (Adlard Coles Nautical, 2nd edn, 1993)

Sleight, S., *Modern Boat Building Materials and Methods* (Nautical Books, 1985: out of print)

Smith, B., *Design Your Own Yacht* (Adlard Coles Nautical, 1987: out of print)

Smith, C.S., *Design of Marine Structures in Composite Materials* (E. & F.N. Spon, 1990)

Teale, J., *How to Design a Boat* (Adlard Coles Nautical, 2nd edn, 1992)

Thornton, T., *The Offshore Yacht* (Adlard Coles Nautical, 1988: out of print)

Timings, R.L., *Engineering Materials*, Vol 1 (Addison Wesley, 2nd edn, 1998) (Vol 2 is out of print)

Warren, N., *Metal Corrosion in Boats* (Adlard Coles Nautical, 2nd edn, 1998)

Professional Boatbuilder (bimonthly trade magazine; PO Box 78, Naskeag Rd, Brooklin, ME 0616-0078, USA)

Glossary

Cross-references to other glossary entries, in their different parts of speech and expressions, are set in italics.

Acetone Solvent particularly effective for cleaning tools soaked in un*cured resins* and for preparing a *GRP* surface before further *laminating*

Aerodynamic Term relating to the behaviour of air (or other gas) under conditions of motion

Allowable stress Design-targeted maximum *stress* in the material of a *structure*; less than the material's breaking *strength* in order to provide a *factor of safety*

Alloy A mixture of metals plus, usually, non-metallic elements

Aloft Up the mast; high up

American Bureau of Shipping [ABS] A classification society that provides a service in regulating the construction and equipping of vessels

Angle of shear Angle of distortion resulting from *shearing stress*

Angle section *Stiffener*, manufactured in long lengths and usually in metal, the section being of L form

Anisotropic Term describing a material that possesses directional properties, notably *strength* and *stiffness*

Annular growth rings A tree's growth rings, approximately circular in form, as seen in a tree *section*

Aramid fibre A synthetic, long-chained aromatic polyamide fibre possessing high *tensile* strength

Argon arc Metal *welding* process in which the weld is surrounded by the inert gas argon

Aspect ratio Ratio of length to width; greater to lesser spacing of *frames* and *longitudinals*

Athwartships At right angles to the centre-line of a boat

At the flywheel Indicating that measured engine *power* is gross, not accounting for the energy used to rotate the transmission or the engine's ancillaries

Backbone Main centreline structural assembly of a yacht of *traditional wood construction*

Backstay *Stay* running from high up the mast to the aft end of a yacht, in order to restrain *downwind* sail loads

Backswept shrouds *Shrouds* attached to the hull aft of the mast step rather than in line with the mast *athwartships*

Ballast keel bolts Fastenings used to attach the ballast keel to the hull of a yacht

Barrel Effect in which the *section* of a relatively short *compressive* member increases when the material exceeds its *elastic limit*

Beam *Structural* member subject to *bending*

Beam shelf Substantial *structural* member, used for boats of *traditional wood construction*, fastened along the upper edges of the hull

Beam theory Engineering theory that permits a prediction of the *structural* behaviour of a *beam* under *bending* loads

Bedding compound Putty-like material used to aid the fit and watertightness of non-glued joints

Bending Consequential curvature in a *structural* member, as a result of loadings perpendicular to the axis

Bending moment [at a section] Sum of the *moments* about the *section* of all the forces acting to one side or the other of it

Bending strength As *flexural strength*

Bias Direction in a fabric at 45 degrees to the *warp* and the *weft*

Bilge Rounded part of the hull where the bottom curves towards the sides

Bilge stringer *Longitudinal* positioned at the *bilge*

Bimetallic corrosion As *galvanic corrosion*

Block coefficient Ratio of the underwater volume of a vessel to the cuboid that surrounds the volume

Body plan A drawing depicting the *sections* of the hull

Bottlescrew Device used to adjust the *tension* of *shrouds* and *stays*

Bow line As for a *buttock line*, but forward of amidships

Bow's notation System of analysis in which the loadings in the members of a *space-frame* may be represented by a complex, complete *vector diagram*, the spaces and *vectors* being labelled appropriately as an aid to its construction

Brake power *Power* of an engine *at the flywheel*

Brittle Term describing a material apt to fracture readily when subject to a sudden load

Buckle Failure of a *strut* when not *in column*

Bulkhead Transverse (usually) partition separating portions of a vessel and providing major *structural* support to *longitudinals* and the hull *skin*

Buoyancy Upthrust, as a result of water pressure; for equilibrium, the buoyancy of the hull is equal to the weight of the vessel

Buoyancy tank Watertight compartment in the hull intended to provide *buoyancy* when the hull is otherwise filled with water

Buttock line Imaginary line on the hull resulting from a vertical cutting plane aft of amidships and parallel to the centreline

Butt Meeting of two *planks* or other members

end to end

Butt joint Joint formed between the ends of two members that come together but do not overlap

Butt strap Member that bridges a *butt joint*, providing *strength*

Cantilever *Fixed-ended beam*, otherwise unsupported

Carbon [fibre] Treated *polyacrylonitrile* fibre, with high *strength* and *modulus*

Carling Construction member running fore and aft to give support to the inner ends of half *beams* in way of the *superstructure*

Carvel System of wood hull construction in which the *planks* are laid flush and edge to edge

Catalyst Chemical agent that initiates the *curing* of *polyester resin* (in context)

Catenary Curve, and hence *structural* configuration, of a flexible member subject to a uniformly-distributed load and resisted by placing the member in *tension*

Caulking Process in which *caulking cotton* is forced into the *seams*, primarily for water-tightness

Caulking cotton Bundled cotton fibres, available in long lengths, for *caulking*

Caulking iron Tool used for driving in *caulking cotton*

Centre of effort Centre of force of the wind in the sails, usually considered when sailing *upwind*

Centre of gravity Point at which the weight of an object may be considered to act

Centre of lateral resistance Centre of force of the water on the hull, keel and rudder combination

Centroid Centre of an area; *centre of gravity* if the area were represented by a material of consistent thickness

C-flex *One-off GRP* construction based upon longitudinal *glass fibre–resin* rods

Chainplate Fitting enabling rigging to be attached to the hull or deck

Chine 1. Corner where adjacent hull *panels*

meet, other than on the centreline; 2. As *chine log*

Chine log The longitudinal member to which the *panels* are fastened at the *chine*

Chopped strand mat Glass-fibre reinforcement material, comprising short *strands* randomly bound with an agent to form a mat, available in different thicknesses (weights)

Classification length Hull length as defined by a classification society

Clew Lower, aft corner of a sail

Clinker System of wood hull construction in which the edges of the *planks* overlap and are through-fastened

Cold moulding Process of *modern wood construction* in which layers of planks of *veneer* are built up using a *resin* adhesive able to *cure* at room temperature

Composite Construction comprising two or more distinct materials

Compound curvature Curvature in more than one direction of a *panel*, as for a sphere

Compressive Able to compress; nature of the forces tending to reduce length in the line of the forces and the accompanying *stress*

Conical projection System employed for the design of *sheet material* boats in which each *panel* takes the form of part of the surface of a cone

Coniferous Type of tree that typically retains its needle-like leaves all the year round

Constant camber Hull design system for *cold-moulded* construction in which *planks* of *veneer*, having identically-shaped edges, are laid on a *mould* with a constant form both longitudinally and transversely

Conversion Sawing of logs into usable boards

Core Lightweight material separating the two *faces* of a *sandwich panel*

Core mat *Plastic*-based, cellular *core* material, able to absorb *resin* which produces a secure connection between the *faces* of a *sandwich panel*

Cor-Ten A type of steel, sometimes used for hull construction, providing slightly greater strength and improved atmospheric corrosion resistance over that of mild steel

Counter stern Characteristic stern which extends beyond and above the *waterline*

Couple Pair of equal forces acting in opposite and parallel directions

Crimp Undulation of individual *yarns* or *rovings* resulting from the weaving of fibre reinforcement fabric

Cross-linked foam Foam, usually *PVC*, of high *strength* and *stiffness*, the result of its cellular structure

Cup *Movement*, producing hollowing in the *section* of a *plank* of wood

Cure Chemical reaction resulting in the solidification of a synthetic *resin*

Cycles [of stress reversal] Number of times the loading and therefore *stress* in a material changes

Cylindrical projection System employed for the design of boats to be constructed from *sheet material* in which each *panel* can be envisioned wrapped around a cylinder, usually of varying diameter

Dart Removal of a V-shaped piece of material from a *panel* where excess occurs as a result of *compound curvature*, the cut edges of the panel then being joined

Deadrise Angle (usually) between one side of the bottom of a hull and the horizontal

Deciduous Term describing trees that shed their leaves before the onset of winter

Deck beam Transverse *structural* member supporting the deck and linking the *gunwales* or *beam shelves*

Deep-V hull Powered craft hull form with an angle of *deadrise* of the order of 25 degrees, carried through to the *transom*

Design load Assumed load on a *structure* to serve as the basis for its design

Design spiral Classic approach to design in which the design considerations are revisited at increasing levels of sophistication and detail

Development Outline of a *sheet material panel* when it is laid flat

Dezincification Loss of zinc, as a result of *galvanic action*, from copper–zinc alloys (such as brass), leaving porous copper

Direct [relationship] As *linear relationship*

Discontinuity Abrupt change in shape, such as at a notch, crack or internal corner, presenting a disruption to the lines of *stress*

Double chine Hull possessing two *chines* per side

Double diagonal System of wood construction in which layers of *planking*, separated by calico, are laid at 90 degrees to each other and at 45 degrees to the centreline

Double inflection Curve having two bends; of S-form

Double shear *Shear* involving two planes

Downwind [sailing] Sailing with the wind

Drape Ease with which fibre-based fabric, impregnated with un*cured resin*, can form around contours

Ductile Term describing a material that *yields* readily when drawn

Durable Term describing wood that is resistant to decay; lesser resistance to decay is given by the categories: non-durable and moderately durable; while very durable indicates wood that is the most rot-proof

Duralumin [Duraluminium] Copper-based aluminium *alloy*

Dynamical loadings Loadings resulting from motion

Egg box [construction] Type of construction involving multiple *stiffeners* interlinked in cruciform fashion, broadly like an egg box

E-glass fibre Most commonly used type of *glass fibre* in *GRP* manufacture, the E symbolizing electrical grade

Elastic limit Maximum *stress* in a material at which the material will return to its original dimensions if the *stress* is removed

Electric arc System of *welding* in which an arc is formed between a *weld* electrode and the metal to be joined, the electrode also serving as a filler rod

Electrolyte Solution permitting the passage of ions in an electrical cell

End grain balsa *Core* material comprising *panels* of balsa sawn across the grain

Endurance limit Level of *stress* below which a material will not fail, regardless of the number of *stress reversals*

Engineering towards failure System of *structural* design in which the limit of acceptability is defined by failure

Epoxy [resin] *Resin* having relatively high *strength*, waterproofness, bonding and *strain* capability; made by condensing diphenylolpropane with epichlorhydrin, the *hardener* producing a rigid network of *polymer* molecules

Equivalent torque Expression, in the form only of *torque*, of the multiple loadings in a component experiencing principally *torsion*

Evergreen Term describing a tree that does not shed its leaves

Extrusion Long length of a required *section* (which may be hollow), manufactured by a process in which a semi-molten billet of metal is pushed through a shaped die or former

Face One or other of the outer layers of a *sandwich panel* (usually in *fibre–resin composite*)

Factor of safety Multiplier of the *working load* to indicate a *design load*

Fail safe Design of a system so that the consequences of failure are relatively minor

Fatigue Reduction of *strength* of a material when subject to *stress reversal*

Fatigue limit As *endurance limit*

Feathered edge Sharp edge produced by a *plain scarph*

Female mould Conventional *mould* inside which *fibre–resin composite mouldings* are *laminated*, producing a good quality exterior finish

Ferric oxide Oxide of iron; rust

Ferro-cement construction Construction comprising a steel framework and *mortar*

Fibreglass Term used historically to describe boats of *GRP* construction

Fibre–resin composite System comprising fibres (such as *glass* or *carbon*) in a solidified *resin* matrix

Fillet Reinforcement on an inside corner between two *panels* or between a *panel* and *stiffener*

Finite element analysis System of computer-based *stress* mapping that examines individual, small elements of the *structure*

Fixed-ended Manner of locating the end of a *beam* or *strut* so that it is as if buried in solid material

Flexural strength *Strength* of a material under *bending*

Floor *Athwartships*, *structural* member linking *frames* and *wood keel* (or other centreline reinforcement)

Foot Lower edge of a sail

Foresail Fore and aft sail set forward of the mast

Forestay *Stay* providing forward support to the mast and to which the *foresail* is attached

Forged Metal that has been hot worked by hammering or pressing in order to impart directional properties in accordance with metal flow

Former Shaped material that provides a suitable form to lend high *strength* and *stiffness* when *laminated*

Framed construction Type of construction comprising an array of supporting members (e.g., *frames*, *longitudinals* and *bulkheads*) covered by a *skin*

Frames Transverse *structural* members (ribs) either sawn from *grown wood* or *laminated*

Gaff-rigged *Rig* having a *mainsail* that is four-sided in profile, the upper edge being supported by a gaff that projects from the mast

Gallery Aperture in a ballast keel which houses the nut that tightens a keel bolt

Galvanic corrosion Corrosion resulting from the close proximity of two different metals in the presence of an *electrolyte*

Galvanic series Rank ordering of metals depending upon their *nobility*

Gap-filling Capability of an adhesive to bridge gaps in joints without noticeable loss of *strength*

Gel coat Outer, unreinforced *resin* layer of a *laminate* for waterproofing and decorative purposes

Generators Projection lines used to define the three-dimensional form of a *panel* (based typically upon a cone)

Glass [fibre] Reinforcement fibre produced by drawing glass very finely

Glass fibre cloth Fabric woven from *yarns* of *glass fibre*

Glass-fibre-reinforced resin *Composite* of *glass fibres* in a *resin* matrix

Glass-fibre tape *Glass-fibre cloth*, woven in narrow widths

Global loads Large-scale loads affecting the whole *structure*

Glued clinker System of *clinker* construction in which the *planks* are glued rather than fastened together

Gooseneck Hinge connecting the boom to the mast

Graphite As *carbon*

Graveyard test Method of measuring the *durability* of wood by burying samples in good soil and assessing the wood samples' decay over a period of time

Green Term describing: 1. *Resin* in the early stages of *curing*; 2. Unseasoned wood

Grown wood Wood selected for its curved grain to match individual *structural* components

GRP Abbreviation for glass fibre-reinforced *polyester*, plastic or *polymer*

Gunwale 1. Upper edge at the side of the hull; 2. *Longitudinal* at this position, usually for *modern wood construction*

Half-breadth plan A drawing of the *waterlines* and *sheerline* of a hull from the centreline outwards

Hanging knee *Knee* disposed vertically

Hardener Component added to *epoxy resin* which serves as part of the chemical reaction (unlike the *catalyst* added to *polyester resin* that initiates *curing*)

Hard spot Localized, stiffened area on the *skin* or *sandwich* of a hull that is less flexible than the surrounding *panel*

Hardwood Wood from broad-leaved trees (usually slow growing, thus producing compact, dense, hard wood)

Heartwood Wood inside the *sapwood* of a tree, used for construction

Head Height of a liquid (e.g., sea water), producing pressure

Heat-treatable Term describing metals that respond to appropriate heat treatment with improved mechanical properties, especially *strength*

Heeling couple Product of the force on the sails at the *centre of effort* (equal to the *hydrodynamic* force at the *centre of lateral resistance*) and the *heeling lever*

Heeling lever Perpendicular distance between the lines of the *aerodynamic* and *hydrodynamic* forces or, in rig analysis, between a heeling force at the *hounds* and the *chainplate*

Hog Centreline *longitudinal* of a wood dinghy or small cruiser

Hogging Tendency for a hull to *bend* upwards in the middle

Honeycomb core *Sandwich core* material (typically of aluminium *alloy* or *aramid fibre paper*), comprising hexagonal or other cells, their axes being through the thickness of the core

Hooked scarph joint Wood joint between two *structural* members, not unlike a *plain scarph*, but zigzagged to lock the joint

Horn timber Structural member running from the *transom* to the *stern post* on a *counter-sterned* craft

Hot moulding System used by Fairey Marine for *moulding* wood boats, involving large ovens to *cure* the adhesive bonding the *veneer*

Hounds Position on the mast at which the main *shrouds* and *forestay* meet

Hydrodynamic Term relating to the behaviour of water (or other liquid) under conditions of motion

Hydrostatic Term describing an environment in which forces are produced by a static water *head*

Impact strength *Strength* of a material or *structure* under impact or sudden load

In column Term describing a *strut* that is essentially straight such that end loads are transmitted without producing a tendency to curve

Interlaminar strength *Strength* between *laminates* of a *fibre–resin* composite, assessed by direct *tension* in a line perpendicular to the plane of the composite or by peeling laminates

International Organization for Standardization International body concerned with the development of standards, such as technical standards for boat construction

Isophthalic [resin] Type of *polyester resin*, named after the *isophthalic acid* that this *resin* contains, which is mechanically superior and more waterproof than the commonly used *orthophthalic polyester*

Isotropic Term describing a material that possesses mechanical properties which are essentially equal in all directions

Keel line Line along the keel, usually the centreline

Kicking strap System for pulling the boom downwards by using a line or wire attached to both boom and mast

Kiln drying *Seasoning* of wood using ovens

Kilogram (kg) *SI* unit of mass (2.205lb)

Knee *Structural* member used to brace the corners formed in a vessel's construction

Laminate 1. Single layer of *fibre–resin composite*; 2. Complete fibre–resin composite; 3. Layered wood, glued together

Laser cut System for cutting *plywood* and other materials using a *numerically-controlled laser*

Leech Aft edge of a sail

Leeward Away from the wind

Lenticular rod rigging Streamlined *shrouds* having a convex lens-shaped *section*

Linear [relationship] Relationship between two variables in which a percentage increase in one produces the same percentage increase in the other

Linear foam Ductile, but low *strength*, *plastic* foam that is non-*cross-linked*

Lines plan Drawing of the lines of a boat, depicting the shape of various cutting planes

Lip Squared-off *section* at each end of a *scarph joint* so that a *feathered edge* is avoided

Lloyd's Register Rules and Regulations Set of requirements developed by the classification society Lloyd's for construction and equipment

Local loading Loading occurring over a small area

Lodging knee *Knee* linking two horizontal *structural* members

Longitudinal *Stiffener* (usually for the hull *skin*), running fore and aft

Longitudinal stability Stability in the fore and aft sense

Loose tenons Rectangular-sectioned pieces of wood inserted into paired sockets in two components in order to prevent relative side movement

Low-carbon steel Steel having a carbon content up to about 0.15 per cent

Luff Leading edge of a sail

Mainsail Principal sail set on the after side of the main mast

Mainsheet Rope system that controls the *mainsail*

Mass Quantity of matter in a body, measured by its resistance to change of motion

Mast pillar Deck to keel support for a deck-stepped mast

Mast step Fitting into which the matching bottom of the mast fits

Mechanical losses Energy losses within a mechanical system (such as result from the friction caused by rotating gears and bearings and the resistance produced by an alternator)

Metallizing Spraying of molten zinc on to heated steel

Micro-balloons Very small, gas-filled *plastic* bubbles added to *resin* to provide a lightweight filler

Micro-cracking Formation of fine cracks in a *fibre–resin composite*

Micro-spheres As *micro-balloons* except that the bubbles are of glass

MIG Acronym for metal inert gas *welding*, involving an electrical current between a mechanically-fed wire and the work piece, the *weld* being surrounded by an inert gas such as argon

Mild steel Steel in which the carbon content is less than about 0.8 per cent

Model Description of the behaviour of a system in words, mathematically or as a diagram, in order to study the relationship or process more easily

Modern wood construction Wood construction involving the extensive use of synthetic *resin* adhesives in favour of fastenings

Modulus As *Young's modulus of elasticity*

Modulus of rigidity Measure of the *stiffness* of a material in *shear*

Moisture content Percentage of moisture contained within a sample of wood to the dry weight of the sample

Moment [of a force about a point] Product of the force and the perpendicular distance from the force to the point

Momentum Product of the mass and the velocity of a moving body

Monocoque Shell that is self-supporting and does not rely on *framing* or *stiffeners*

Mortar Mix of cement and sharp sand (having angular grains that lock together)

Mould Pattern from which a hull or another component can be built

Moulded Type of construction, based upon a

mould, involving: 1. A *fibre–resin composite*; 2. *Laminated* wood *veneers*

Movement Change in the dimensions of wood with change in *moisture content*

Multi-axial [fabric] Fabric comprising multiple layers of glass or other fibre reinforcement with varied directional orientation

Multi-chine Hull form possessing several *chines*

Multi-conical Hull *panel* design in *sheet material* based upon multiple cones having *generators* in common

Neutral axis Axis perpendicular to the *bending* forces (in the case of a *beam*) and passing through the *centroid* of the *section*

Neutral surface Surface or plane passing through the *neutral axis* of a beam at all *sections* along its length and thus remaining unchanged in length when bent

Newton (N) *SI* unit of force and weight; rigorously, the force required to accelerate a mass of 1kg by 1 m/s; equivalent to 4.45lb force

Noble Indication of the relative tendency of a metal to resist *galvanic corrosion*

Node Intersection, as where the *structural* members of a *space-frame* meet

Normalize Process in which a metal is heated and cooled naturally

Numerical control Approach in which components are shaped by machine from numerical data in the form of *offsets*

Offsets Co-ordinates of points defining a line

One-hundred-year-wave Wave of a height occurring on average once every hundred years

One-off Term describing the building of a single boat without intention for multiple production

Orthophthalic [resin] Widely-used *polyester resin*, made by a combination of maleic and phthalic anhydrides with a glycol

Orthotropic As *anisotropic*

Osmosis Process in which water-soluble material in a *fibre–resin composite* draws water through micro-pores in the surface as a result of a pressure differential, resulting in entrapped cavities filled with contaminated water that then form blisters on the surface

Oxidize To combine with oxygen

Panel 1. Area of hull *skin* bounded by elements of the framework; 2. Length of mast between supports (e.g., deck, *shrouds*, *stays* or *spreaders*)

Parabeam [trade name] Form of *sandwich construction* in which the *glass fibre faces* are separated by pillars of *glass fibres*, the whole being impregnated with *resin*

Patch Sail cloth reinforcement in the corner of a sail

Perishable Description for wood of low *durability*

Phosphor bronze *Alloy* of copper, tin and phosphorus

Pin-ended [strut] A *strut* in which the ends are not constrained

Pinned *Modelling* of a *space frame* in which the *structural* members are regarded as being able to rotate freely relative to each other at the *nodes*

Plain sawn Description for wood *planks* in which the *annular growth rings* run approximately across the width

Planking Lengths of wood that constitute the *skin* of a *framed* wood boat

Planing craft Craft that produce significant *hydrodynamic* lift at speed

Plastic Synthetic *polymer* that can be moulded while in an appropriate state

Plug Full-sized model of a hull, deck, etc. from which a female *mould* can be produced

Plywood *Sheet material* manufactured by gluing together layers of *veneer* with the grain running alternately along and across the sheet

Poisson's ratio Ratio of a material's lateral contraction to longitudinal extension when subject to longitudinal *stress*

Polar second moment of area Measure of the

resistance of a shaft to twisting as a function of its *sectional* shape

Polyacrylonitrile Starting material for the manufacture (with pyrolysis) of *carbon fibre*

Polyester [resin] Type of *thermoset*, used extensively in the boat building industry for *GRP* construction

Polyethylene Tough, translucent *thermoplastic*, best known under the trade name Polythene

Polyethylene fibre Fibre produced from *polyethylene*, having good mechanical properties but a tendency to creep

Polymer Compound made up of large molecules composed of many repeated simple units

Polyurethane Type of *plastic* used significantly for surface coatings, glues and foams

Polyvinyl chloride [PVC] *Thermoplastic* material produced by the *polymerization* of vinyl chloride

Power Rate of doing work or consuming energy, measured in watts (W)

Pre-impregnated materials [pre-pregs] *Fibre–resin composite* in which the precise amount of *resin* is incorporated in the reinforcement and is *cured* subsequently by heat only

Pressure Force per unit area, usually of a fluid

Pre-tensioning *Tensioning* a *tie* before any external load is applied

Principal stresses The largest single *stress* representative of two or more individual *stresses*, simultaneously applied

Production Construction of more than one boat to the same design and specification

Profile plan Drawing of the side view of a hull (usually with keel and rudder), depicting the *sheer*, *keel*, *buttock* and *bow lines*

Proof stress *Stress* in a material at a particular value of percentage *strain*, applied where the *yield* point is indistinct

Quarter sawn Description for wood *planks* in which the *annular growth rings* run perpendicular to the width

Radial Direction perpendicular to a tree's *annular growth rings*, viewed in *section*

Radian Angular measure; formally, the angle subtended at the centre of a circle by an arc equal to the radius of the circle

Rake [of mast] Lean of the mast in the fore and aft sense

Reaching Point of sailing with the wind abeam

Recreational Craft Directive [RCD] European Union directive specifying a range of requirements with which boat builders must comply

Reinforced plastic Generally used term to describe a *fibre–resin composite*, normally *GRP*

Resin 1. Name given to many *polymers* (e.g., synthetic adhesives, surface finishes and *plastics*); 2. Substance naturally exuded from trees

Resorcinol formaldehyde Fully waterproof, two-component *resin* adhesive for wood

R-glass fibre *Glass fibre* possessing superior mechanical properties to *E-glass fibre* (and having a specification similar to the better known *S-glass fibre*, developed in the USA)

Rig *Spars*, sails, *shrouds*, *stays* and ropes of a sailing craft

Righting couple Product of the weight of a boat numerically (equal to the *buoyancy*) and the *righting lever*

Righting lever Perpendicular distance between the lines of the forces given by the weight of the boat and the *buoyancy*

Ring frame *Frame* that runs continuously around the hull and deck

Roll centre Point about which a vessel rolls such that only rotational movement is apparent

Rotational moulding Moulding technique in which a female *mould* is coated with *structural plastic* by bi-axial rotation

Roving Bundle of up to a hundred *strands* of reinforcement fibre (usually *glass*)

Ruling lines As *generators*

Running backstay Readily adjustable *backstay*, usually running aft from the *hounds* or an intermediate position on the mast

Sacrificial anode Metal of low *nobility* (such

as zinc) that will corrode, in the presence of sea water, in favour of other metals in the vicinity

Sacrificial protection   Means of reducing the extent of *galvanic corrosion* by placing a *sacrificial anode* on the hull underwater

Sagging   Tendency for a hull to *bend* downwards in the middle

Sandwich construction   Construction involving *faces* (normally of *fibre–resin composite*) bonded to a lightweight *core*

Sapwood   Wood just inside the bark of the tree, not suitable for construction because it lacks *durability*

Scarph joint   Tapered joint to connect two members of similar *section*

Score   Portion of wood removed from a *structural* member (e.g., a *beam shelf*) to create a joint (e.g., a *skewed dovetail*)

Seam   Space between the *planks* of a *carvel*-built boat

Season   Removal of natural moisture from *green* wood

Second moment of area   Measure of the resistance of a *beam* or *strut* to *bending* or *buckling* as a result of the *sectional* shape

Section   Plane considered perpendicular to the main axis (of a hull, *beam* or *strut* for instance)

Section modulus   Ratio of the *second moment of area* of a *section* to the distance from the *neutral axis* to the outer surface of the *section*

S-glass fibre   Abbreviation for *structural glass fibre*; *glass fibre* having mechanical properties superior to *E-glass fibre*

Shackle   Link to connect fibre and wire ropes to fittings, and for many other purposes

Shear   Deformation in which two parallel planes remain parallel but move relative to each other

Shear pin   Easily replaced component (used with outboard engines) intended to *shear* when subject to abnormal loads, in order to avoid more extensive failure

Shear strength [of a material]   *Strength* of a material in *shear*

Sheerline   Line depicting the intersection of the deck and topsides at all points fore and aft

Sheet material   Constructional material available in sheet form (e.g., *plywood* and steel)

Short grain   Grain direction that does not run along the length, or follow the curve, of a wood member

Shroud   Means of providing *athwartships* support to a mast (usually in the form of wire rope)

SI   Abbreviation for Système International d'Unités, a standardization of units, based upon metric measurements

Single chine   Term describing a hull having one *chine* on each side

Single shear   *Shear* involving a single plane

Skeg   *Structure* projecting from the hull directly ahead of the rudder to provide support to the rudder and protect it

Skewed dovetail   Specific joint used between the *deck beams* and *beam shelf* on craft of *traditional wood construction*

Skin   Outside covering (e.g., *planking*) of a hull

Slamming area   Area of the hull subject to sea water impact in waves (mainly in the bow)

Sleeved   Term describing the reinforcement of an *extrusion* by sliding a length of slightly larger or smaller *sectioned extrusion* outside or inside the first

Snape   *Lip* used for the *stem* to *wood keel* joint

S-N curve   Graph describing the level of *stress* (S) that produces failure in a material when a sample has experienced a specific number (N) of *stress reversals*

Softwood   Wood from the needle-leaved *coniferous* trees

Solvent-based   Term describing surface finishes and adhesives that contain solvents (e.g., spirit-based rather than water)

Space-framed construction   Construction based upon *struts* and *ties*

Spade rudder   Rudder not supported by a *skeg*

Specific modulus   As *specific stiffness*

Specific stiffness *Stiffness* of a material relative to its density

Spile Process in which a board of wood is marked for cutting to fit a complicated shape (e.g., an adjoining *carvel plank*)

Spinnaker pole track Track attached to the forward side of a yacht's mast so that the spinnaker pole height can be varied

Spreader *Strut* attached to the mast and used to spread the main *shrouds*

Sprung Process in which *sheet material*, especially metal plate, has been bent into place when within the material's *elastic limit*

Stainless steel Steel containing at least 11 per cent chromium (18 per cent being normal for marine use) to provide resistance to corrosion

Station Longitudinal location of a *section* of the hull

Stay Means of providing fore and aft support to a mast (usually in the form of wire rope)

Stayed Term describing a mast that is supported by *shrouds* and *stays*

Steam bent Term describing wood that has been steamed so that it *bends* more readily

Stem Forward constructional member where the hull sides meet at the bow

Stern post Near vertical *structural* member at the aft end of the hull on which the rudder may be hung

Stiffener General term to describe *structural* members that support the *skin* or other unsupported constructional panels

Stiffness Measure of a material's resistance to *strain*, or a *structure's* resistance to *deformation*

Stitch and glue Method of construction in which *plywood panels* are first wired (or similar) together and *fibre-glass-taped* (with *resin*) on both sides of the corners to make the joints

Stitched fabrics Multiple layers of directional fibre reinforcement, stitched together, thus avoiding *crimp*

Stock [of rudder] Part of the rudder to which the blade is attached

Stopwater Softwood dowel used at points in joints, intended to swell and limit water ingress

Strain Amount of deformation relative to the extent of the material over which the deformation occurs; *tensile strain* is expressed as extension relative to original length

Strain energy Energy transferred to a material and stored in the material when it is deformed

Strand Bundle of about two hundred reinforcement fibres

Strap knee/floor *Knee/floor* constructed from metal

Strength 1. Maximum *stress* a material can withstand; 2. Measure of the capability of a *structure* to withstand loads

Stress Loading per unit area within a material

Stress concentration Localized high *stress* in a structure caused by a *discontinuity* of form

Stress concentration factor Measure of the acuity of a *stress concentration*; ratio of the stress with and without the *stress concentration*

Stress reversal Change of *stress* in a material as a result of loading variation

Stringer *Longitudinal*, usually of small *section*

Strip planking System for *planking* using edge-glued, narrow, wood *planks*

Structural efficiency Measure of the relative *strength* and *stiffness* of a *structure* or material for its weight

Structure Assembly of components (or a single component) intended to withstand loads

Strut *Structural* member that is long relative to the size of the *section*, subject to *compressive* (end) loads that tend to cause *buckling*

Stud Fixing attached with some permanence to one component and tensioned by a nut after passing through another component

Superstructure Raised area above the deck, increasing interior headroom

Tabernacle *Structure* mounted on the deck of some small yachts into which the mast is fitted, so enabling convenient lowering and raising

Tackle Arrangement of rope running through blocks (pulleys) in order to haul a load greater than the pull on the rope

Tack welds Infrequent, short *welds* made in order to hold two plates in position prior to welding the join fully

Take up Absorption of water by a boat of *traditional wood construction* (causing swelling of the *planking* and the sealing of the *seams*)

Tangential Direction along the *annular growth rings* with respect to the *section* of a tree

Tension Nature of the load tending to stretch a *structural* member

Thermoplastic Type of *plastic* that softens when warmed

Thermoset Type of *plastic* that remains rigid once set and does not soften when warmed

Tie *Tensile* member

Timbers *Steam-bent*, small-*sectioned frames*

Thwart *Athwartships* seat in a small boat

To class Term describing the construction of a vessel so that it meets the requirements of one of the classification societies

Toggle Metal link (usually for attaching a *bottlescrew* to a *chainplate*)

Toggle pin Pin (often termed a clevis pin) to provide attachment to a *toggle*

Top hat stiffener *Stiffener* used in *fibre–resin composite* construction, the *section* taking the form of a top hat

Topside Side of a vessel above the *waterline*

Torque Turning *moment*

Torque curve Graph depicting the *torque* produced by an engine at different rotational speeds

Torsional Effect of *torque* on a component; twisting

Tortured plywood method Technique for design and construction in which *plywood* is forced to take up an element of *compound curvature*

Traditional wood construction Early, largely superseded, wood boat construction in which adhesives are not used (though, since the introduction of *resin* adhesives, curved members are often *laminated*)

Transom Flat, or slightly curved, *structure* extending across the stern of a hull

Transverse stability Stability in the *athwartships* sense

Tri-axial Term describing three-layered reinforcement fabric, each layer being oriented differently (typically at 0, 60 and 120 degrees)

Trichloroethane Agent of value for conditioning a surface prior to further *laminating* in order to achieve a good bond

True length Actual length of a line in three-dimensional space

Trussed structure *Space-framed structure* designed to support a load

T-section *Stiffener* having a *section* in the shape of a T

Ultimate tensile strength [of a material] *Tensile stress* that produces failure in a sample of the material

Una rig *Rig* having a *mainsail* and no others

Unidirectional [reinforcement] Term describing reinforcement possessing *strength* and *stiffness*, effectively in one direction only

Unstayed Term describing a mast that resists loads as a *cantilever*; possessing no *shrouds* nor *stays*

Upwind [sailing] Sailing as close to the wind as possible

Urea formaldehyde Waterproof, two-component, *resin* adhesive for wood

Urethane acrylate Flexible adhesive for bonding the foam *core* to the outer *face* of a moulded *sandwich*

Vacuum bagging Technique for consolidating *fibre–resin composites* (especially *sandwich construction*) and *moulded* wood *veneer* by removing most of the air from a bag surrounding the *moulding*

Vector Quantity defined by magnitude and direction

Vector diagram Depiction of the forces (assumed in equilibrium) at a *node*, expressed as *vectors* and arranged to form a complete diagram

Velocity ratio   Ratio of the distance the rope end of a *tackle* is pulled to the distance the load moves

Veneer   Thin sheet of wood, either sliced *tangentially* or sawn *radially* from the log

Vinyl ester   *Resin* having the characteristics of both *epoxy* and *polyester resins*

Warp   *Roving* or *yarn* running along the length of a fabric

Waterline   Line along the hull of a boat at the surface of the water

Weft   *Roving* or *yarn* crossing the *warp* of a fabric

Weld distortion   Distortion arising in the vicinity of a *weld* as a result of the localized, extreme heat

Welded mesh   Steel lattice welded at its intersections (thus providing a stronger reinforcement for *ferro-cement construction* than hitherto used chicken wire)

Welding   Technique for joining metals in which the edges to be joined are melted and fused, usually with like filler material

Weld penetration   Depth to which the metal to be joined is melted and fused when *welding*

Wet out   Impregnate fibre-reinforcement material with liquid *resin*

Wind   Twist in a component

Windward   Towards the wind

Wood floor   *Floor* fashioned from *grown wood* or *laminated* to shape

Wood keel   Major part of the *backbone* of a yacht of *traditional wood construction*, running fore and aft between the *sternpost* and *stem*

Working load   Load to which a *structure* is subjected in normal conditions of use

Woven rovings   *Rovings* woven together to make a fabric

Yarn   Twisted *strands* of reinforcement fibre

Yield strength [of a material]   Minimum level of *stress* at which a material continues to deform with no increase in load

Young's modulus of elasticity   Measure of the *stiffness* of a material, defined by the ratio of *stress* to *strain*

Index